ANTHOLOGY OF EASIER CLASSICAL PIANO

174 FAVORITE PIANO PIECES BY 44 COMPOSERS

Lower Intermediate to Intermediate Level

EASIER CLASSICAL PIANO

ISBN 978-1-4803-5263-6

In Australia Contact:
Hal Leonard Australia Pty. Ltd.
4 Lentara Court
Cheltenham, Victoria, 3192 Australia
Email: ausadmin@halleonard.com.au

Visit Hal Leonard Online at
www.halleonard.com

CONTENTS

(Continued on next page)

(Continued on next page)

Minuet in G Major

BWV Appendix 116

Composer Unknown

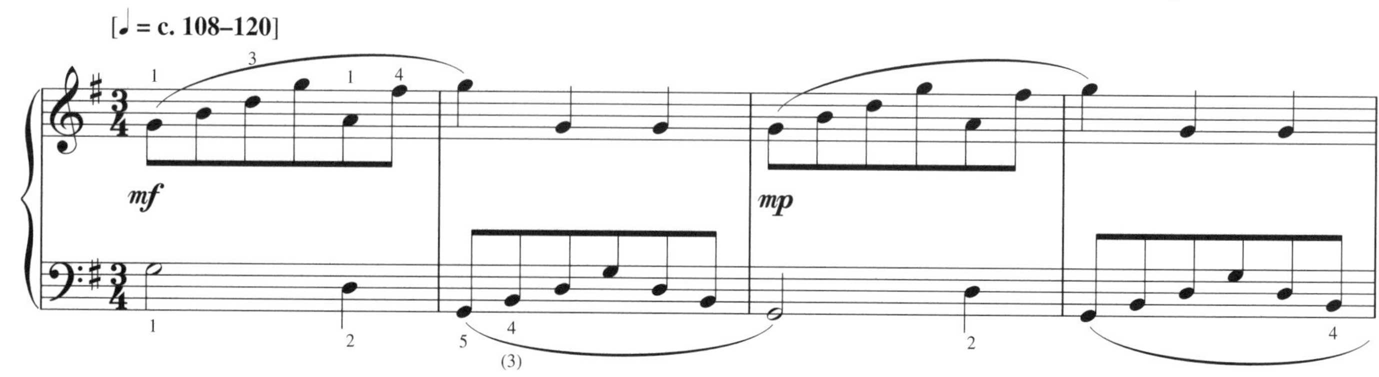

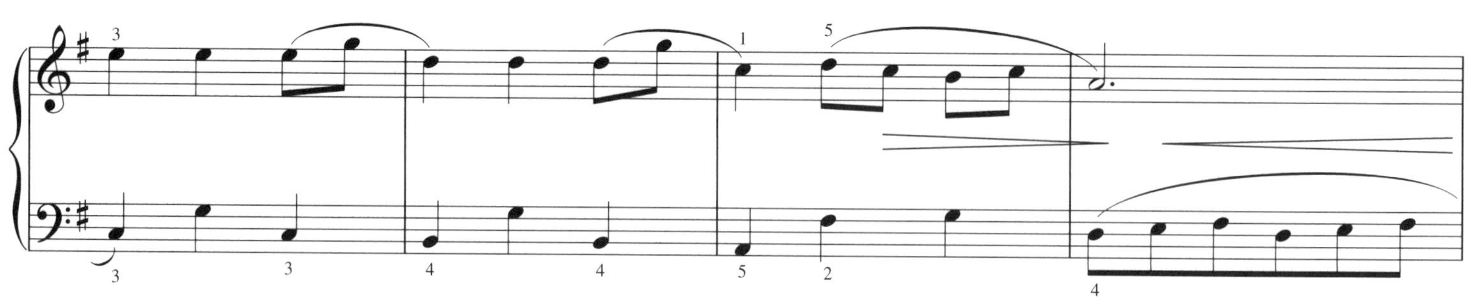

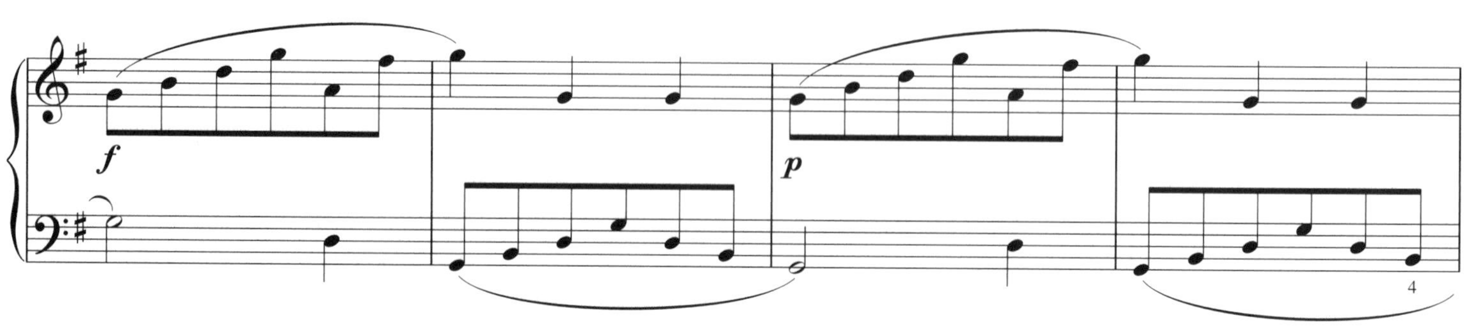

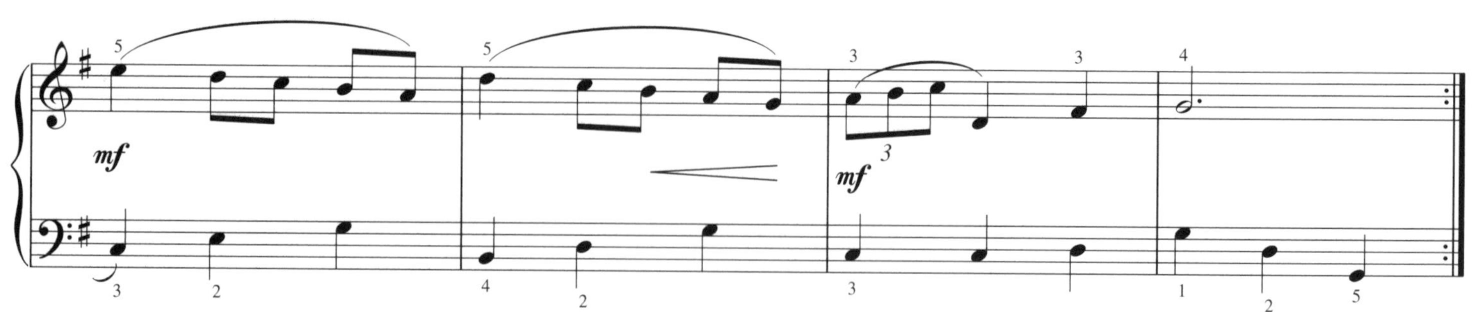

p
mf
mf
p
poco cresc.
mp
mf
mp

Minuet in C minor

BWV Appendix 121

Composer Unknown

Musette in D Major

BWV Appendix 126

Composer Unknown

Minuet in D minor

BWV Appendix 132

Composer Unknown

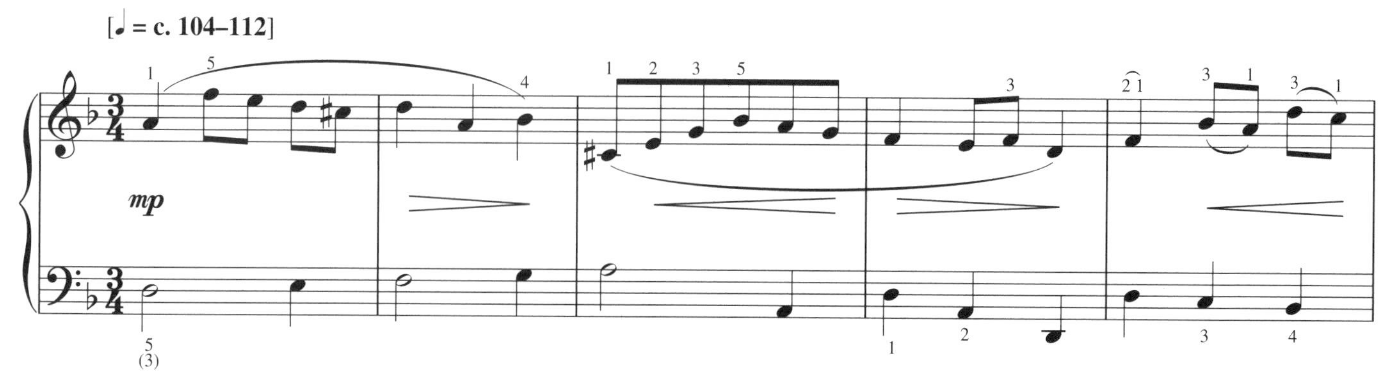

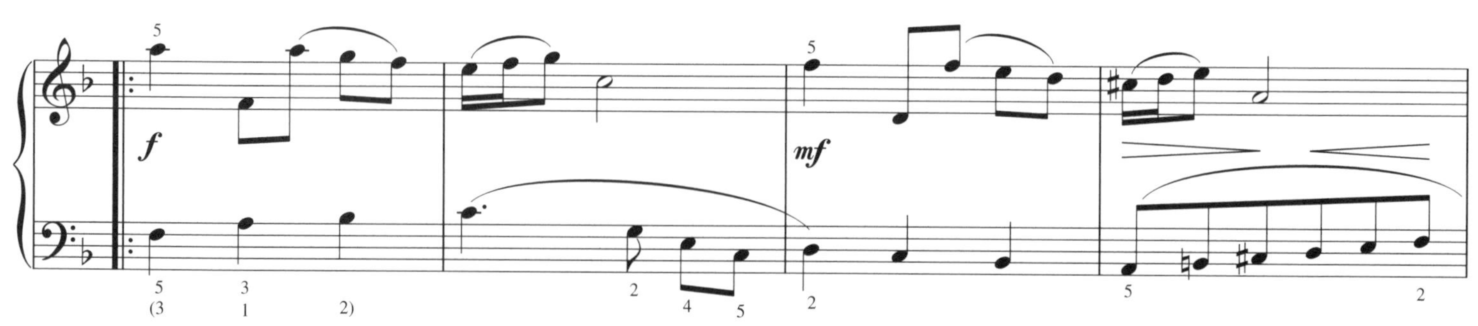

March in D Major

BWV Appendix 122

Carl Philipp Emanuel Bach
1714–1788

March in G Major

BWV Appendix 124

Carl Philipp Emanuel Bach
1714–1788

13
mf – p

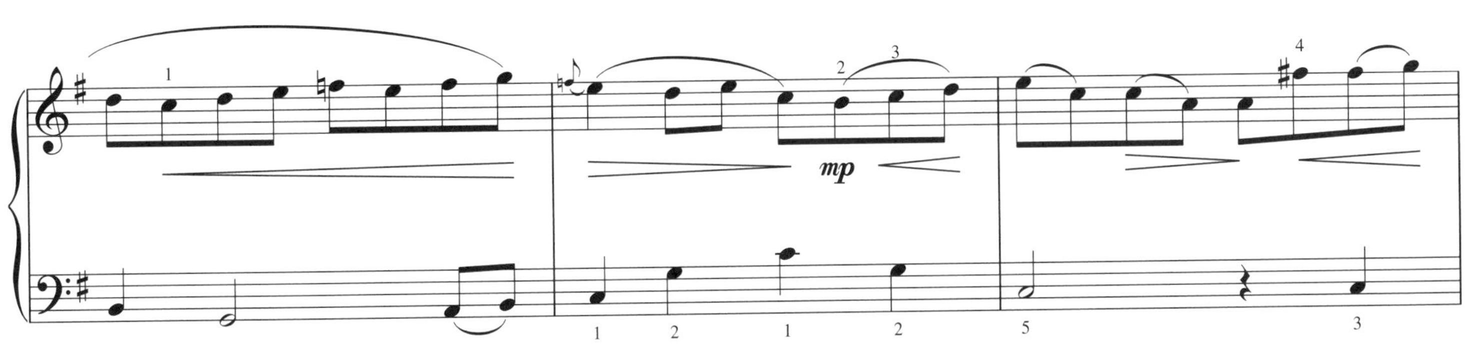
mp

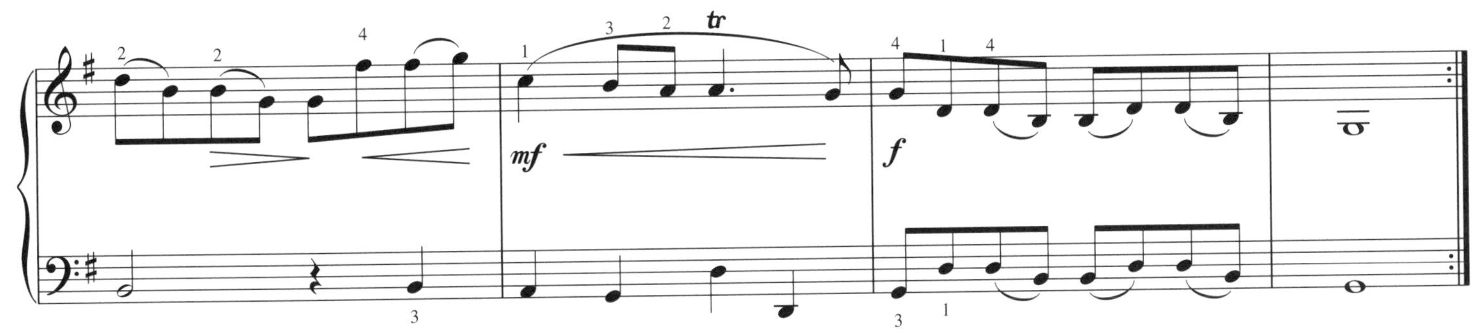
tr
mf
f

Solfeggietto in C Minor

H. 220

Carl Philipp Emanuel Bach
1714–1788

LH over RH
[p]
[f]

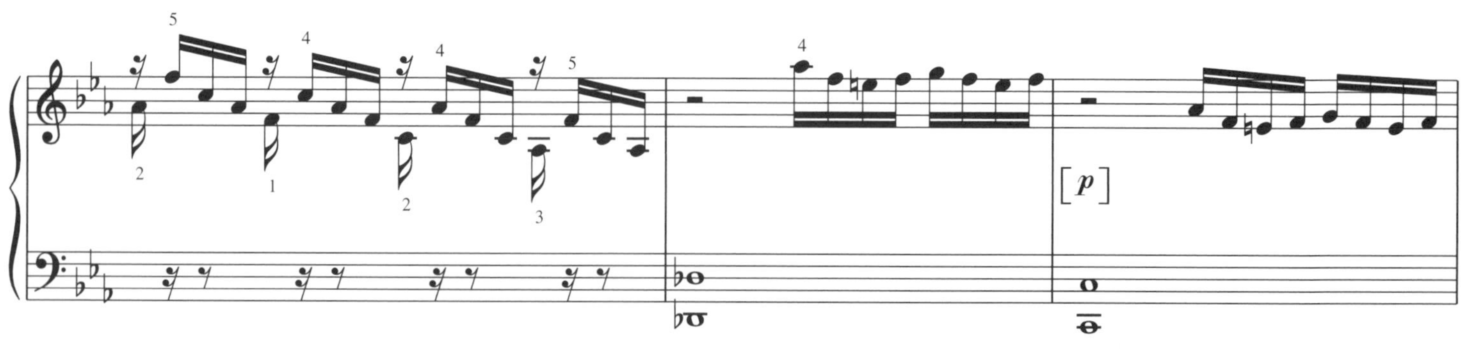
[p]

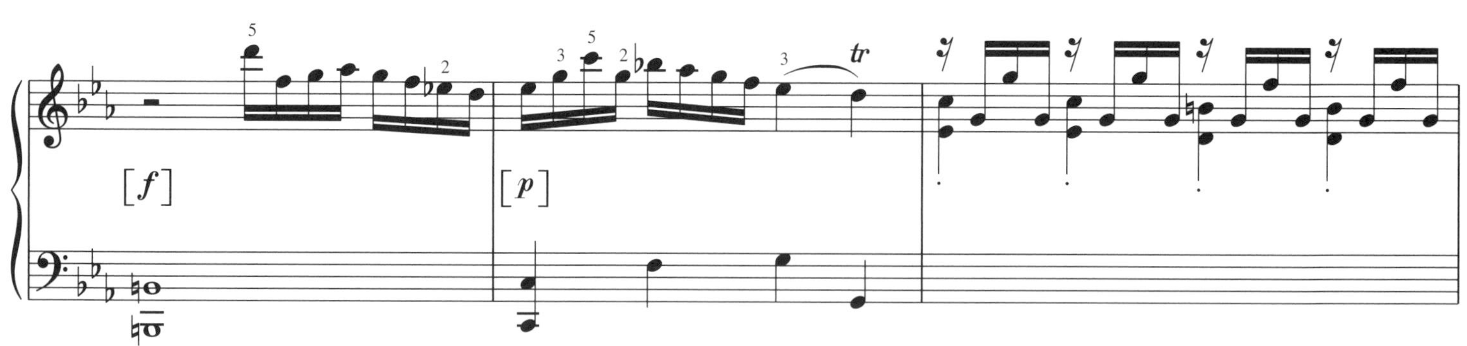
[f]
[p]
tr

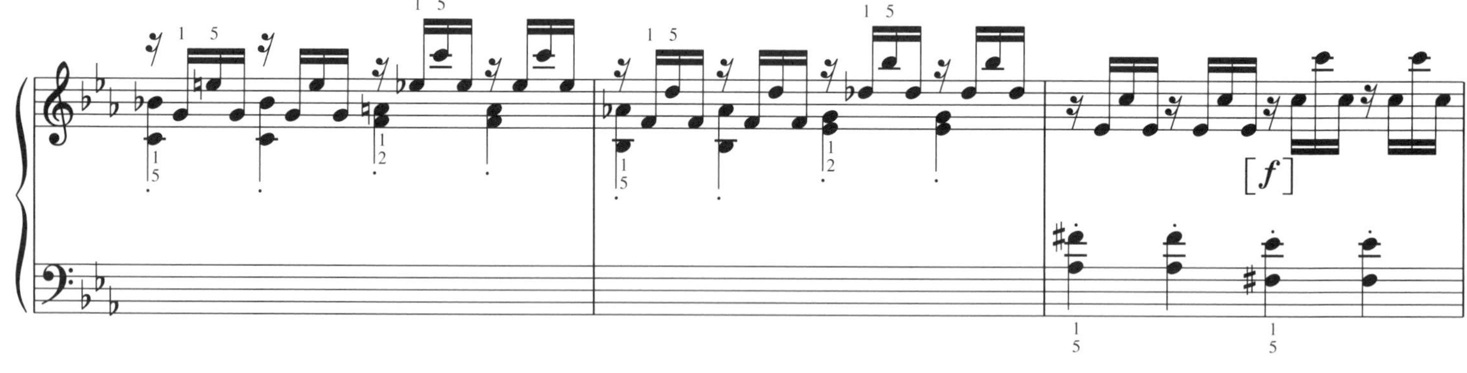
[f]

[p]

Prelude in C Major

from *The Well-Tempered Clavier,* Book I

BWV 846

Johann Sebastian Bach
1685–1750

2
3

1
2
4
3
3

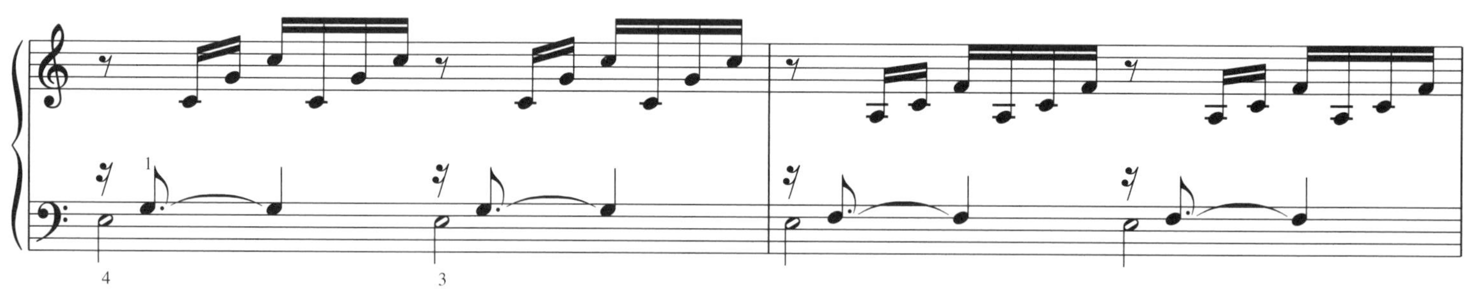
1
4
3

[rit.]

Prelude in C Major

BWV 924

Johann Sebastian Bach
1685–1750

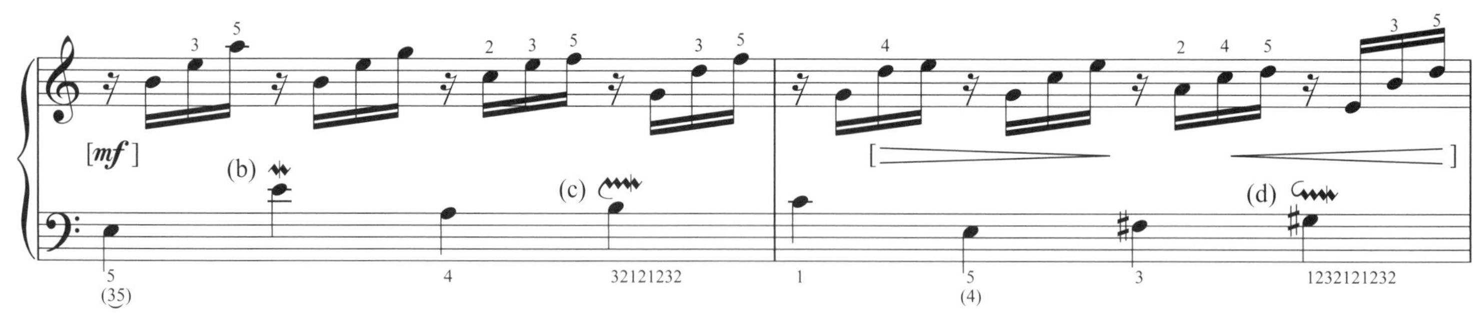

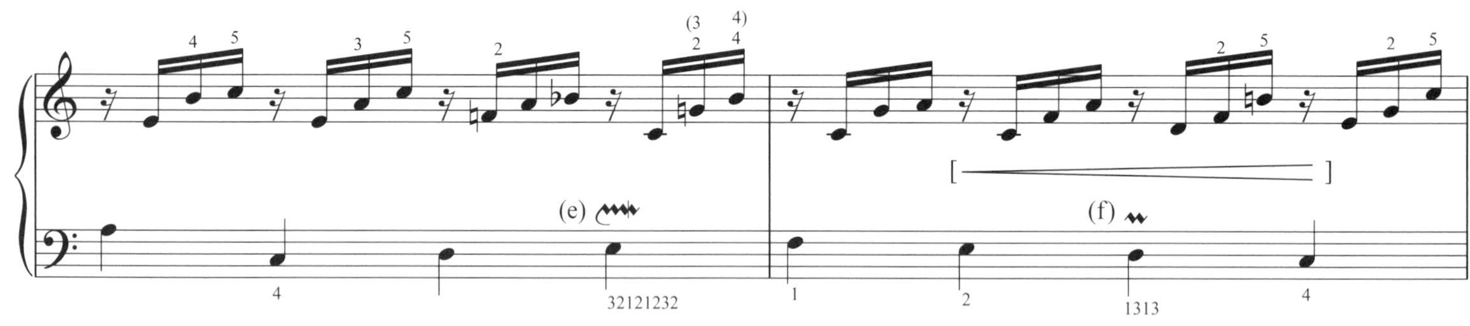

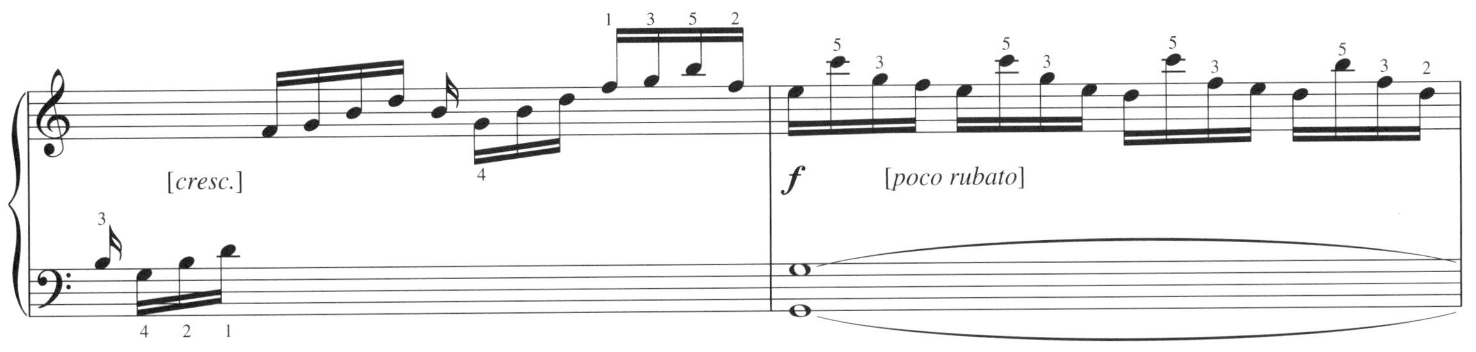
[cresc.]
f
[poco rubato]

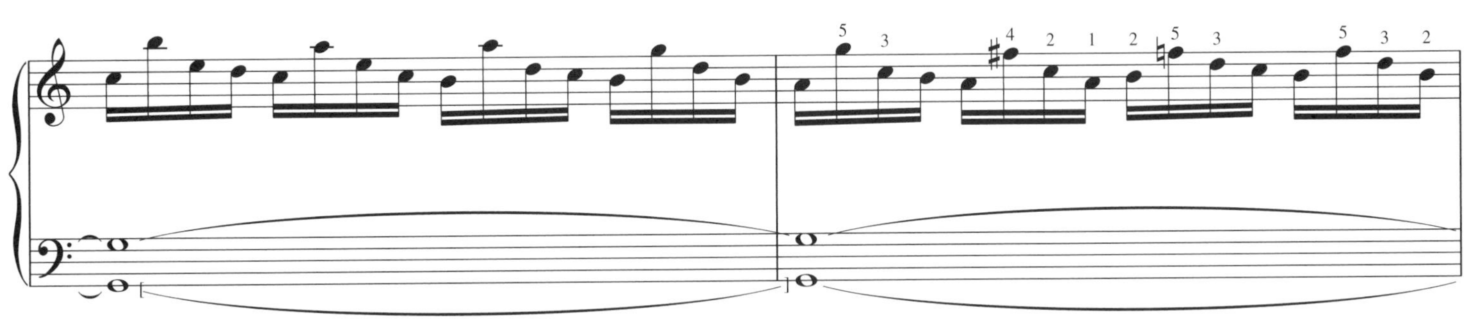

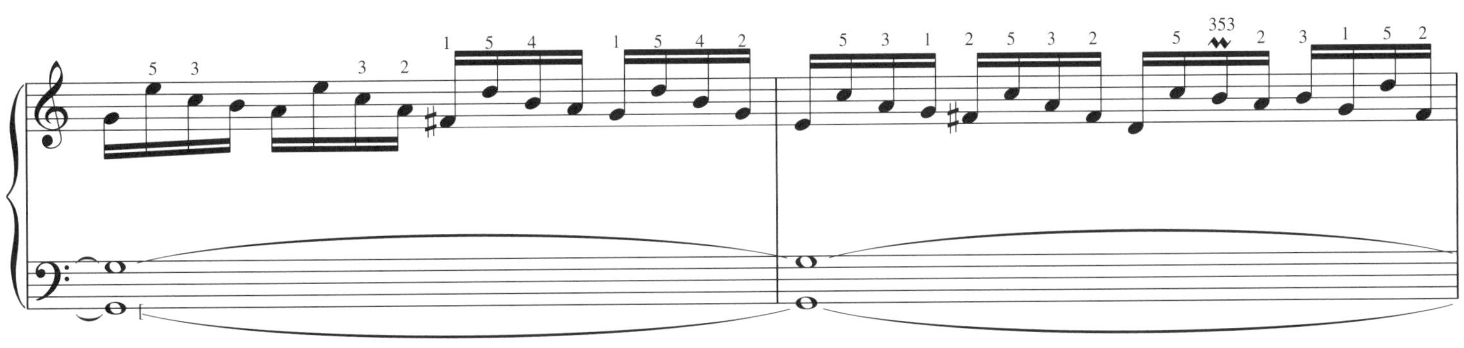

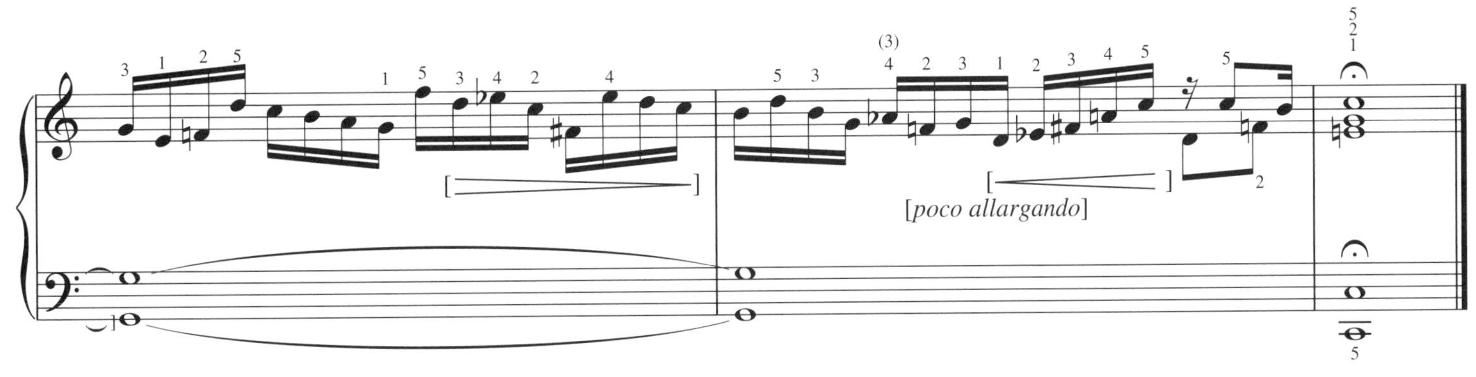
[poco allargando]

Prelude in C Major

BWV 939

Johann Sebastian Bach
1685–1750

Prelude in C minor

BWV 999

Johann Sebastian Bach
1685–1750

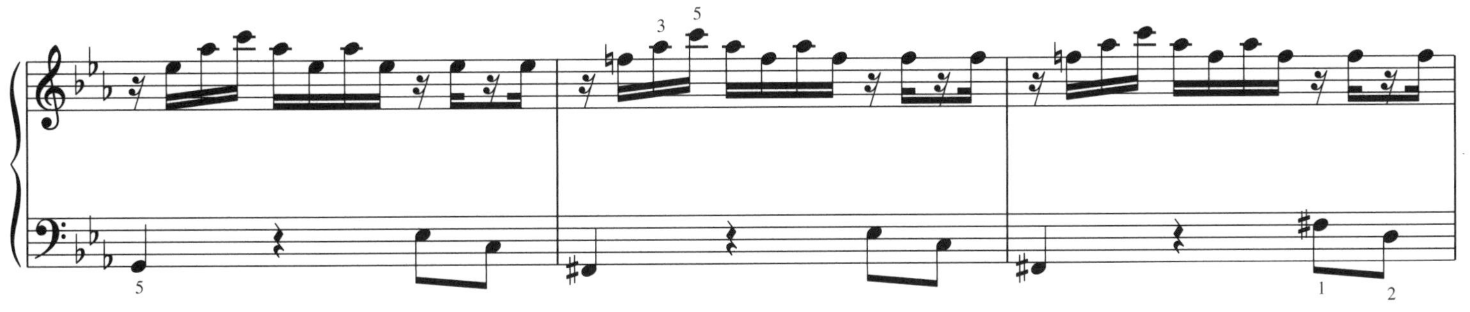

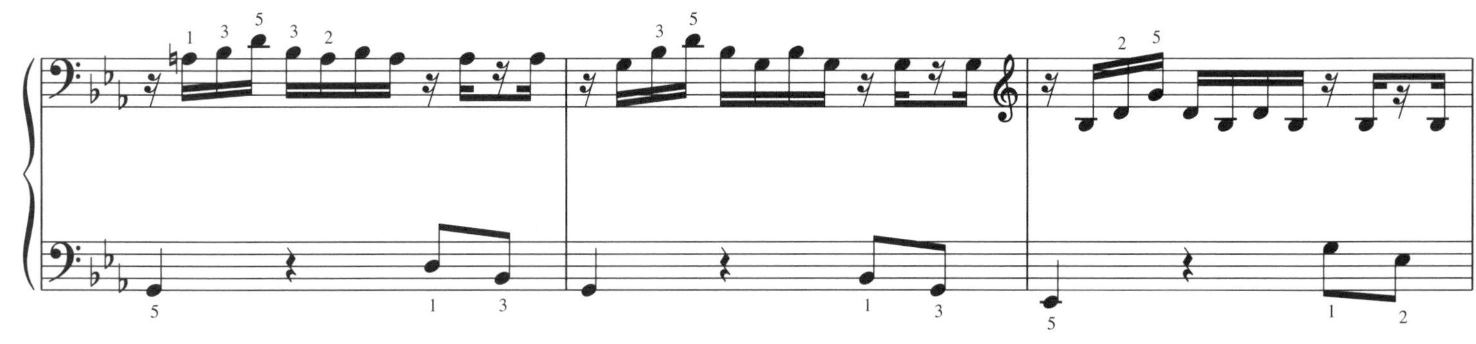

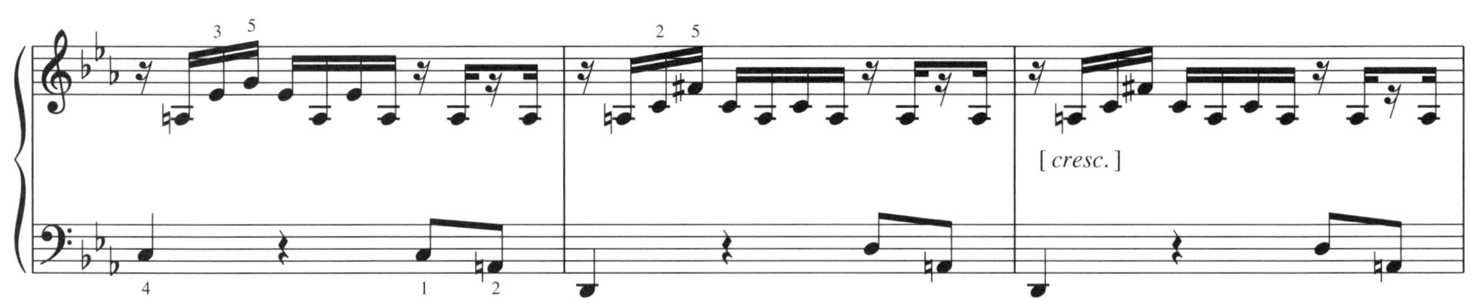
[cresc.]

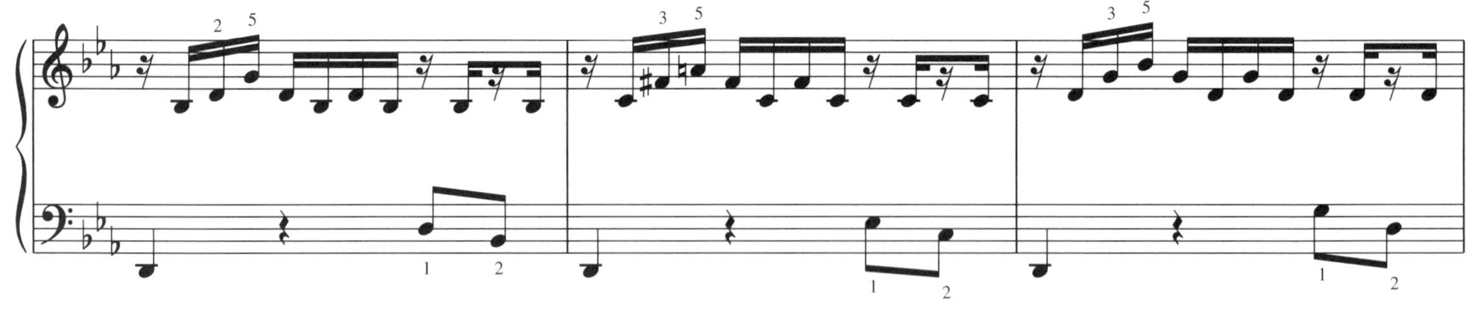

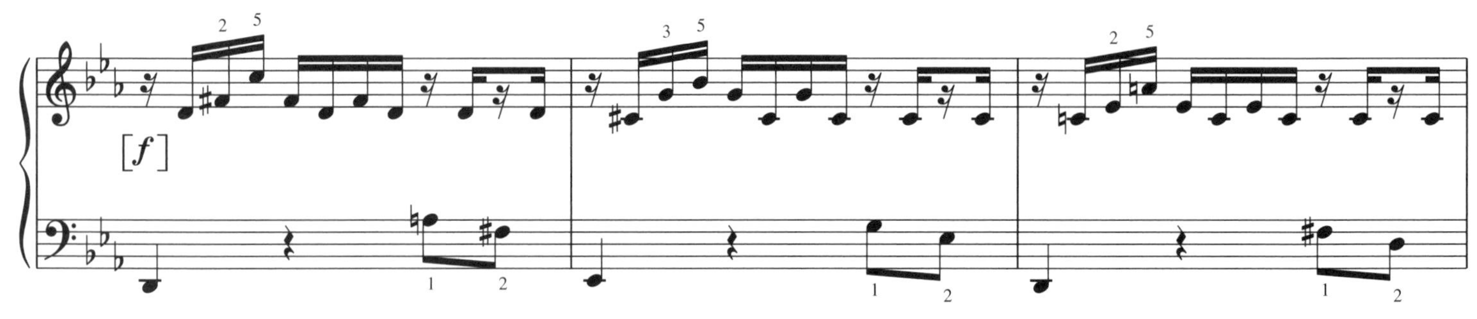
[f]

[decresc.]

[mp]

Allegro in A Major

Wilhelm Friedemann Bach
1710–1784

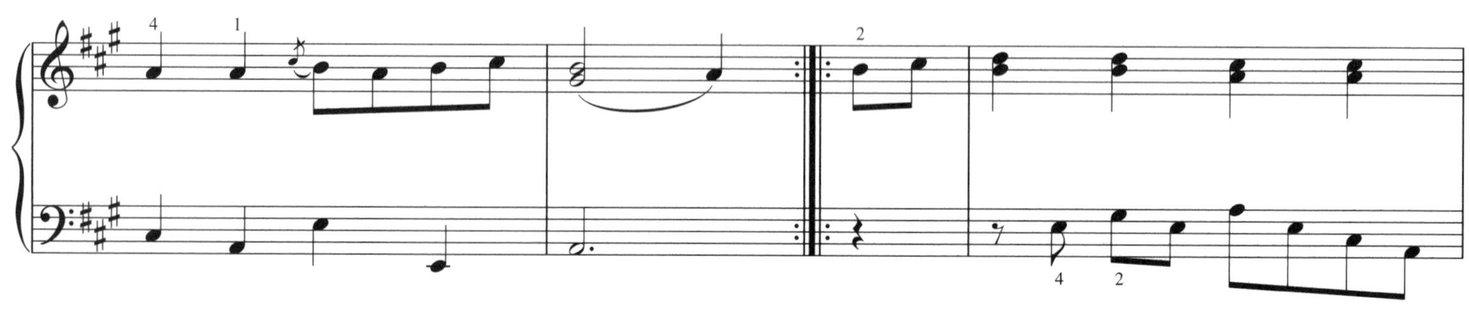

Fine

D.C. al Fine

Bagatelle in C Major

Op. 33, No. 2

Ludwig van Beethoven
1770–1827

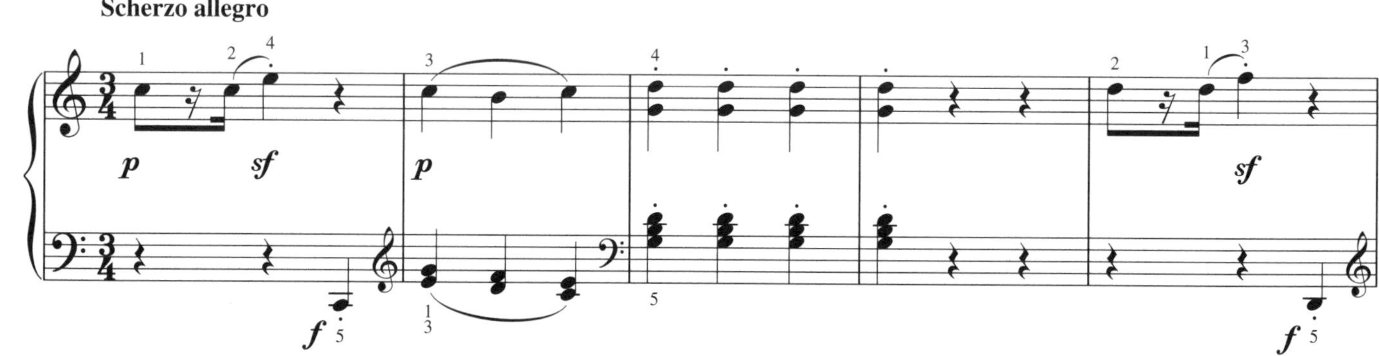

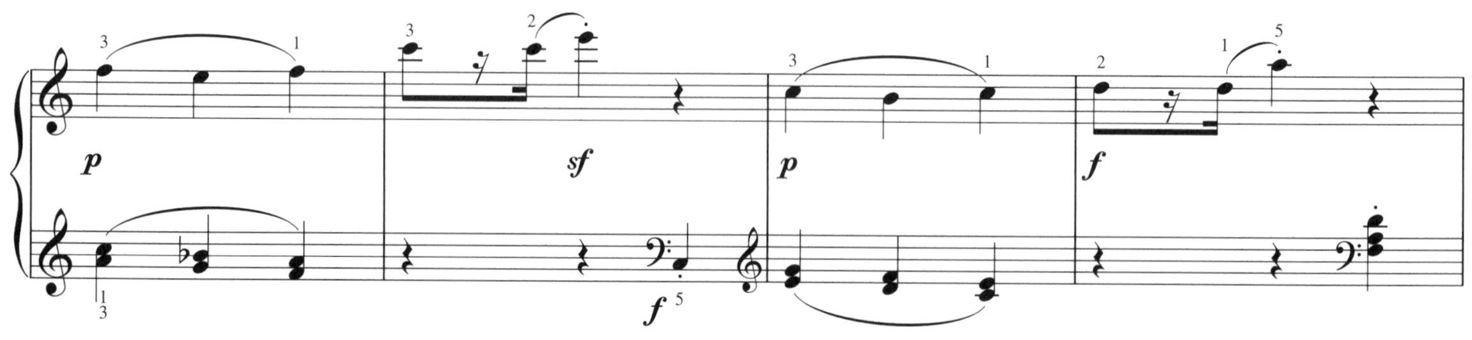

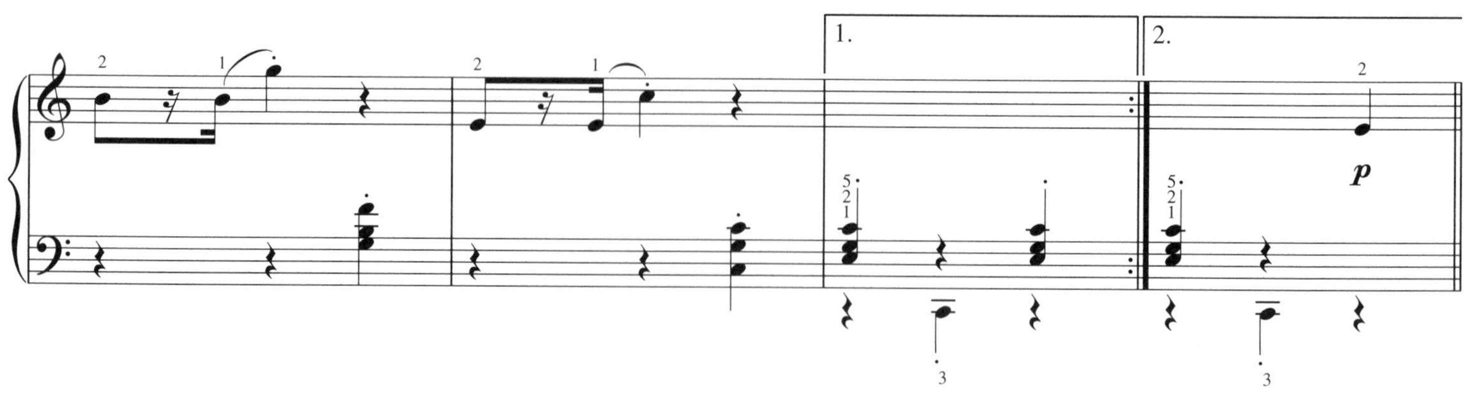

Minore
[pp]
cresc.
ff
p
cresc.
1.
p
2.
p
p
sf
p
f

51
TRIO
cresc.
(cresc.)

63
p
sf
68
sf
sf
cresc.
(cresc.)
sf
sf
sf
sf
sf
sf
1.
2.
p
sf
p
f
sf
p
f

sf
p
sf
p
f
f
p
sf
3
p
sf
p
f
sf
p
1
3
sf
p
1
2
1
5
f
2
1
5
f
2
1
sf
3
3
p
f

sf
p
f
cresc.
(cresc.)
decresc.

Bagatelle in F Major

Op. 33, No. 3

Ludwig van Beethoven
1770–1827

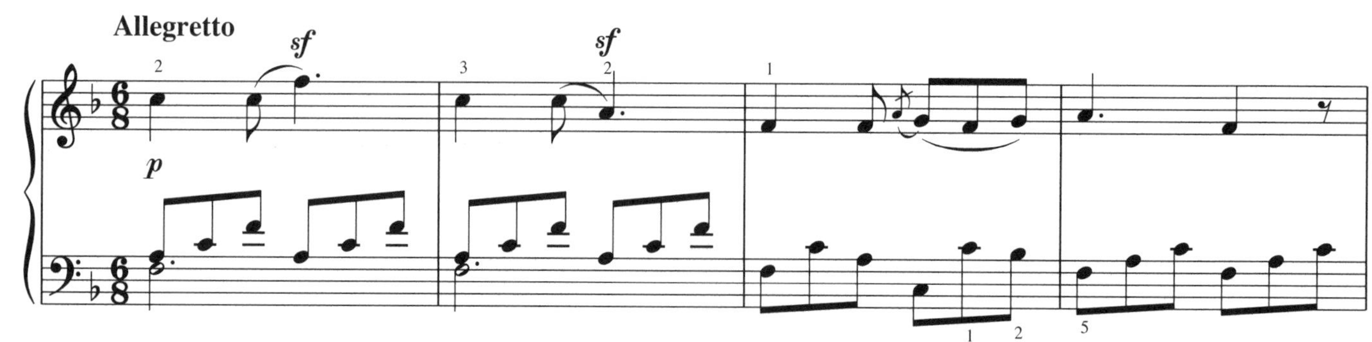

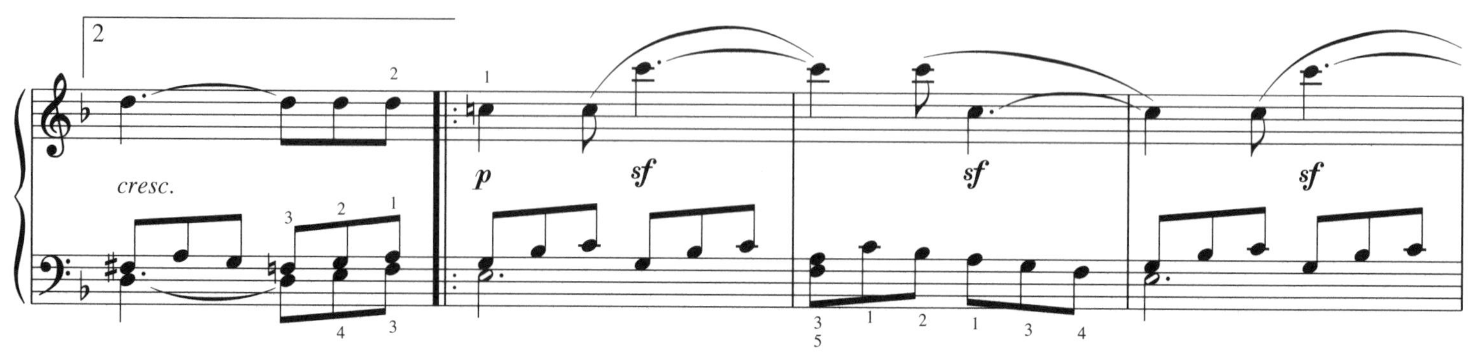

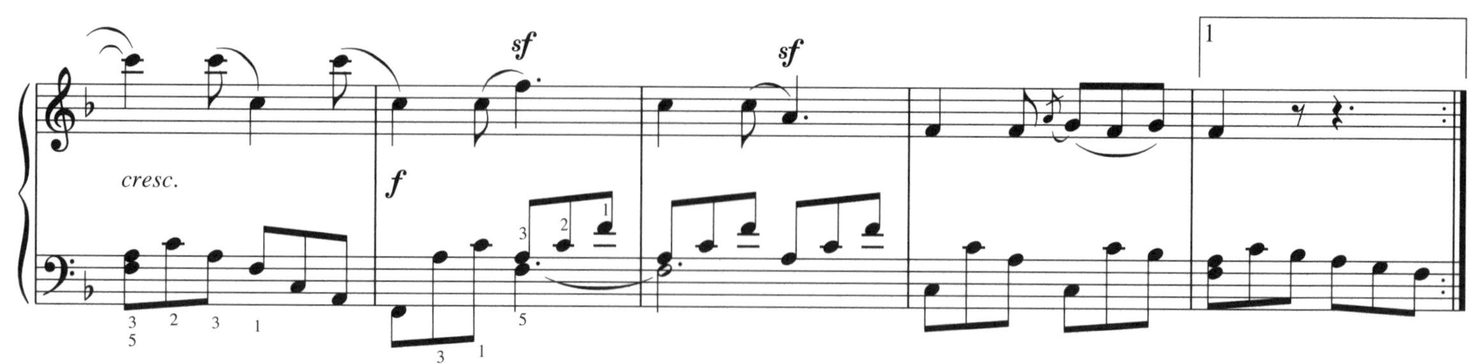

2
p
cresc.
f
ff
decresc.
p
sf
sf

pp
cresc.
sf
sf
p
pp
cresc.
p
sf
sf
sf
cresc.
sf
sf
f
p

p
sf
sf
cresc.
sf
sf
f
p
cresc.
f
ff

German Dance in C Major

WoO 8, No. 1

Ludwig van Beethoven
1770–1827

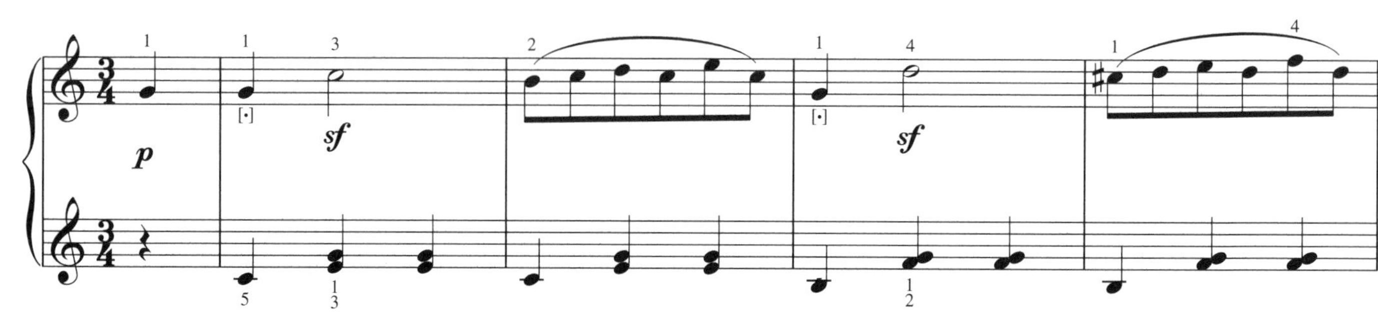

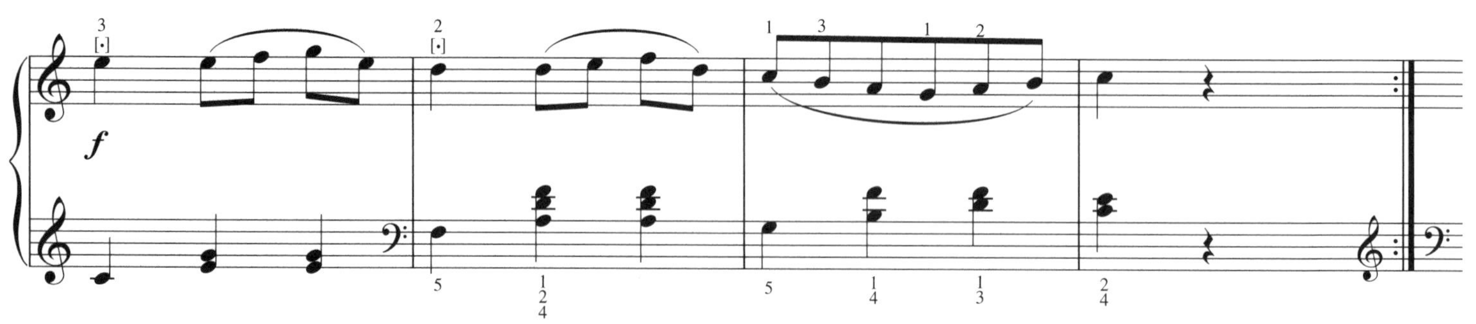

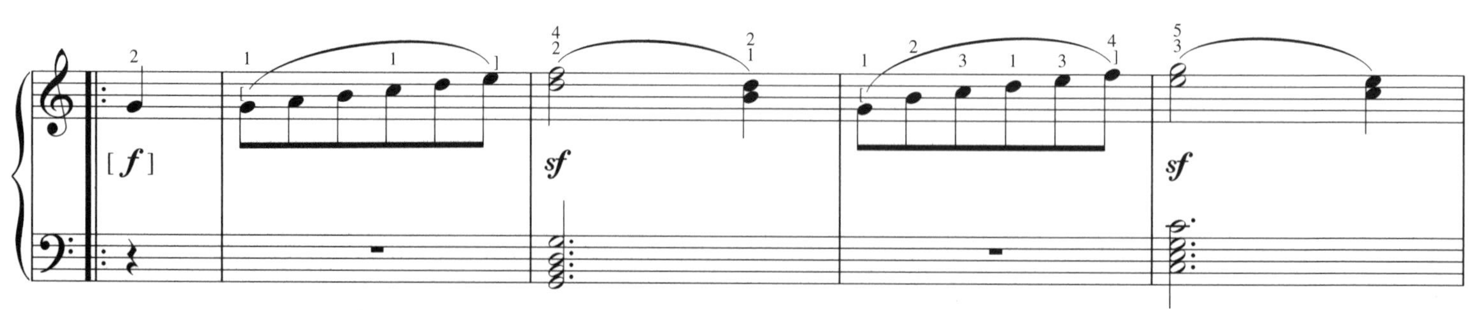

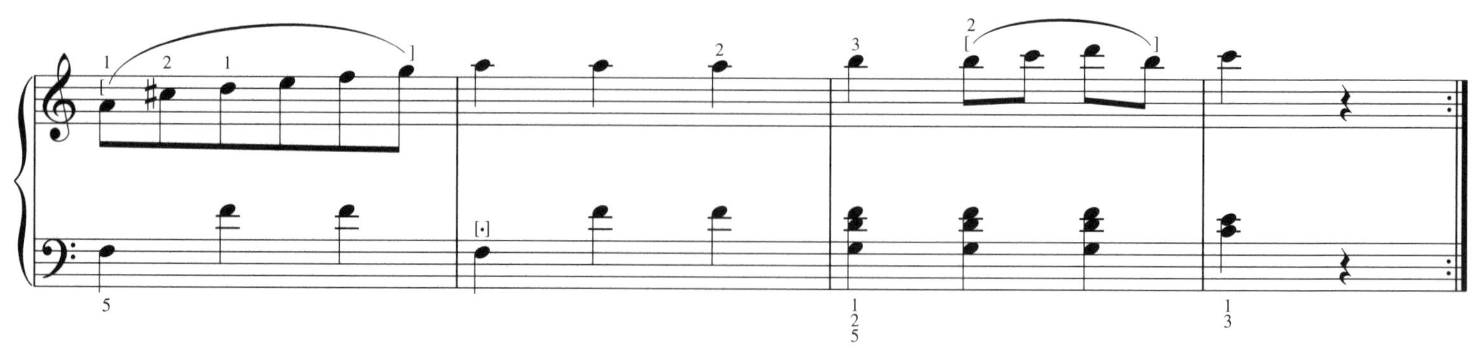

Minuet in G Major

WoO 10, No. 2

Ludwig van Beethoven
1770–1827

TRIO
p
p
mf
mf
p

p
mf
mf
f

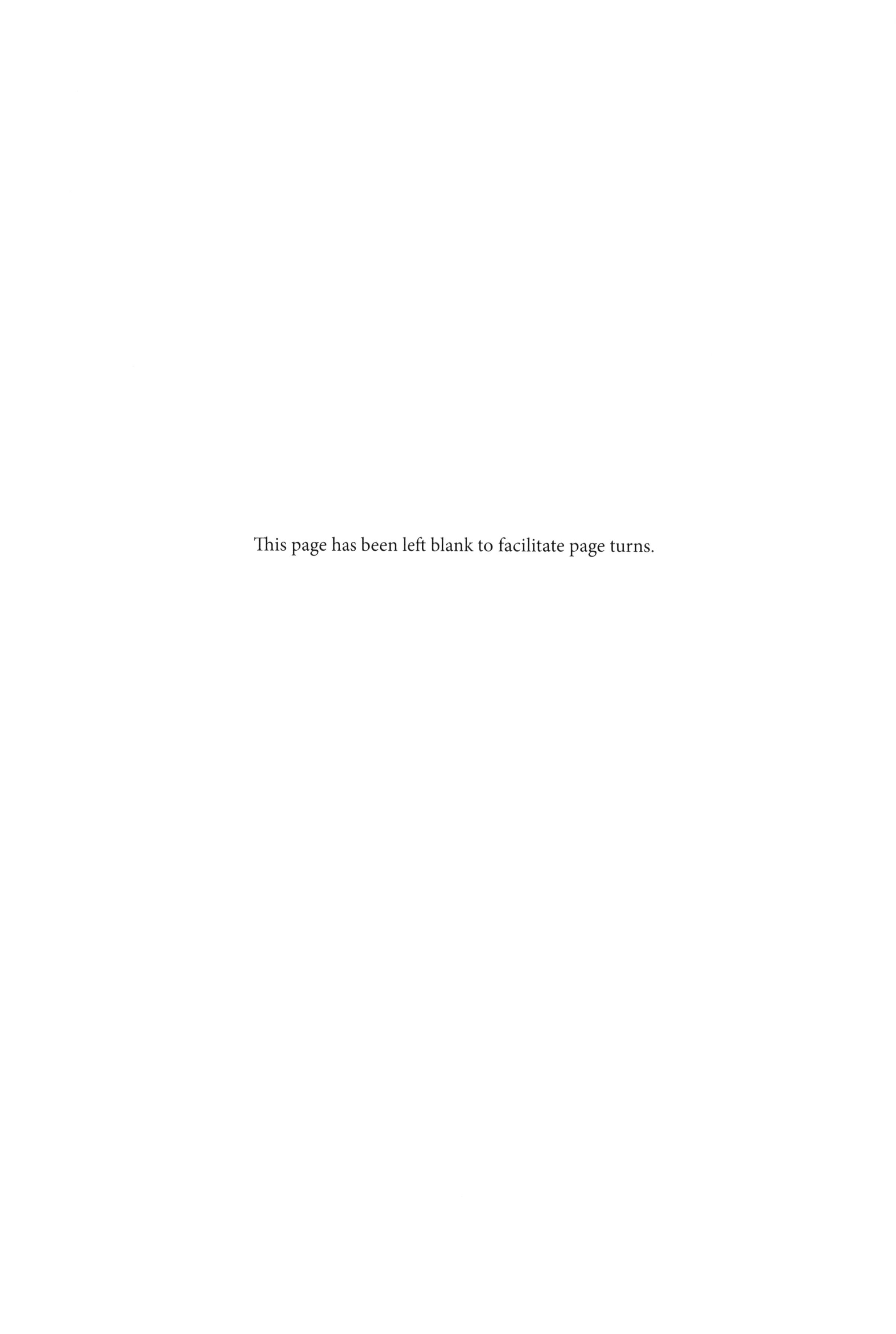

This page has been left blank to facilitate page turns.

Ländler in D Major

WoO 11, No. 4

Ludwig van Beethoven
1770–1827

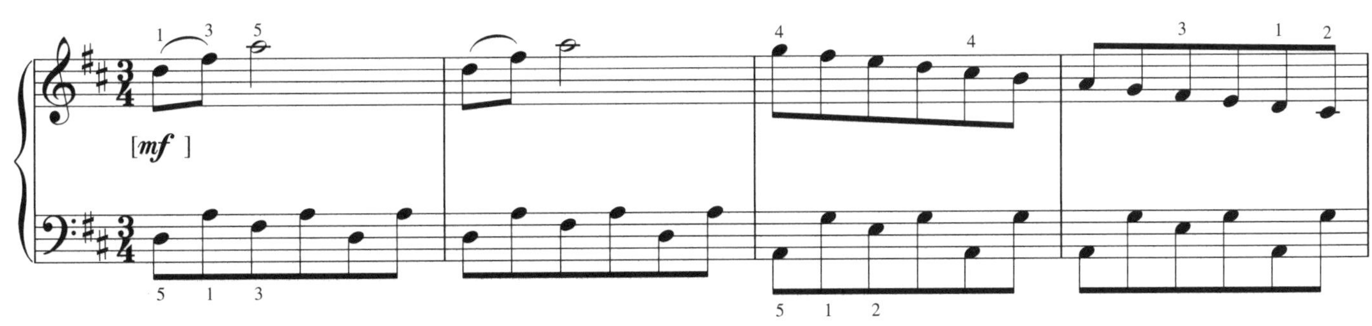

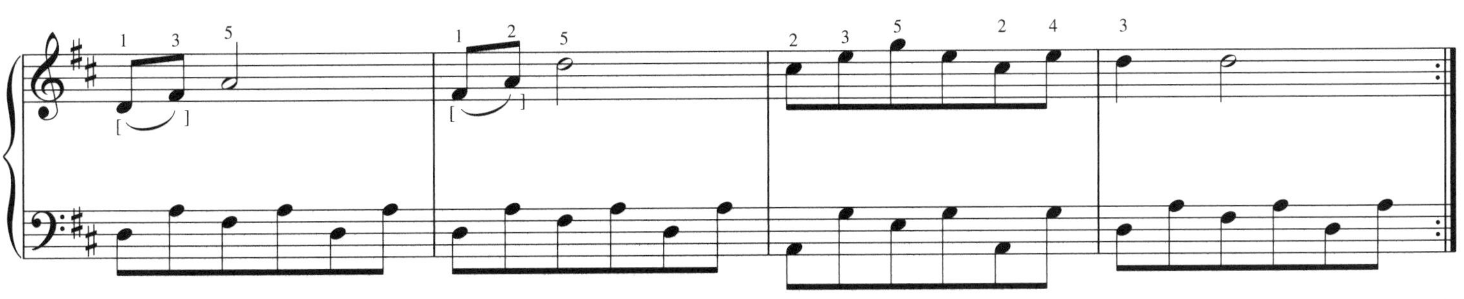

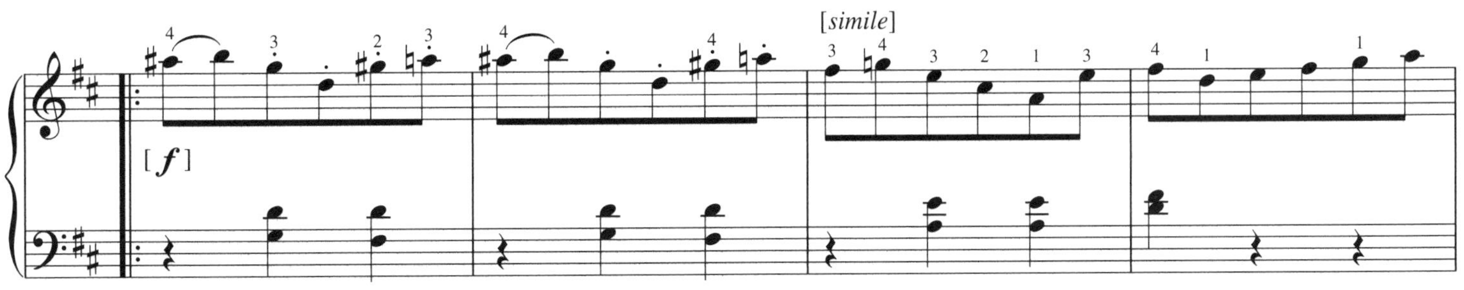

Ländler in D Major

WoO 11, No. 7

Ludwig van Beethoven
1770–1827

[simile]
sf
[sf]
tr

German Dance in B-flat Major

WoO 13, No. 2

Ludwig van Beethoven
1770–1827

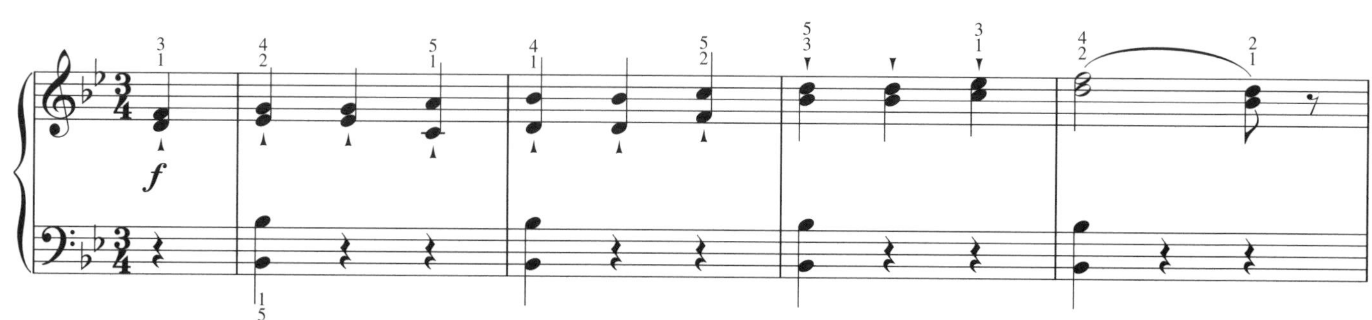

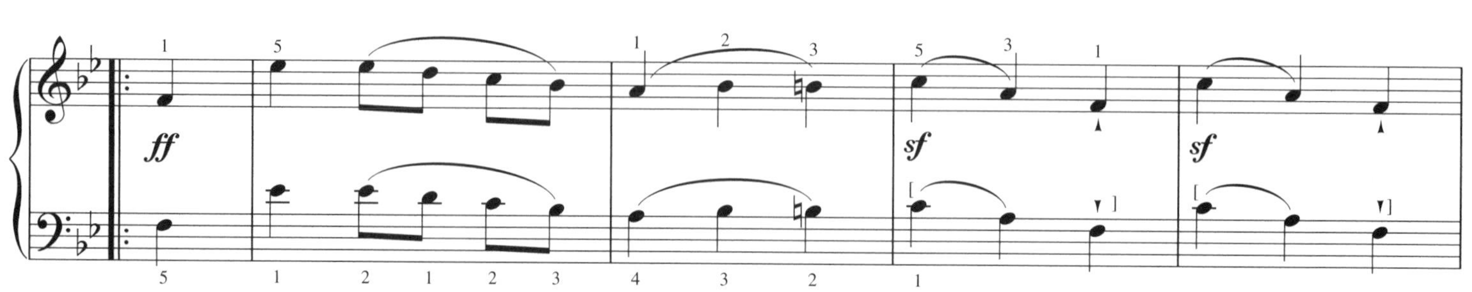

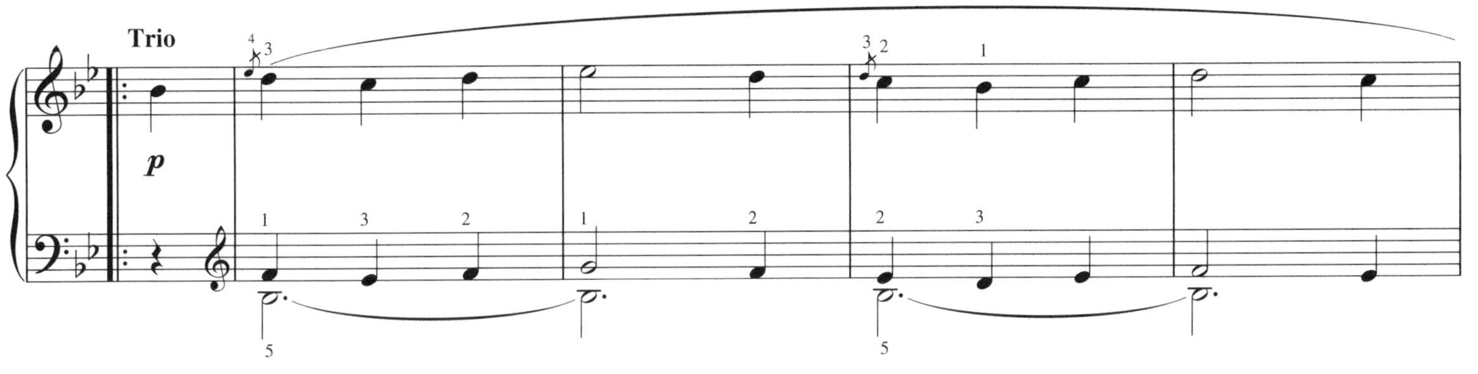
Trio
p

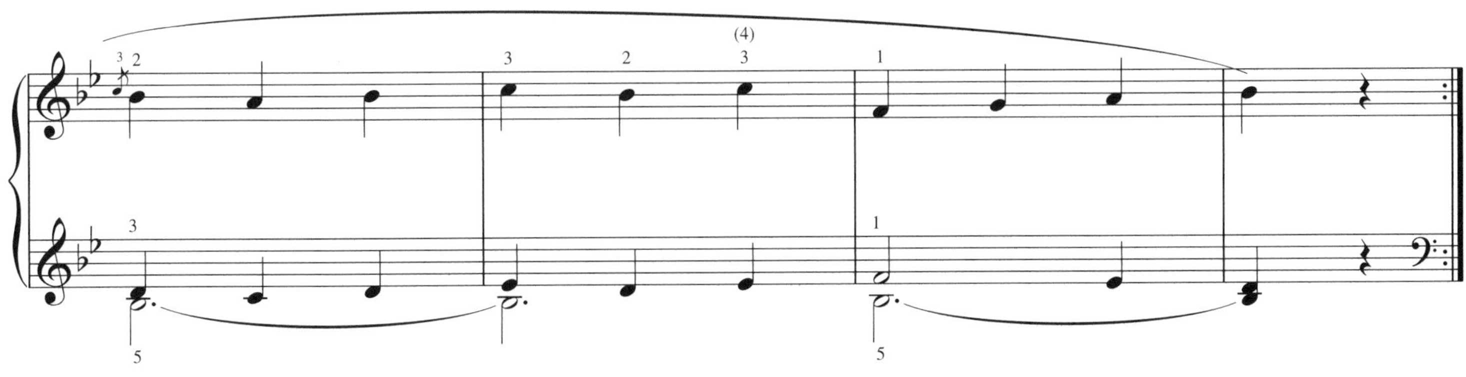

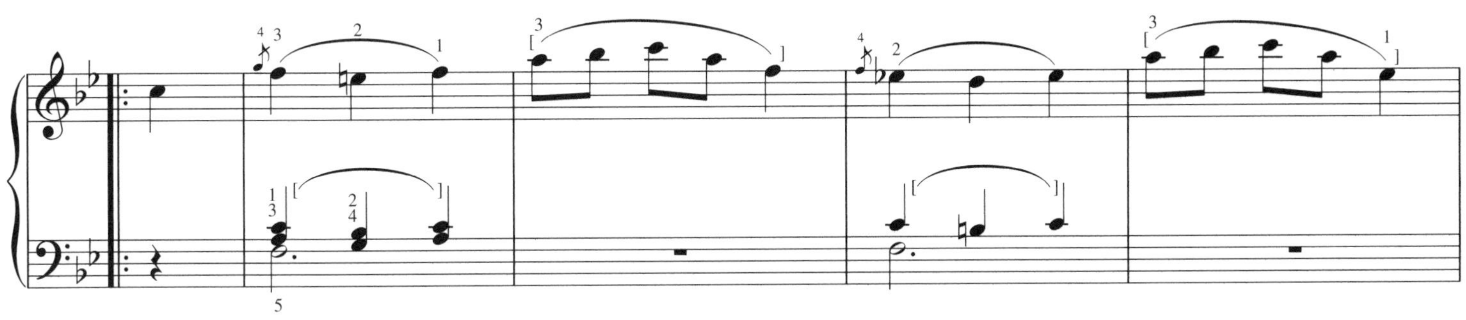

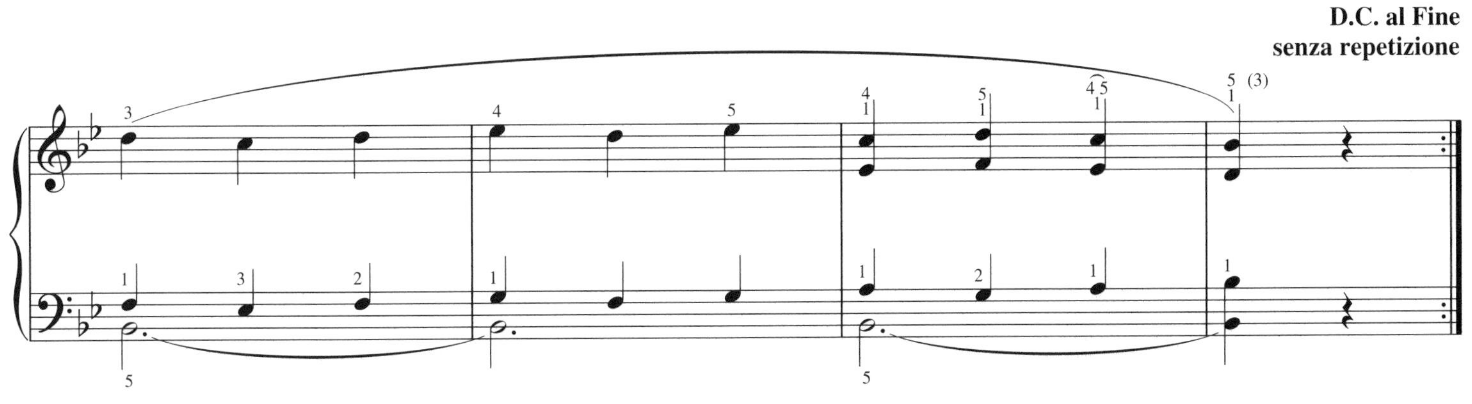
D.C. al Fine
senza repetizione

Six Country Dances

WoO 15

Ludwig van Beethoven
1770–1827

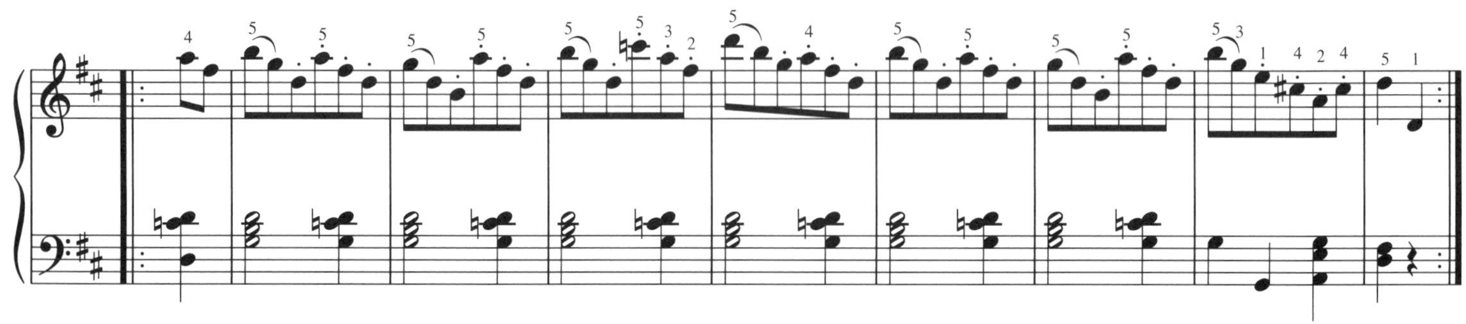

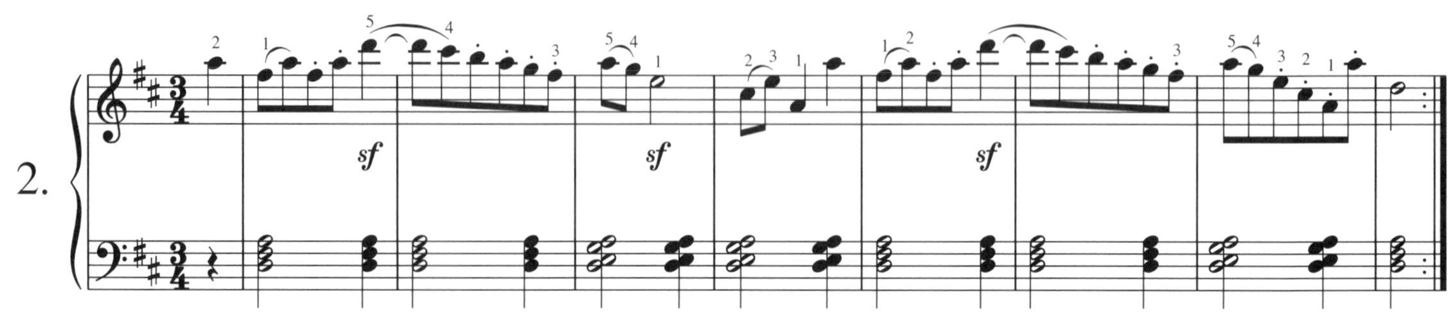

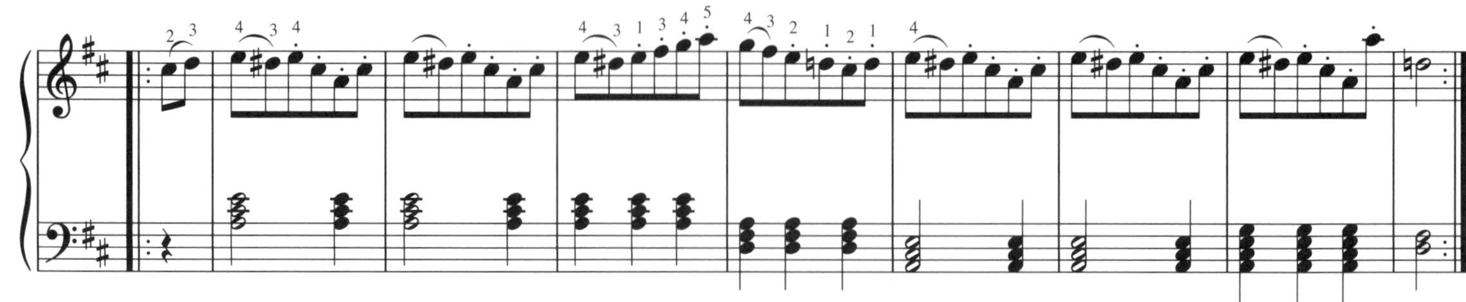

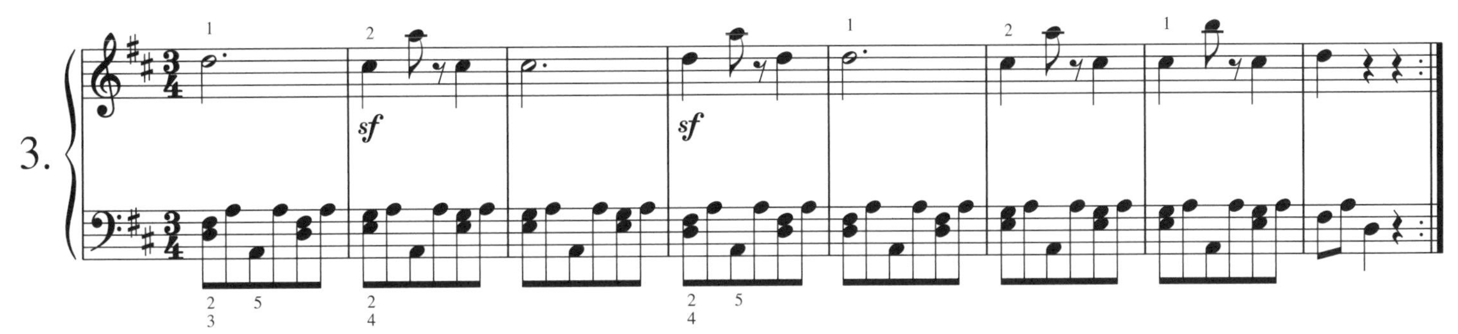
3.
sf
sf

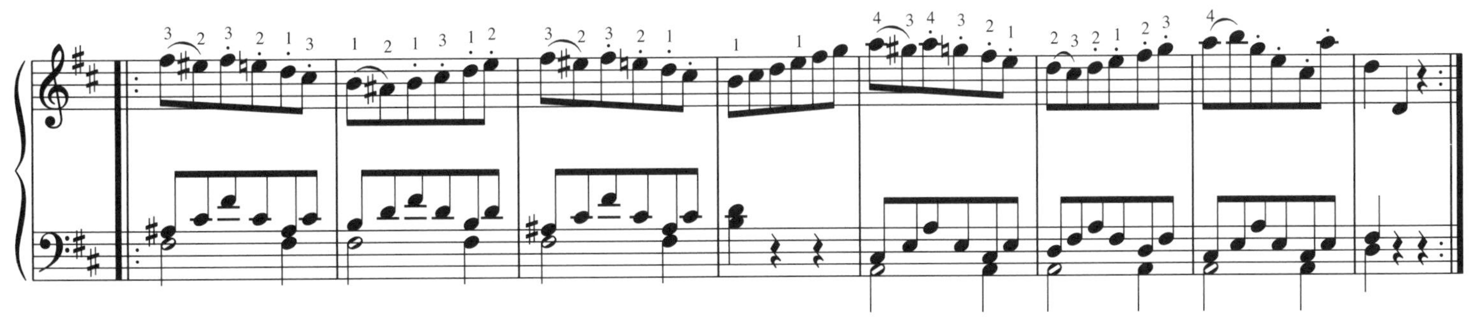

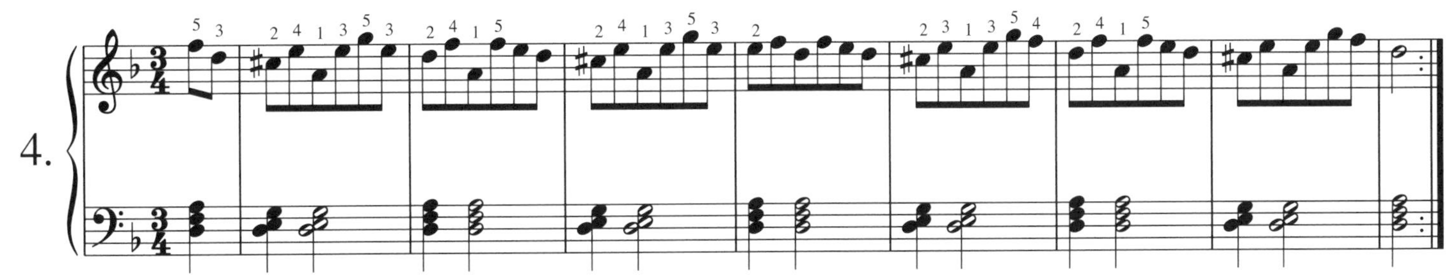
4.

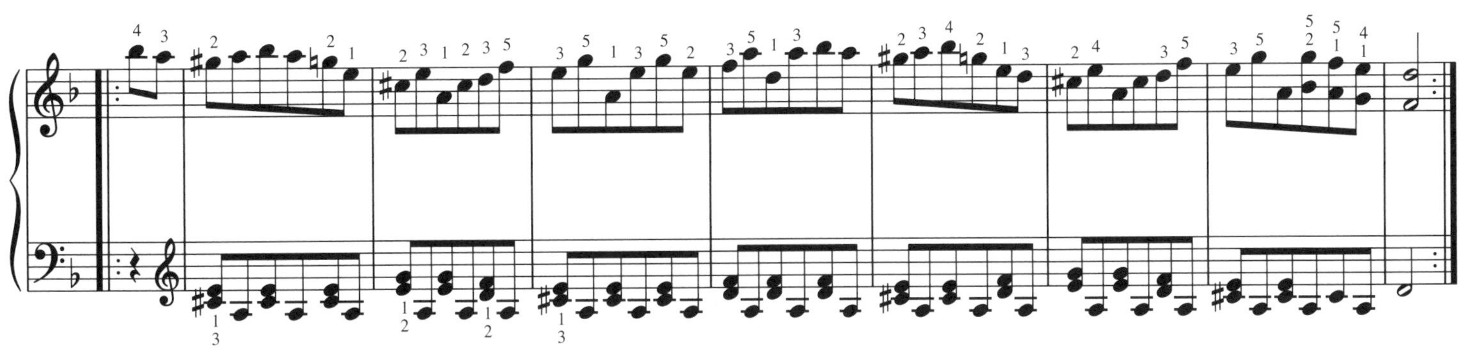

5.
sf
sf
sf
sf
sf
sf
sf
sf
sf
sf

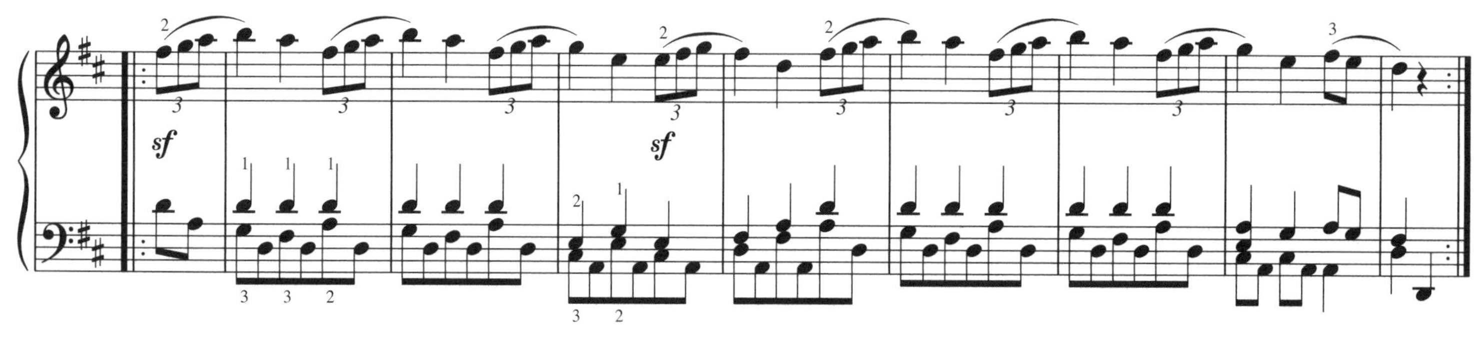
sf
sf

6.

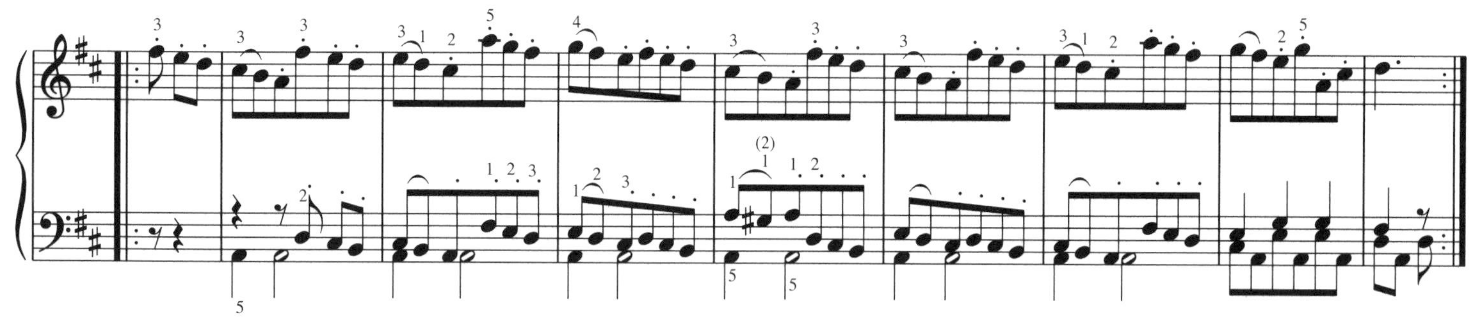

CODA

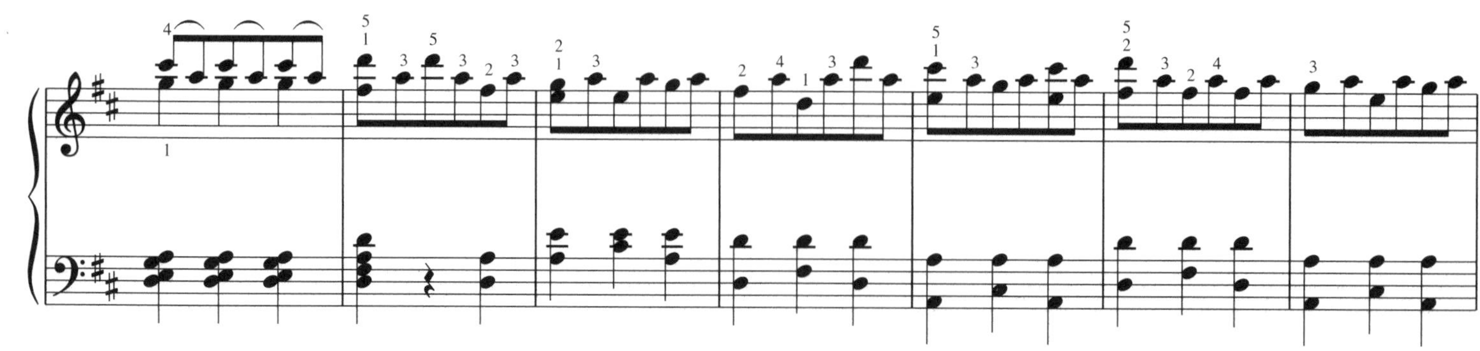

sf
sf
sf
sf
sf
sf
f

Contredance in C Major

WoO 14, No. 1

Ludwig van Beethoven
1770–1827

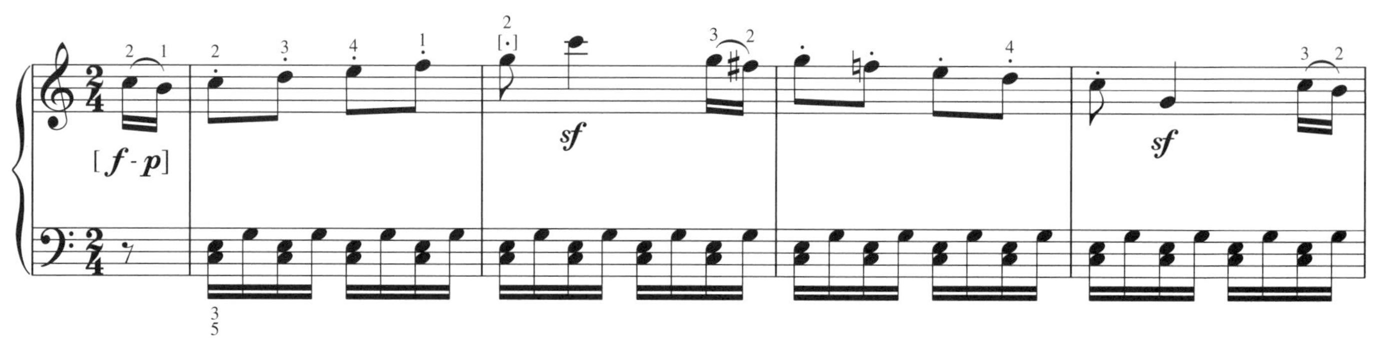

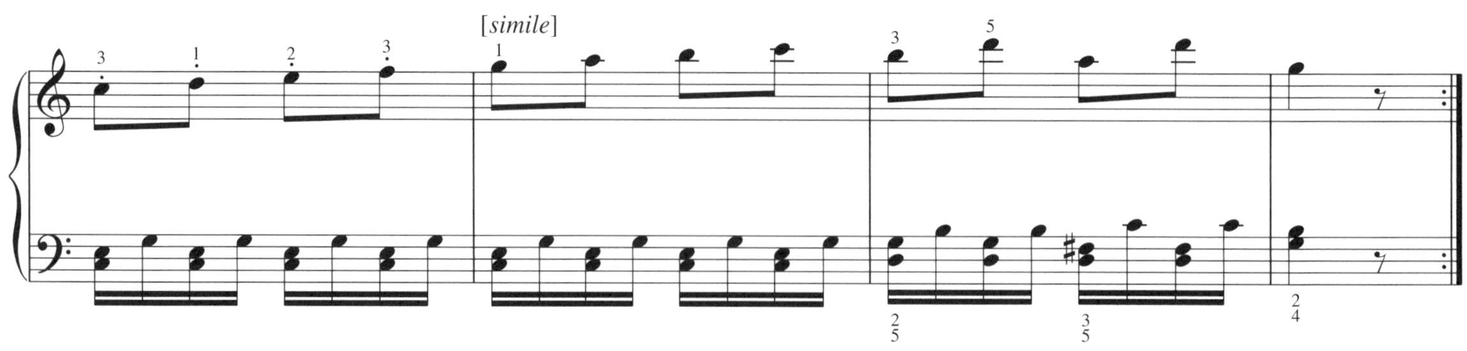

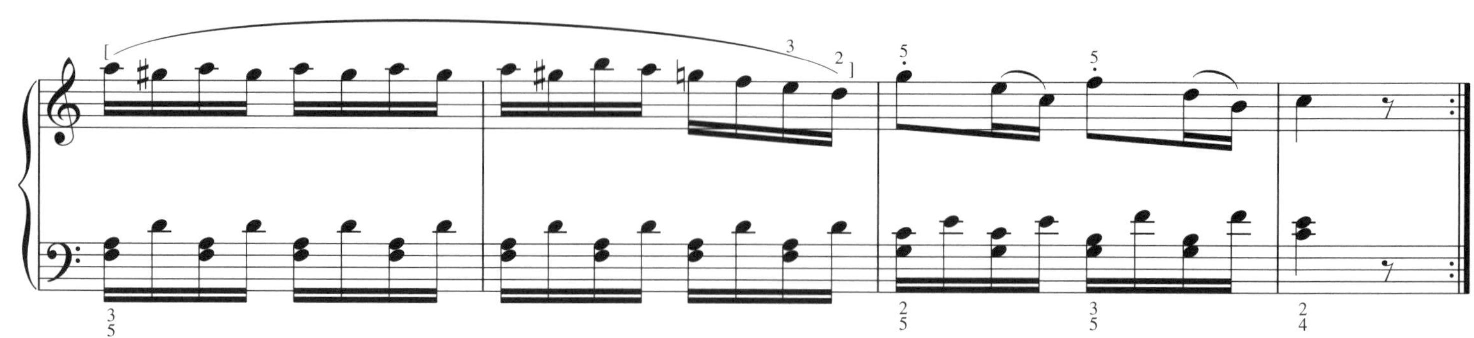

Ecossaise in G Major

WoO 23

Ludwig van Beethoven
1770–1827

Ecossaise in E-flat Major

WoO 83

Ludwig van Beethoven
1770–1827

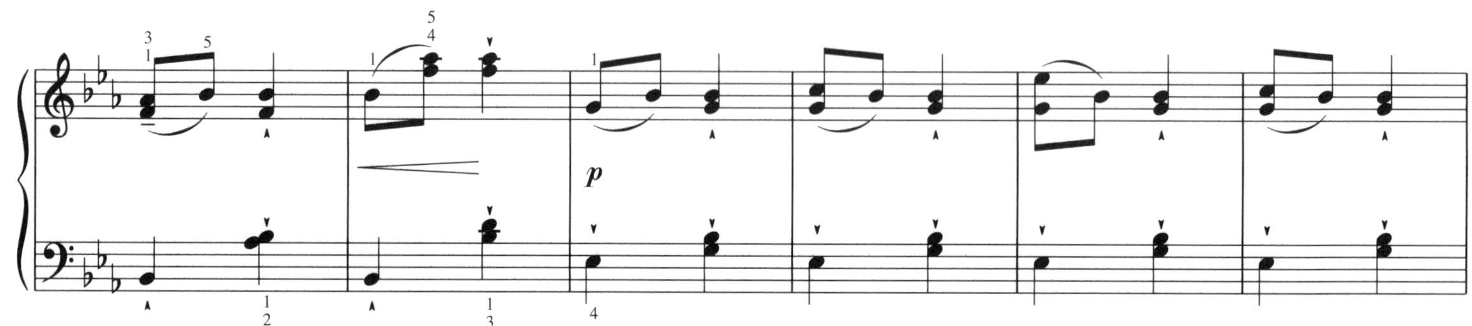

dim.
p
p
f

mp
dim.
p
f
Ped.
p
f
p
allarg.
p a tempo

espressivo
p
Ped.
p
p
poco a poco accel.
Tempo I
mf risoluto

fz
p con grazia
mf
p
leggero
p
mf
p
p
poco rit.
a tempo
cresc. molto
f
p subito
dim.

pp
mf
fz
fz
mf
f
fz
fz
molto cresc.
mf
fz
fz
rit.
fz
fz
fz
fz
a tempo

Sonatina in G Major

Anh. 5, No. 1

Ludwig van Beethoven
1770–1827

Moderato

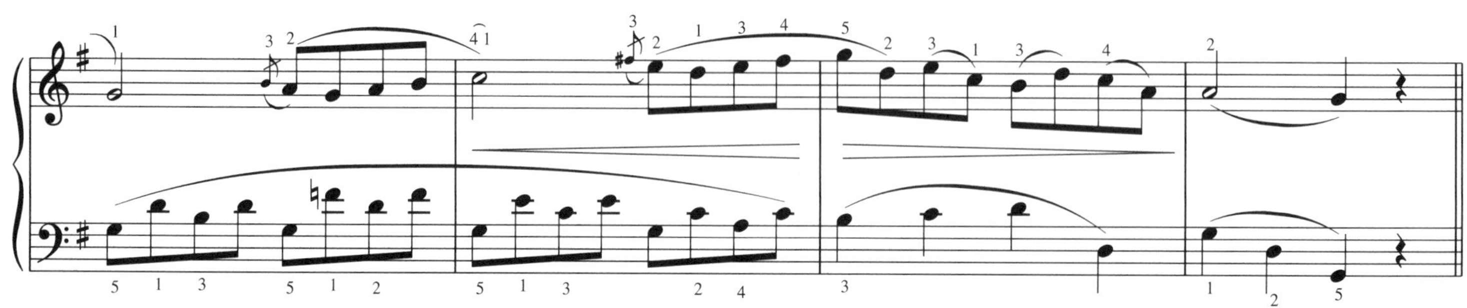

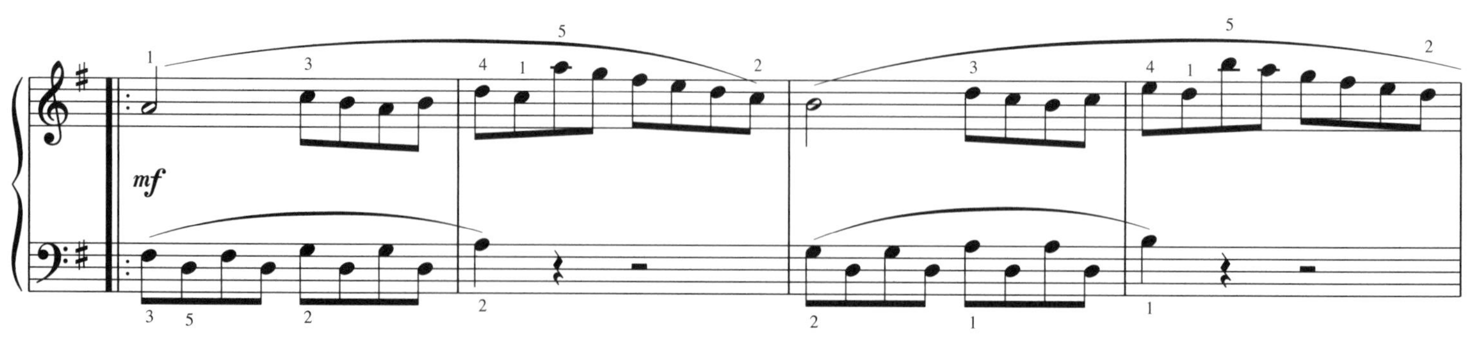

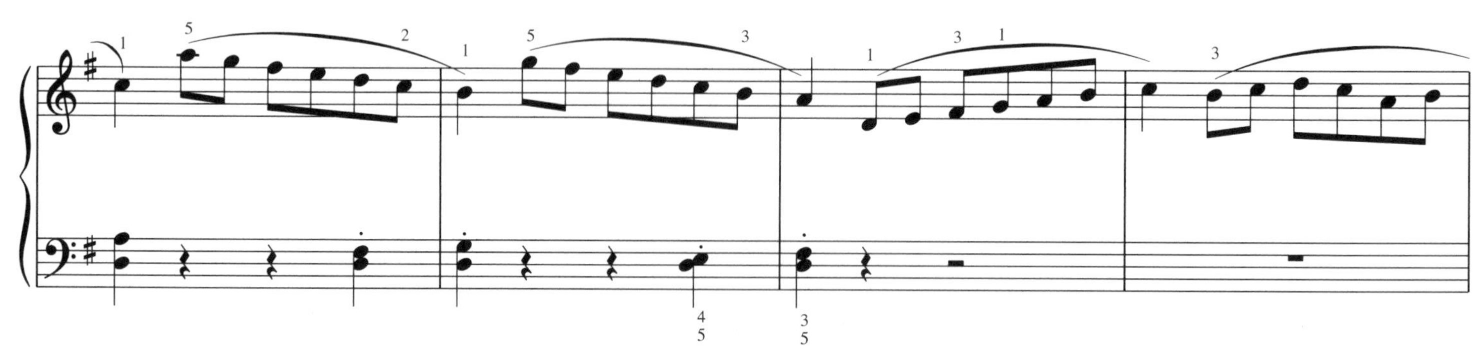

dolce

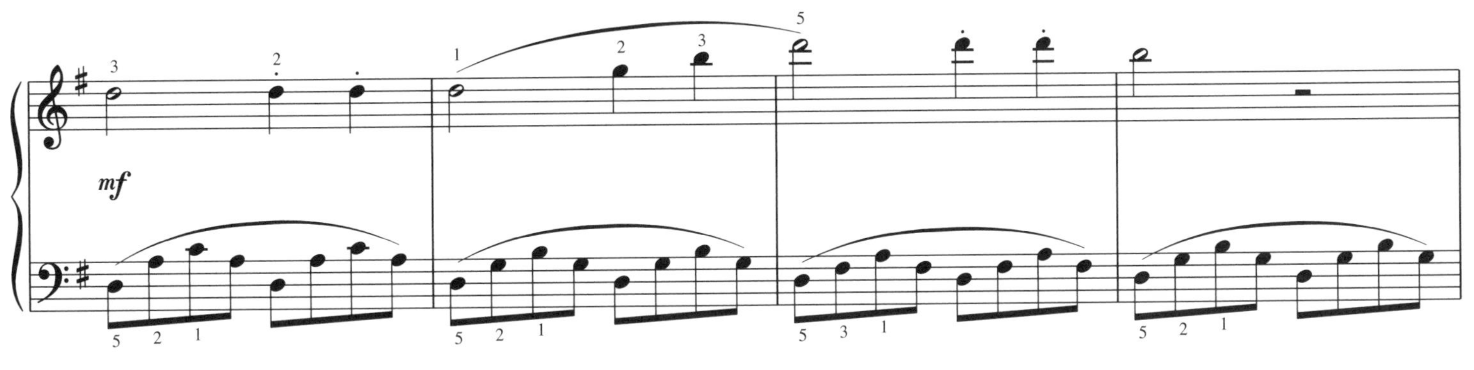
mf

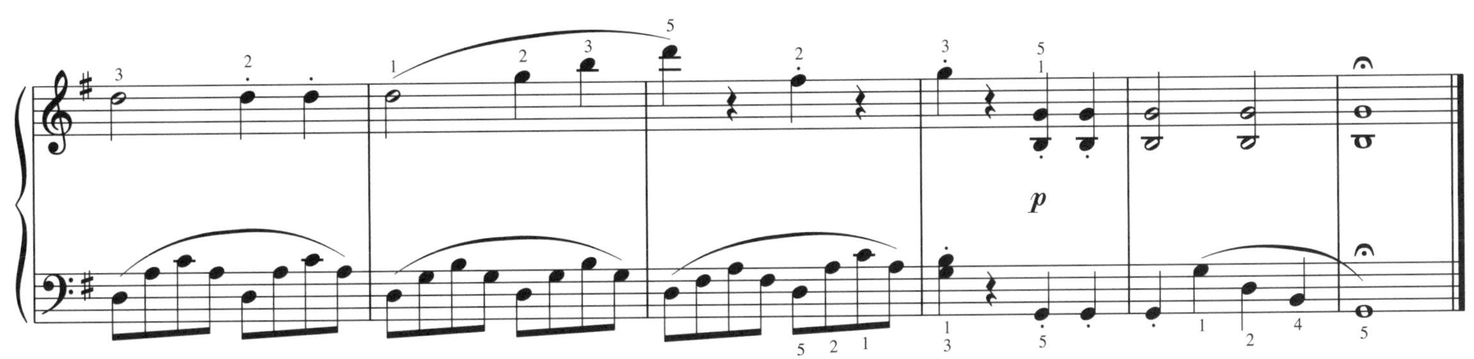
p

Romanza

Allegretto

a tempo
dim. e rit.
p
p
cresc.
f
p

Ecossaise in E-flat Major
WoO 86

Ludwig van Beethoven
1770–1827

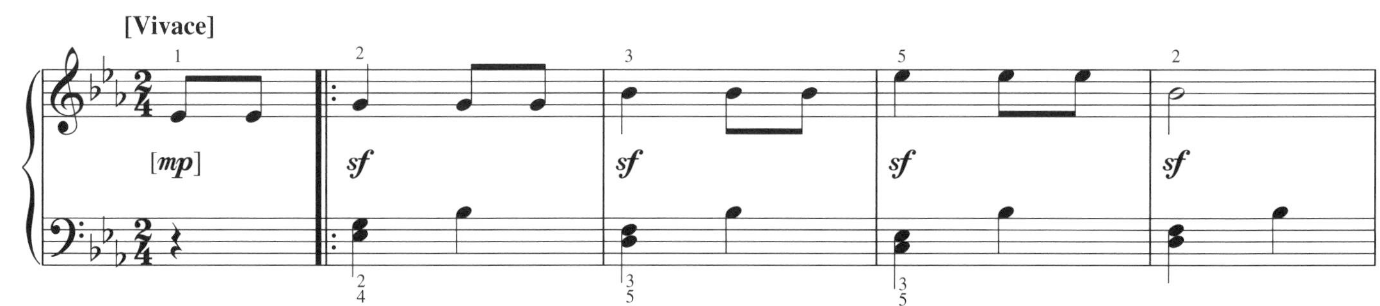

Sonatina in F Major

Anh. 5, No. 2

Ludwig van Beethoven
1770–1827

p
f

dim.
p
dolce

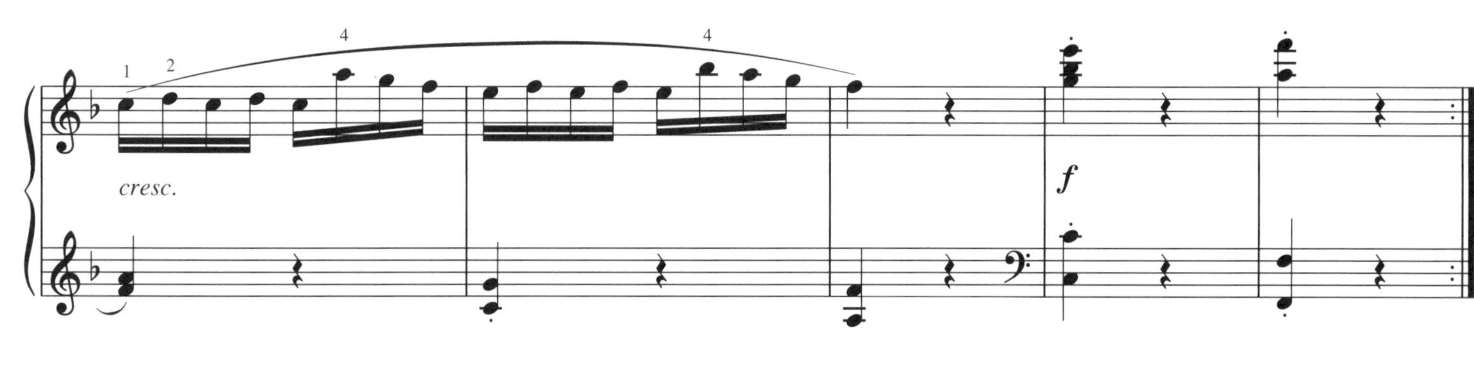

Rondo

Allegro

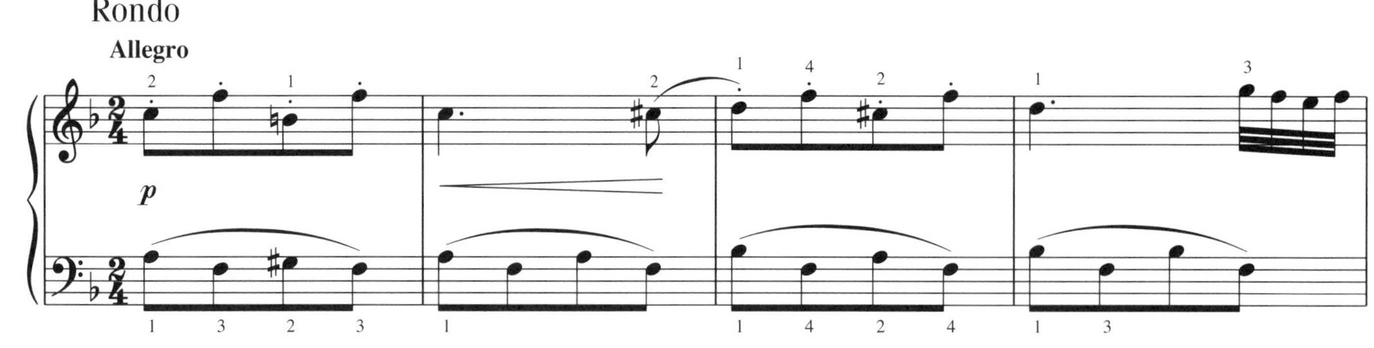

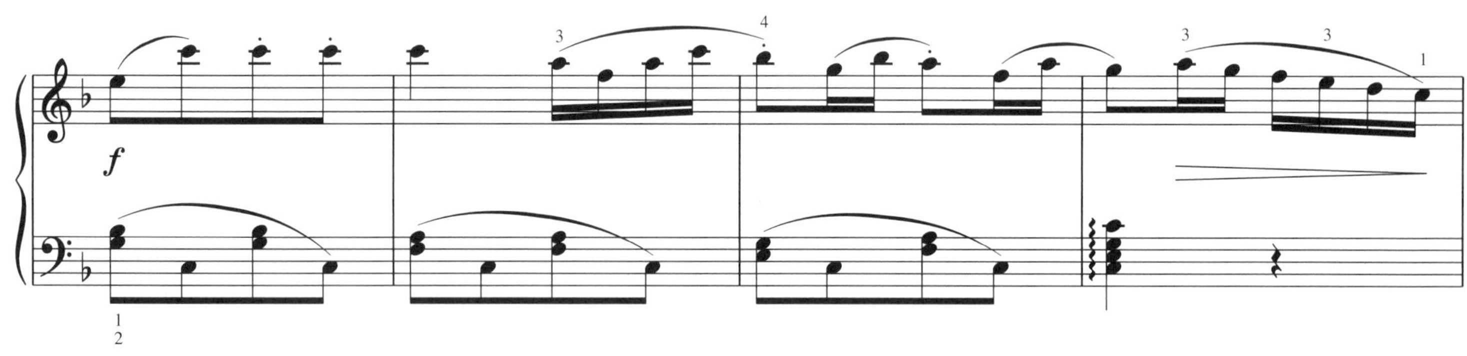

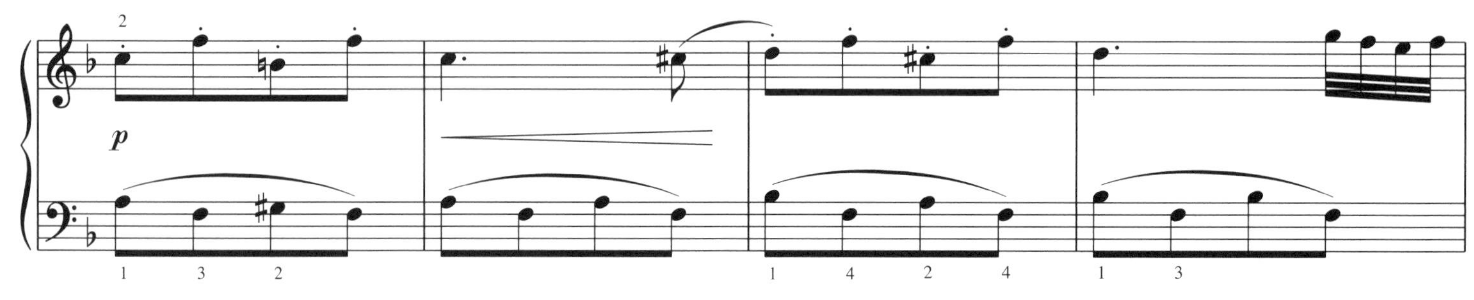

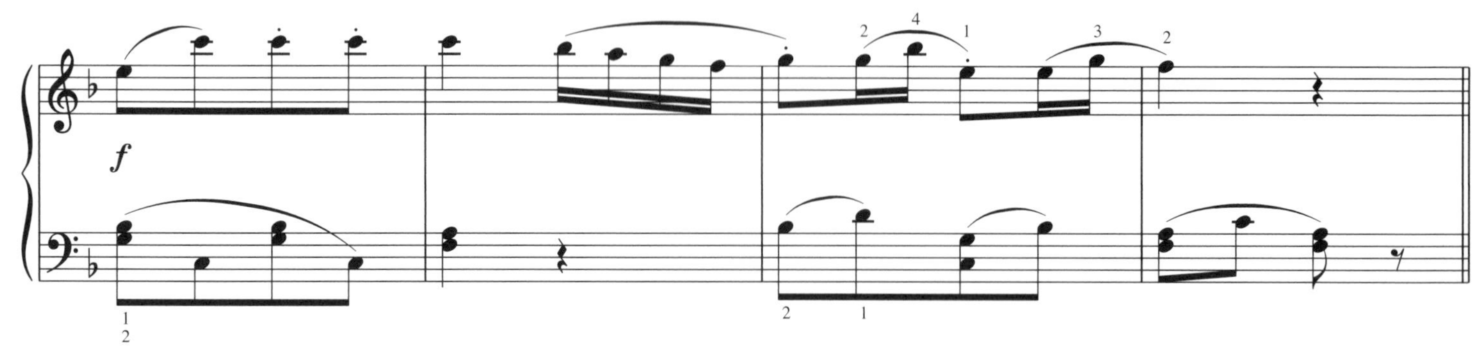

f

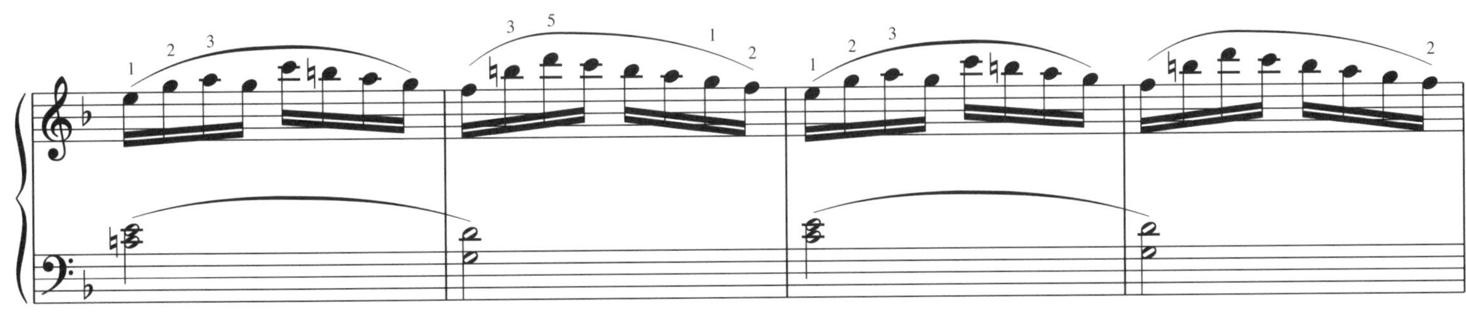

dim.

p

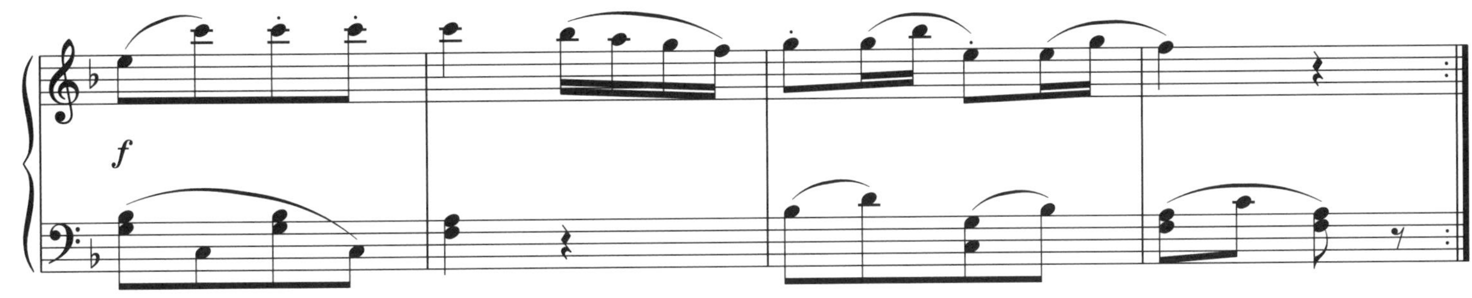
f

p
mf
p

freely
cresc.
a tempo
p
mf
p
mf
p
f

Courante in C Major

John Blow
c. 1648–1708

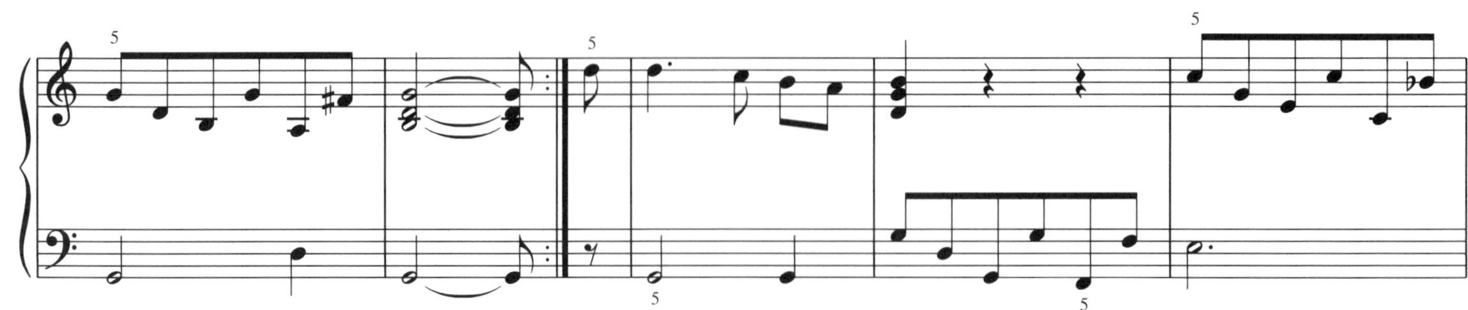

Prelude in C Major

John Blow
c. 1648–1708

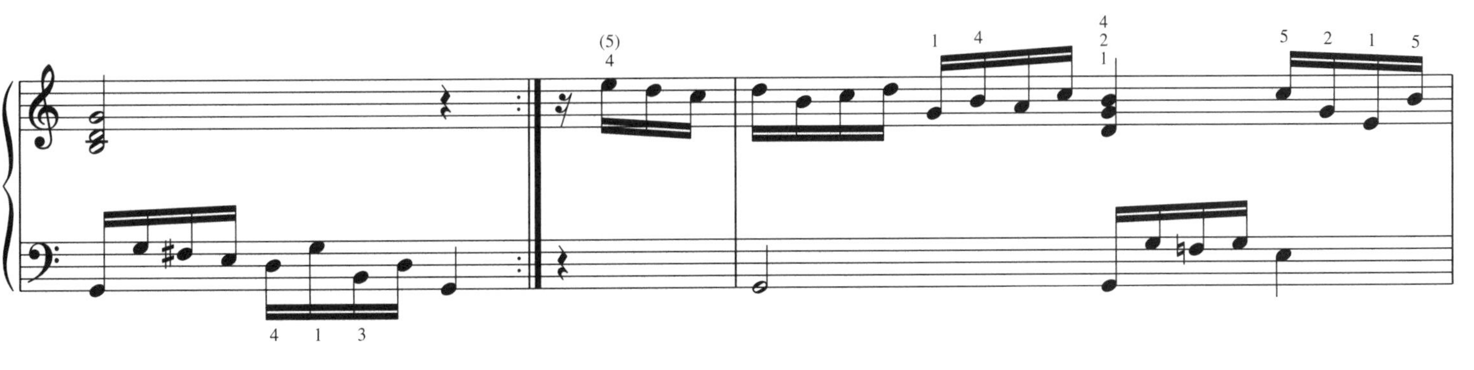
(5)

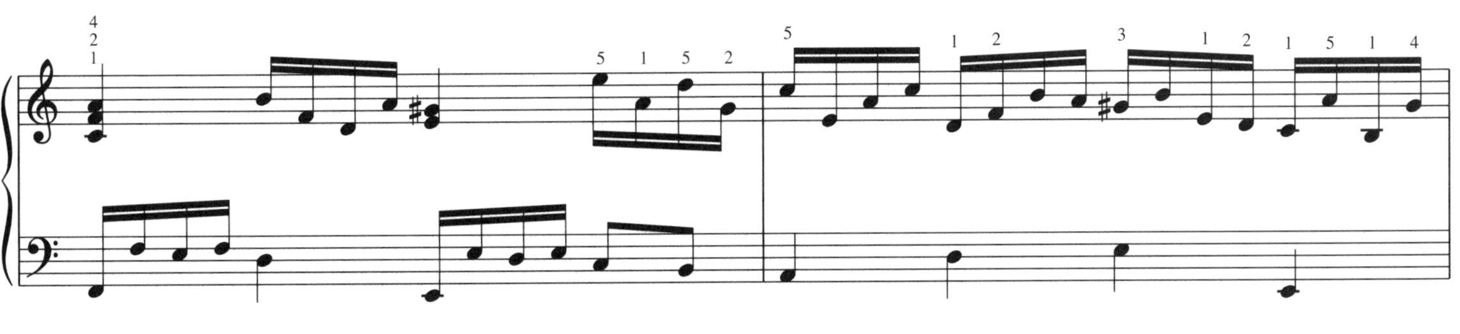

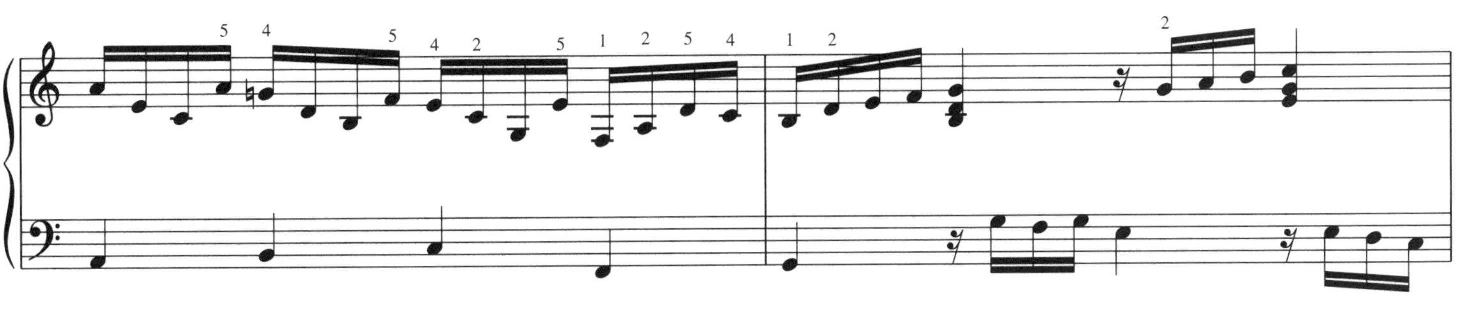

Sincerity

from *25 Progressive Studies,* Op. 100, No. 1

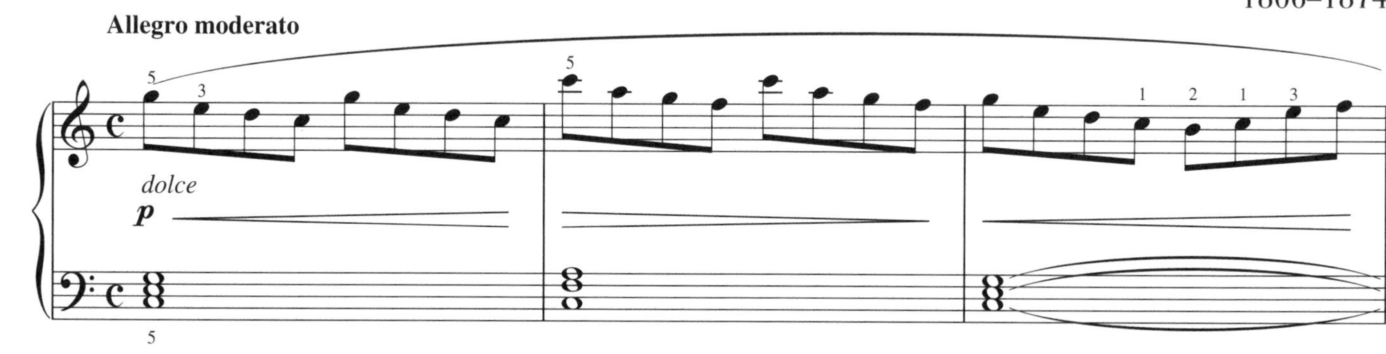

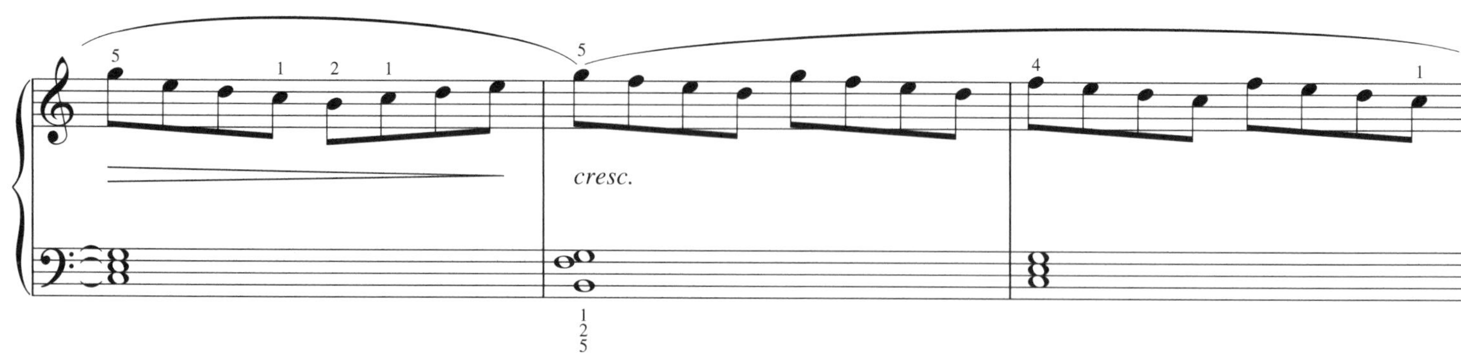

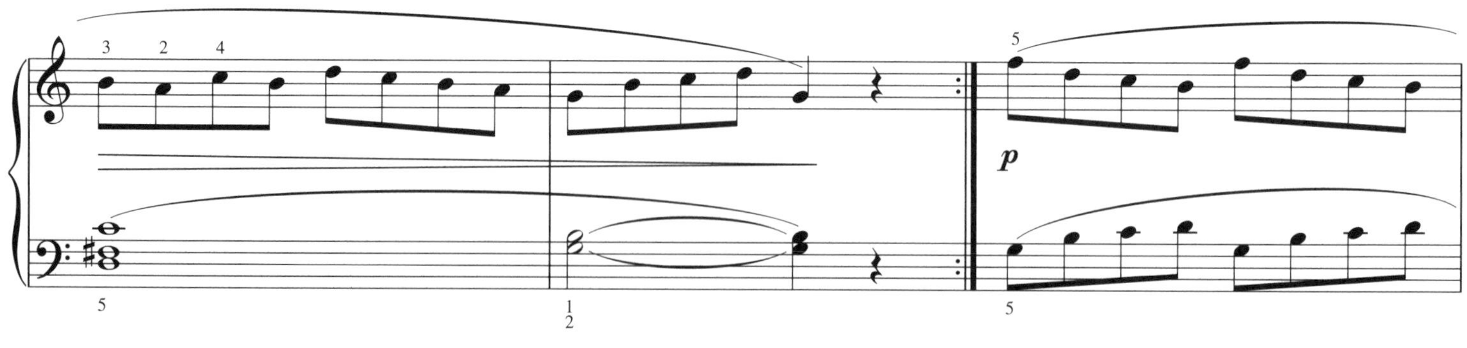

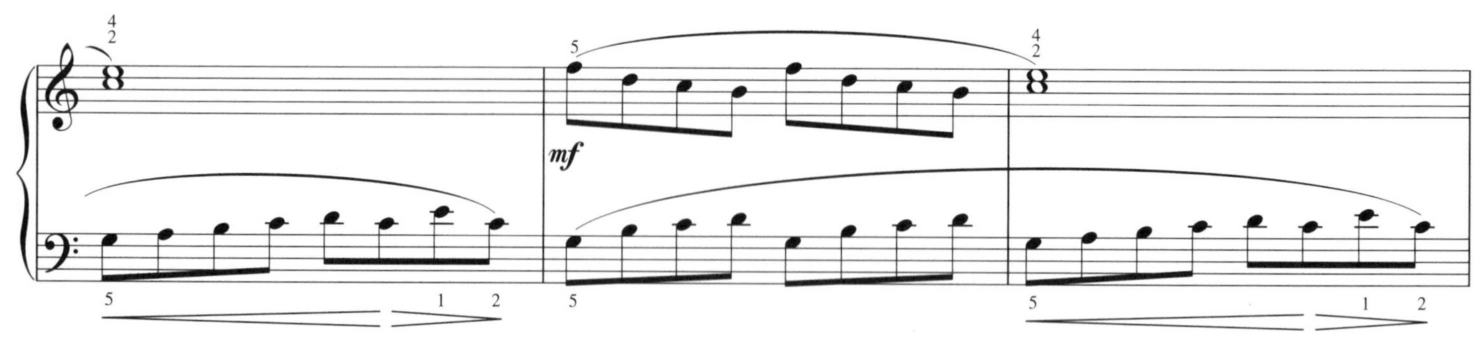

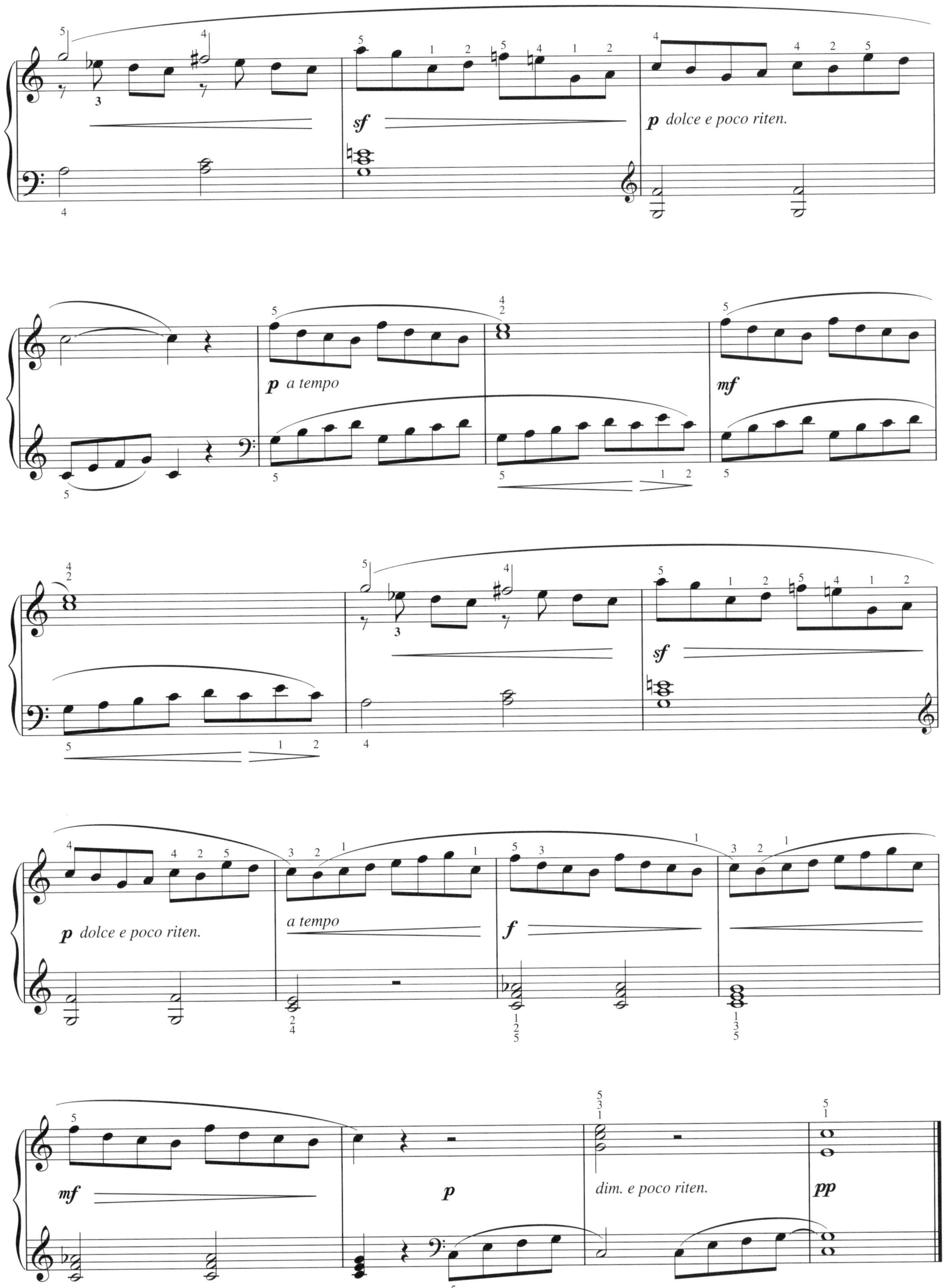
sf
p dolce e poco riten.
p a tempo
mf
sf
p dolce e poco riten.
a tempo
f
mf
p
dim. e poco riten.
pp

Arabesque

from *25 Progressive Studies,* Op. 100, No. 2

Johann Friedrich Burgmüller
1806–1874

Pastorale

from *25 Progressive Studies,* Op. 100, No. 3

Johann Friedrich Burgmüller
1806–1874

Innocence

from *25 Progressive Studies,* Op. 100, No. 5

Johann Friedrich Burgmüller
1806–1874

Progress

from *25 Progressive Studies,* Op. 100, No. 6

Johann Friedrich Burgmüller
1806–1874

The Limpid Stream

from *25 Progressive Studies,* Op. 100, No. 7

Johann Friedrich Burgmüller
1806–1874

The Chase

from *25 Progressive Studies,* Op. 100, No. 9

Johann Friedrich Burgmüller
1806–1874

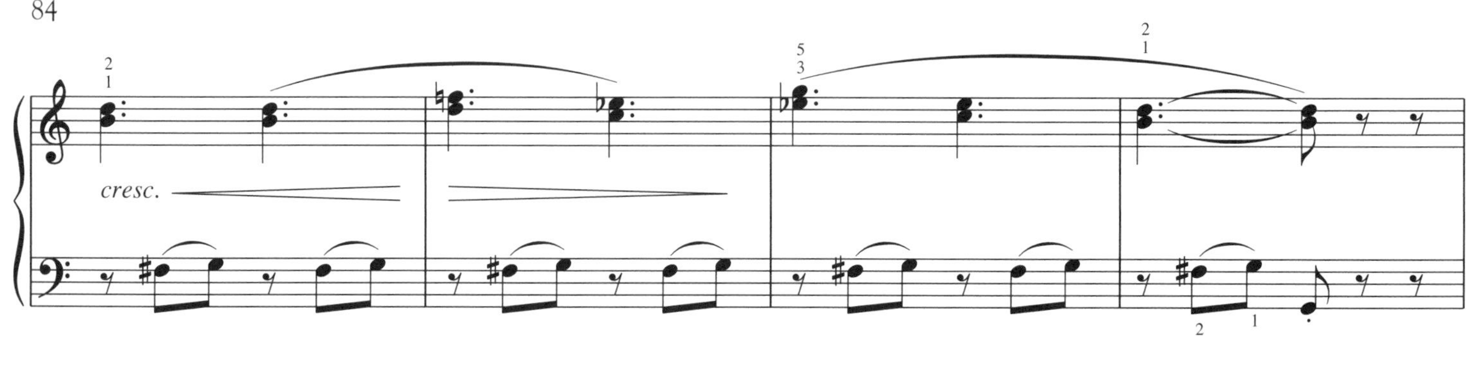
cresc.

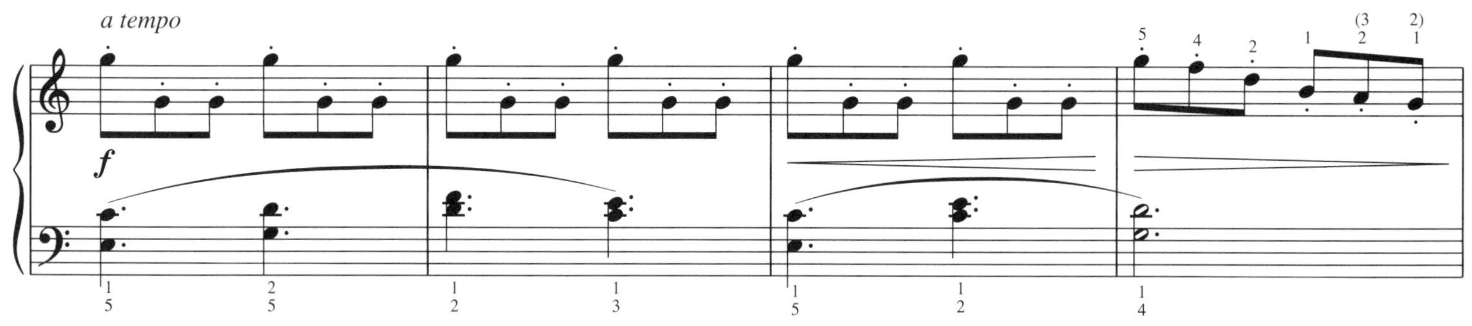
a tempo
f

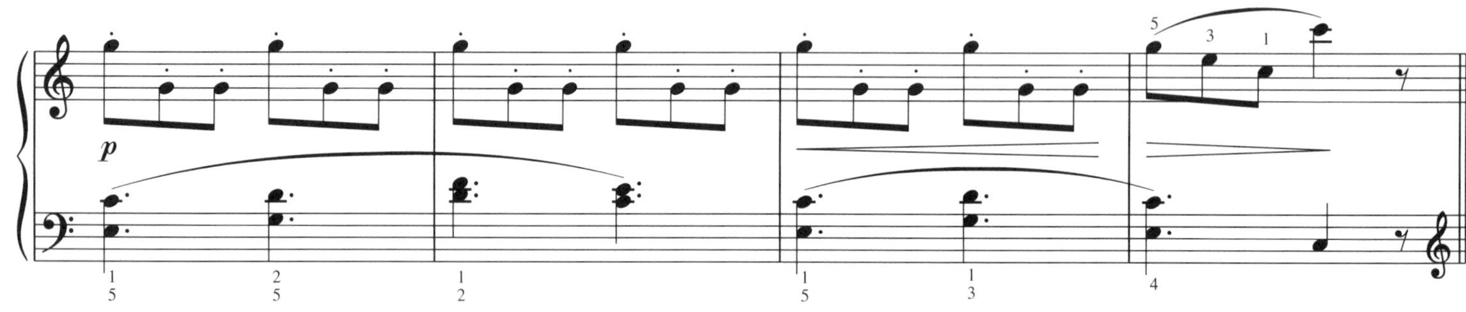
p

p dolente

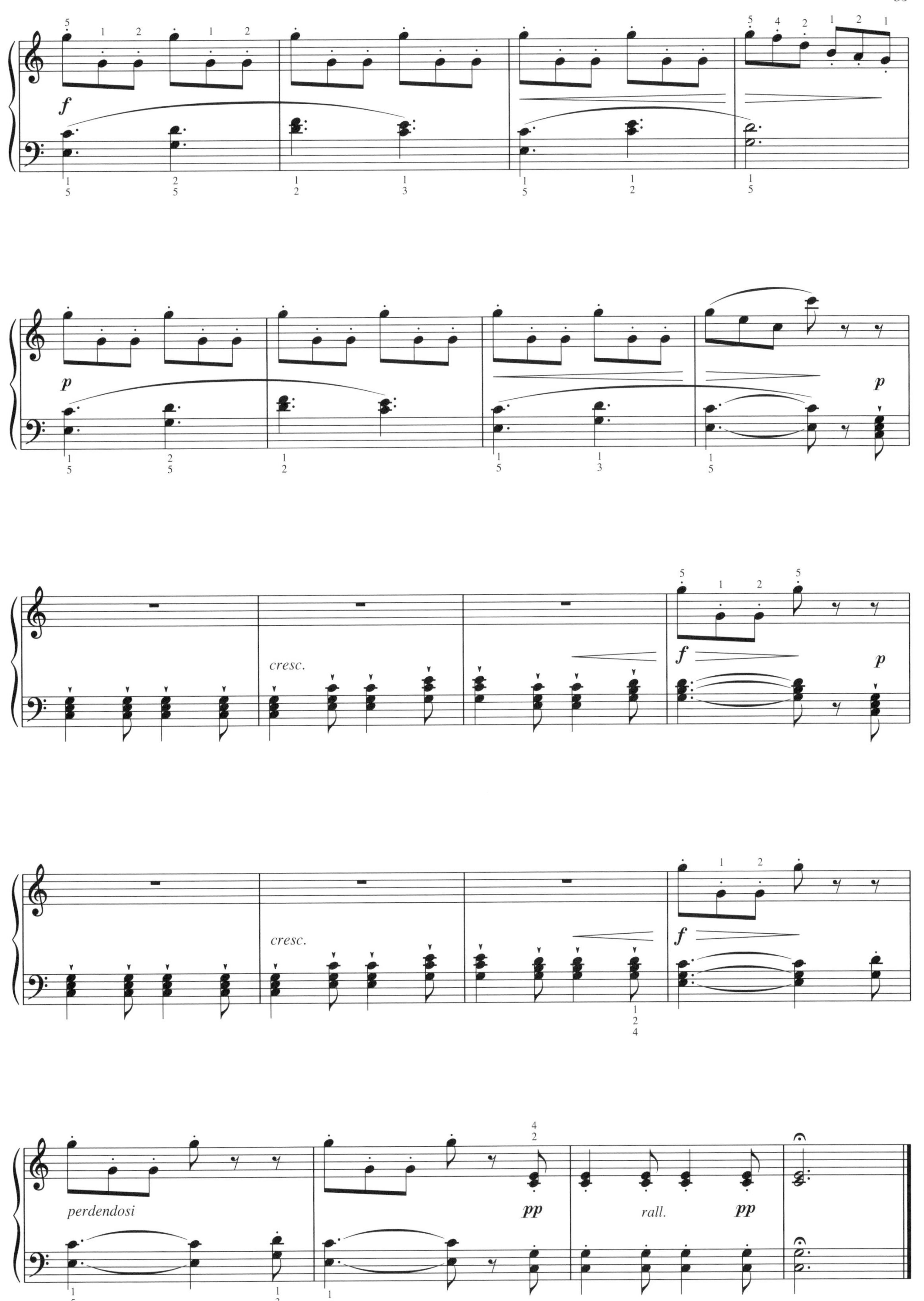
f
p
p
cresc.
f
p
cresc.
f
perdendosi
pp
rall.
pp

Austrian Dance

from *25 Progressive Studies,* Op. 100, No. 14

Johann Friedrich Burgmüller
1806–1874

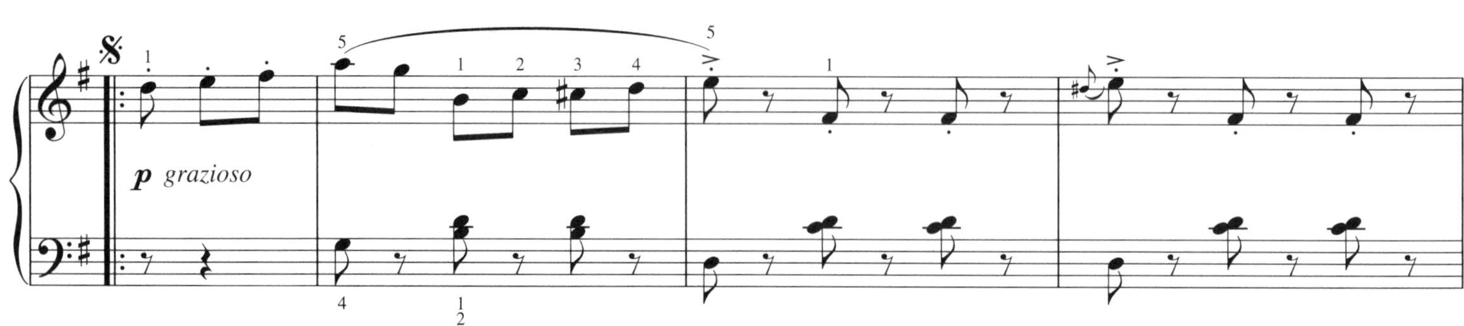

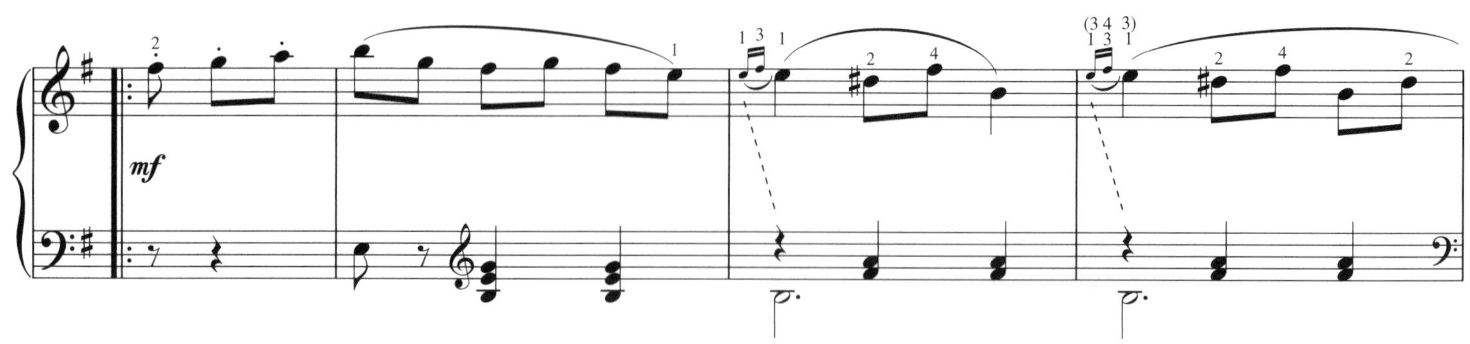

riten.
dim. e rall.
p a tempo
dolce
Fine
f
f deciso
D.S. al Fine
senza repetizione

Inquietude

from *25 Progressive Studies,* Op. 100, No. 18

Johann Friedrich Burgmüller
1806–1874

dim. e poco rall.
p
a tempo
cresc.
1
2
f
dim.
p

Ave Maria

from *25 Progressive Studies,* Op. 100, No. 19

Johann Friedrich Burgmüller
1806–1874

Andantino
p religioso
p
dim. e ritenuto
pp

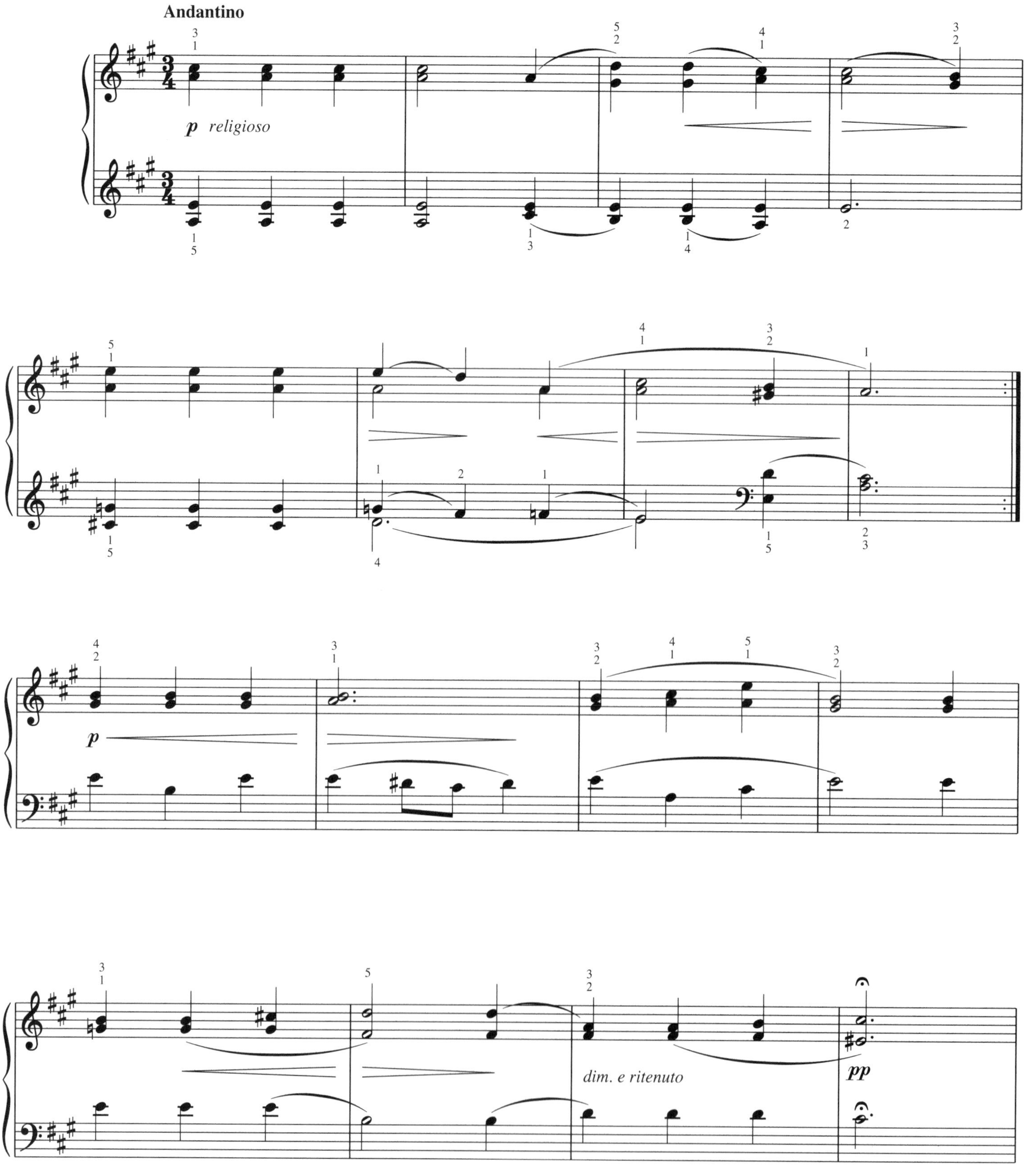

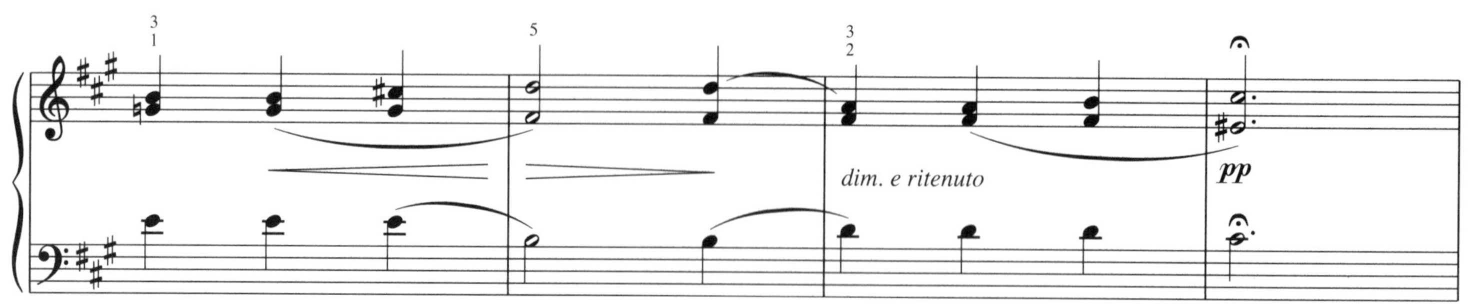

a tempo
p
dim. e poco riten.
pp

Harmony of the Angels

from *25 Progressive Studies,* Op. 100, No. 21

Johann Friedrich Burgmüller
1806–1874

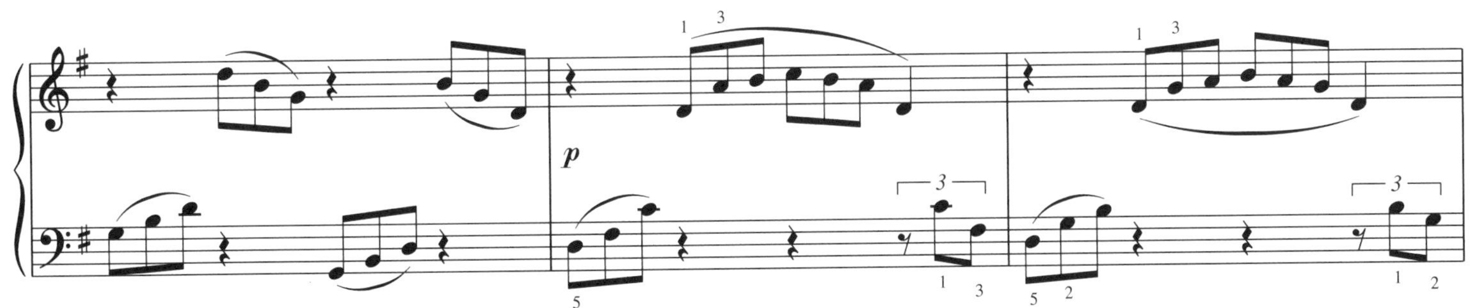

Più lento

The Return

from *25 Progressive Studies,* Op. 100, No. 23

Johann Friedrich Burgmüller
1806–1874

f
p
f
cresc. assai
sf
pp
dim. e poco riten.

Canaries

Jacques Champion de Chambonnières
c. 1602–1672

Sarabande in G Major

Jacques Champion de Chambonnières
c. 1602–1672

Prelude in E minor

Op. 28, No. 4

Frédéric Chopin
1810–1849

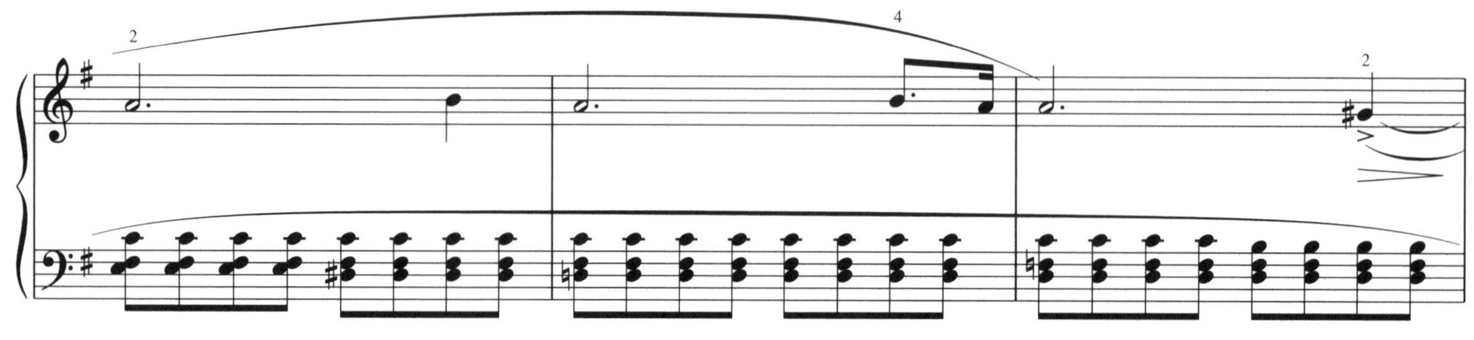

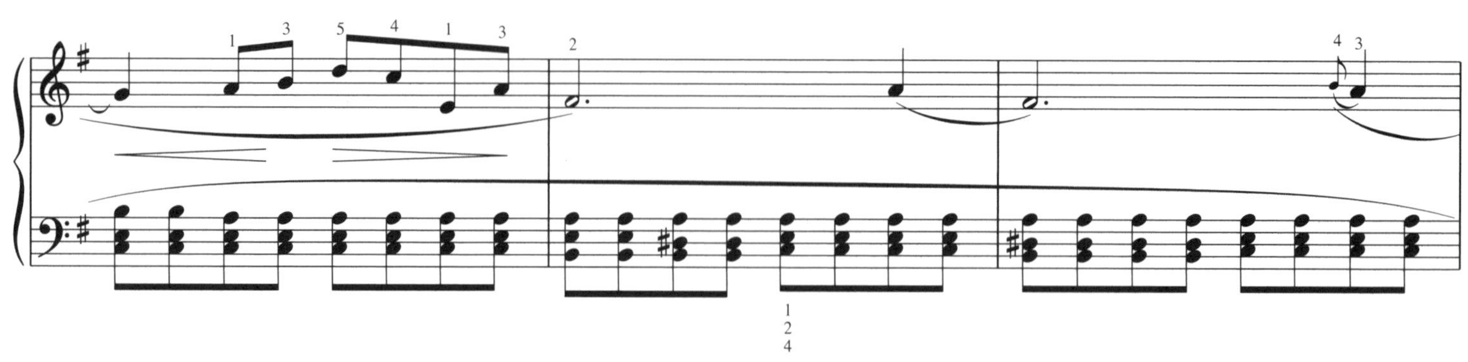

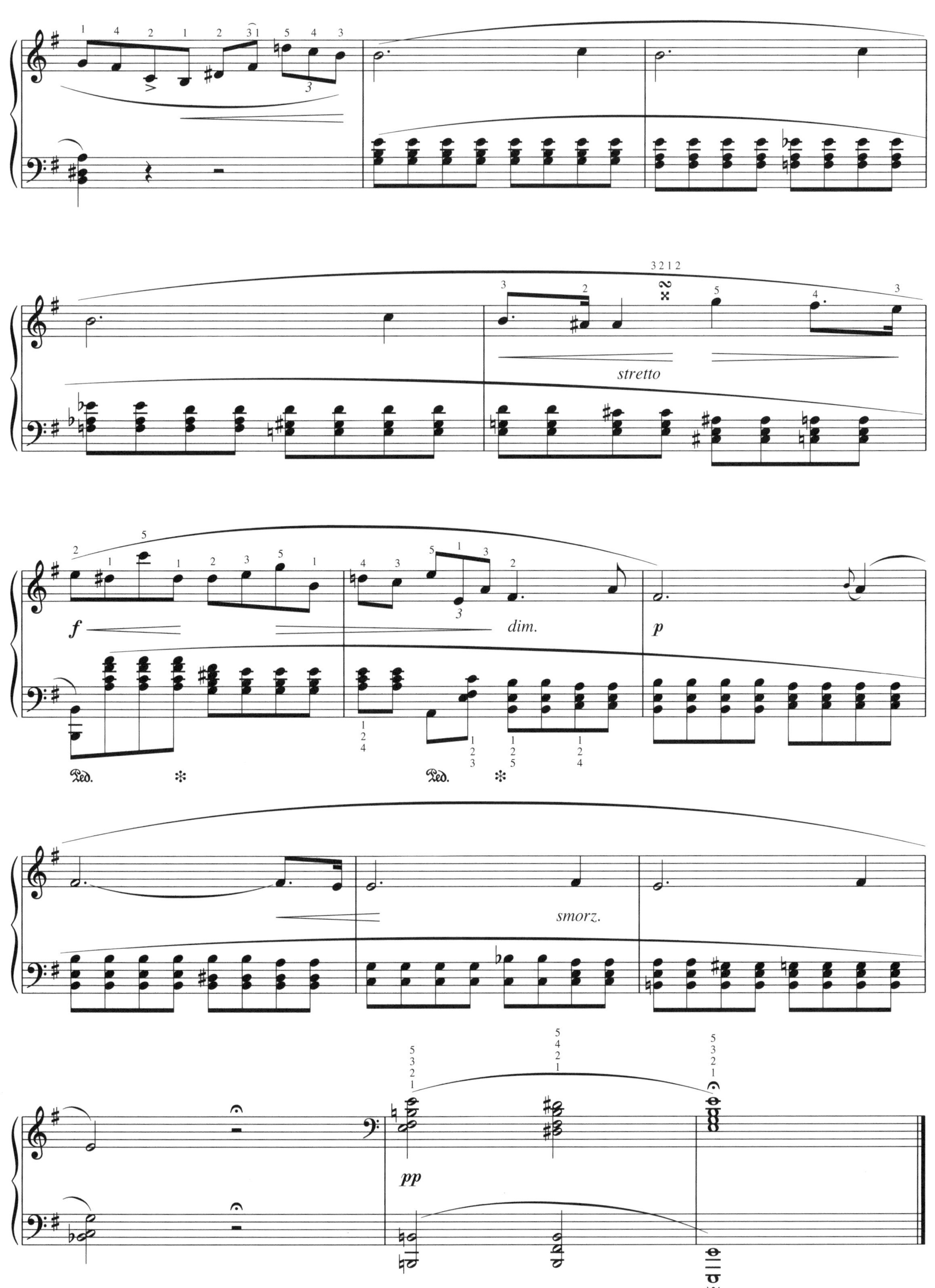

stretto
f
dim.
p
smorz.
pp

Prelude in A Major

Op. 28, No. 7

Frédéric Chopin
1810–1849

Mazurka in F Major

Op. 68, No. 3 (Posthumous)

Frédéric Chopin
1810–1849

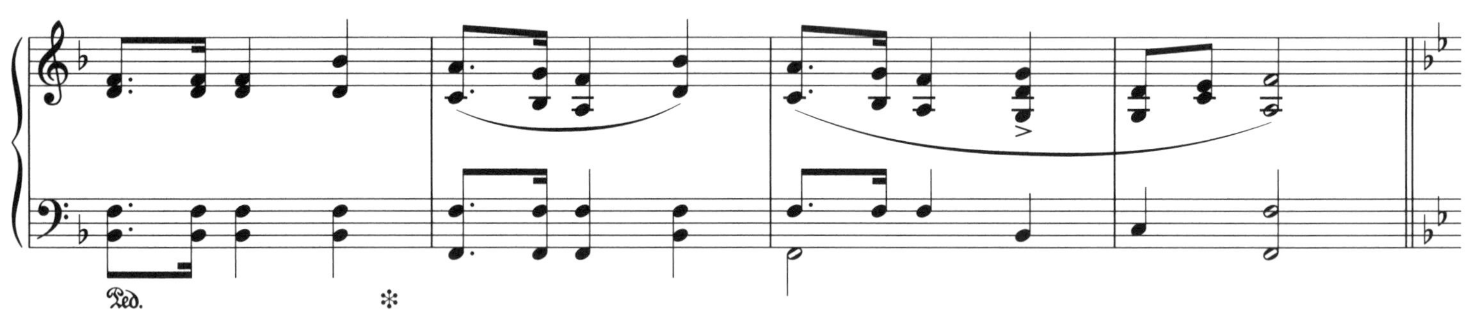

Poco più vivo

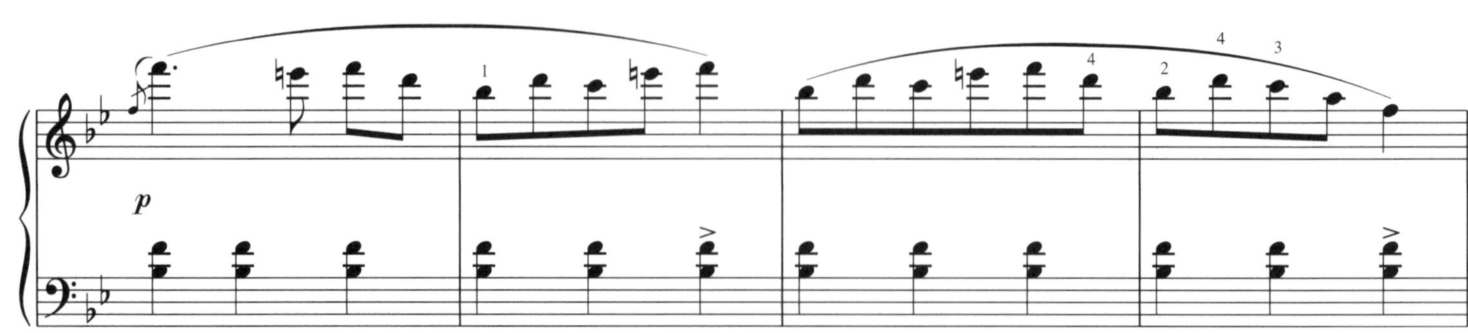

rit.

Tempo I
f

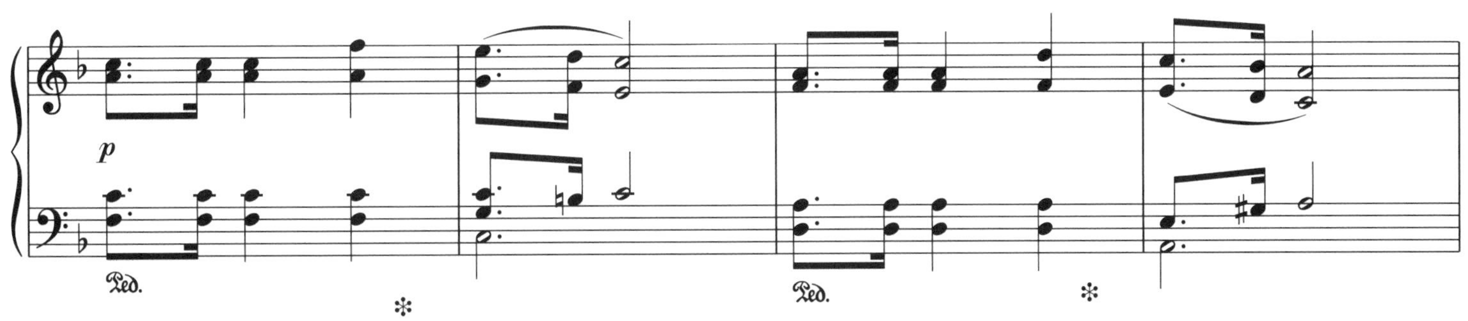
p

Sonata in G Major

Domenico Cimarosa
1749–1801

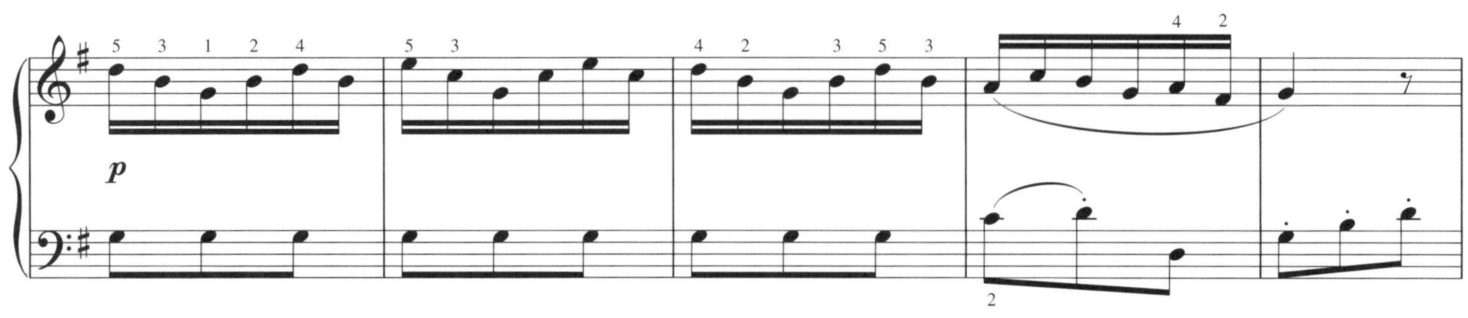

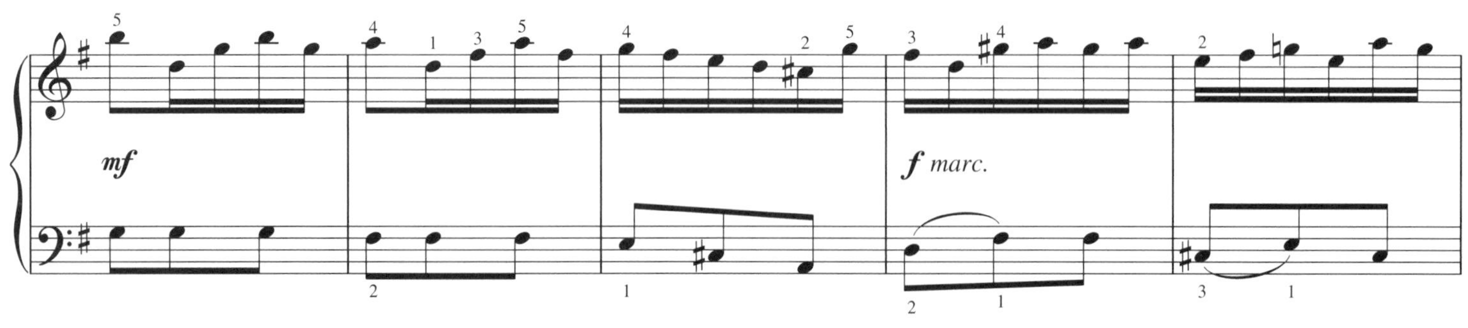

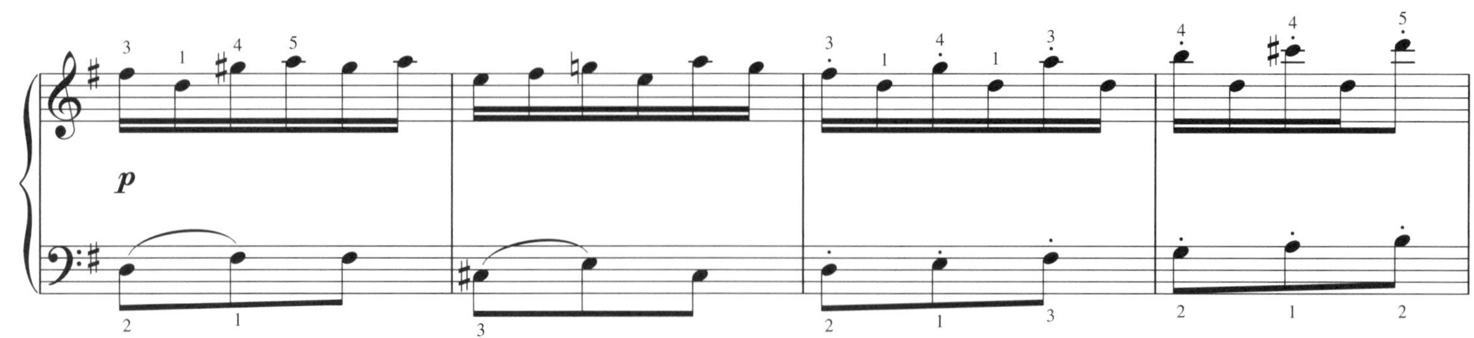

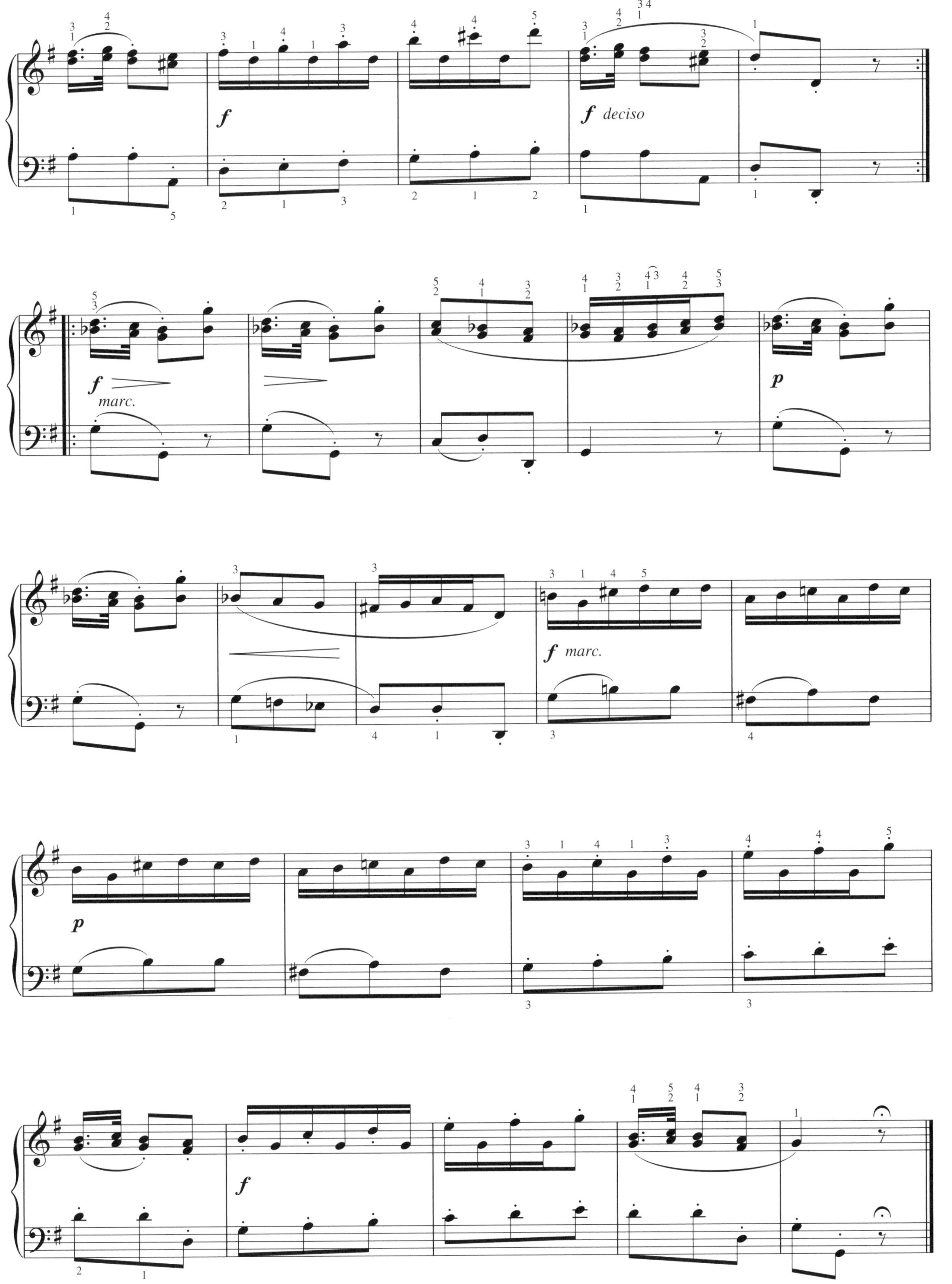
f
f deciso
f
marc.
p
f marc.
p
f

Sonatina in C Major

Op. 36, No. 1

Muzio Clementi
1752–1832

I

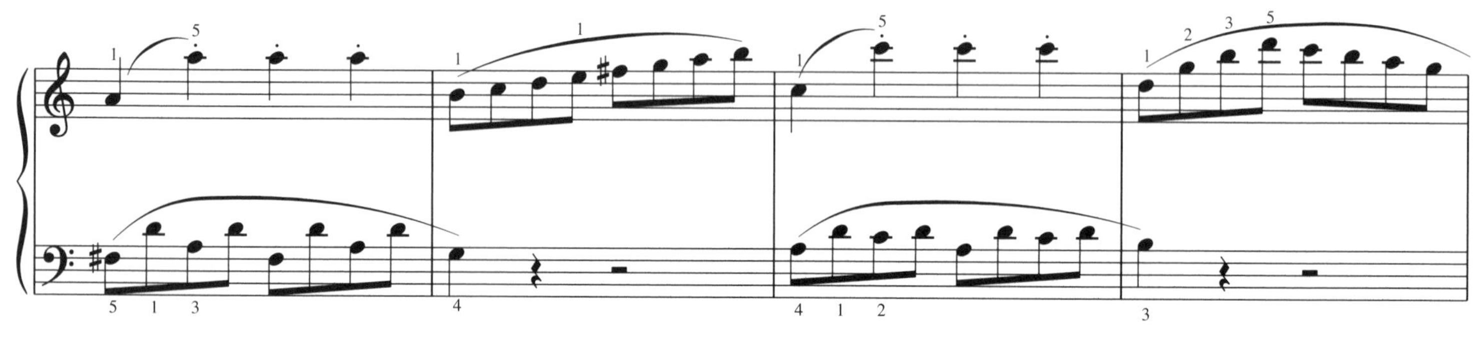

[f]
[p]
[cresc.]
[f]

II

dolce
f
III
Vivace
p
f
p

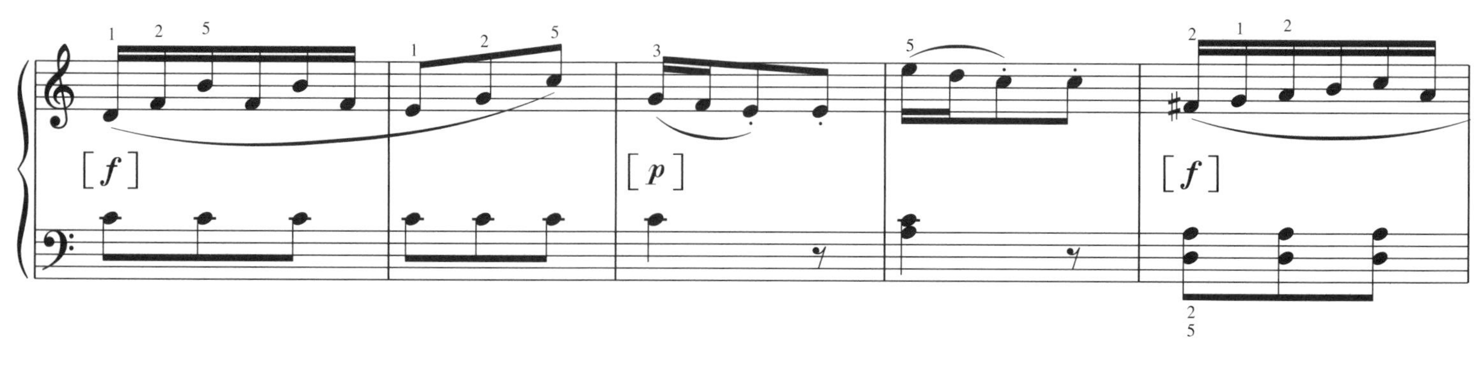
[f]
[p]
[f]

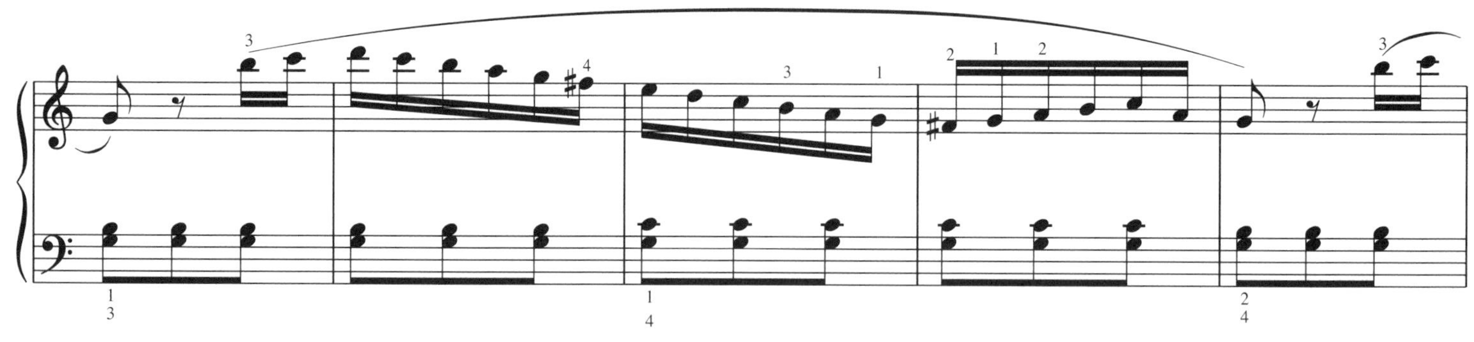

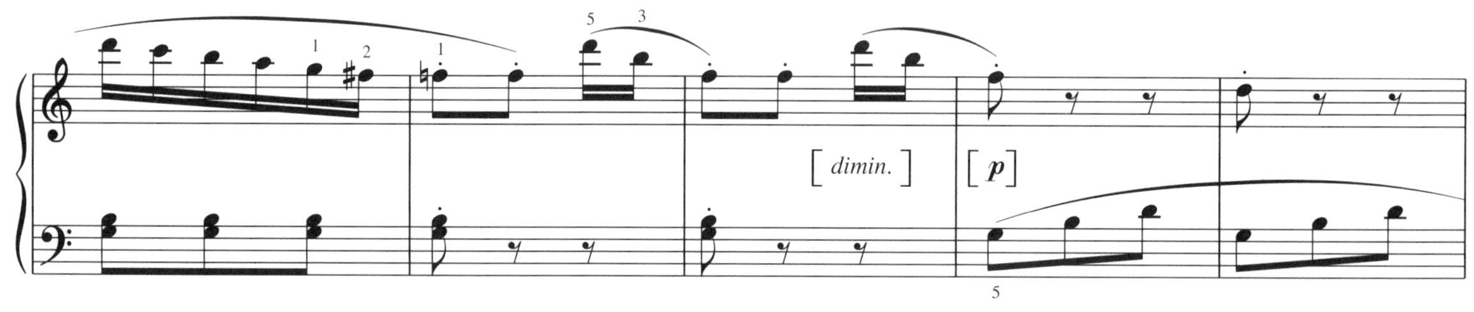
[dimin.]
[p]

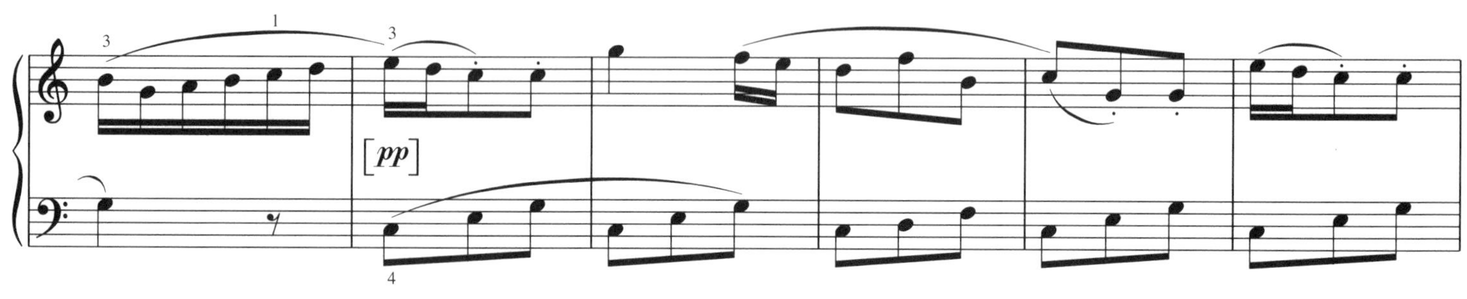
[pp]

[f]

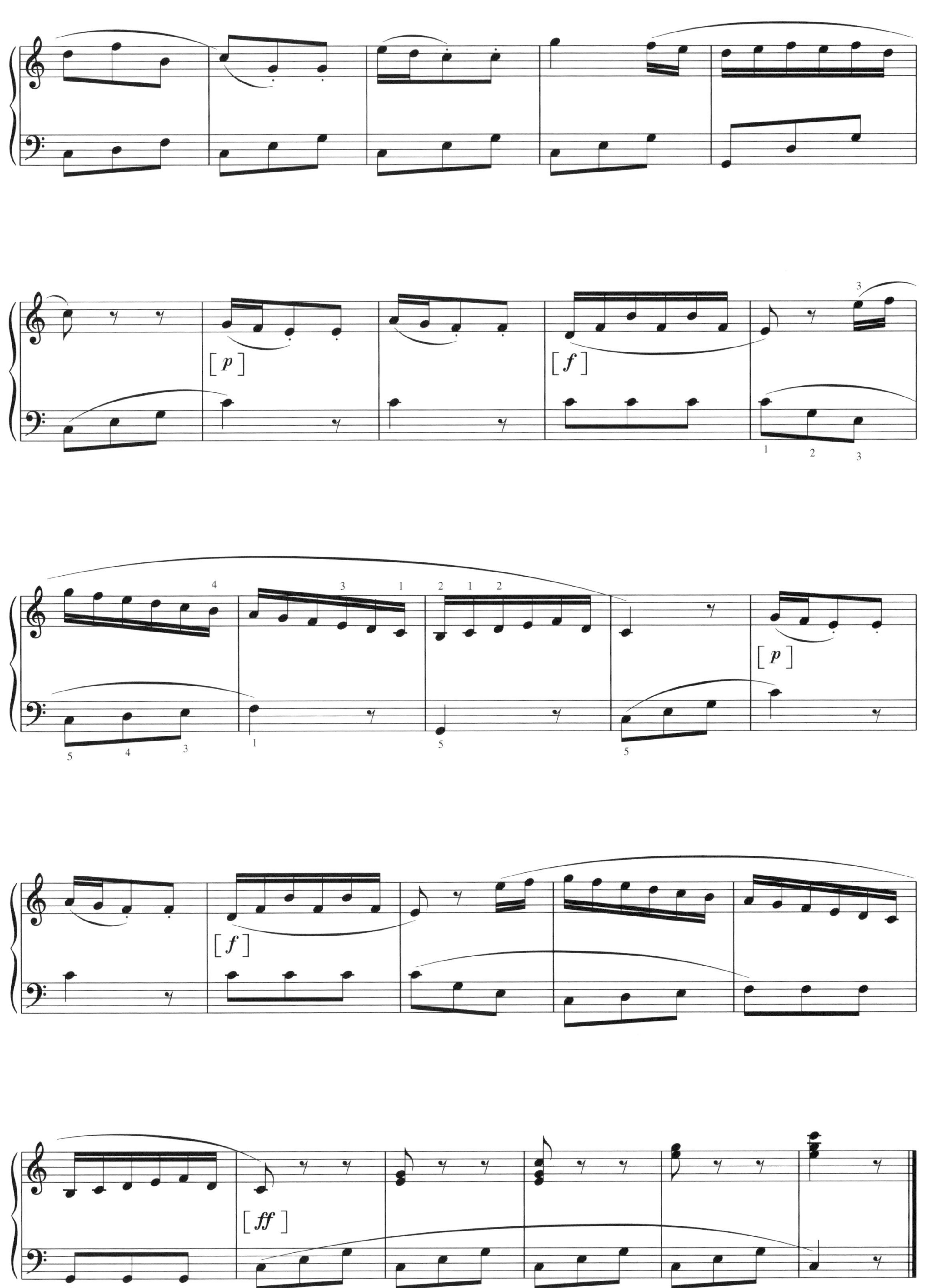
[p]
[f]
[p]
[f]
[ff]

Arietta in C Major

from *An Introduction to the Art of Playing on the Pianoforte,* Op. 42

Muzio Clementi
1752–1832

Sonatina in C Major

Op. 36, No. 3

Muzio Clementi
1752–1832

I

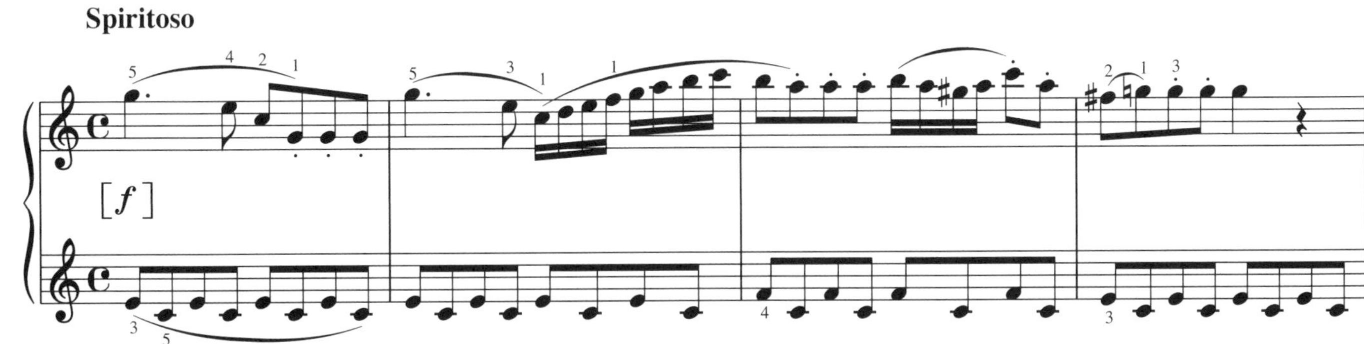

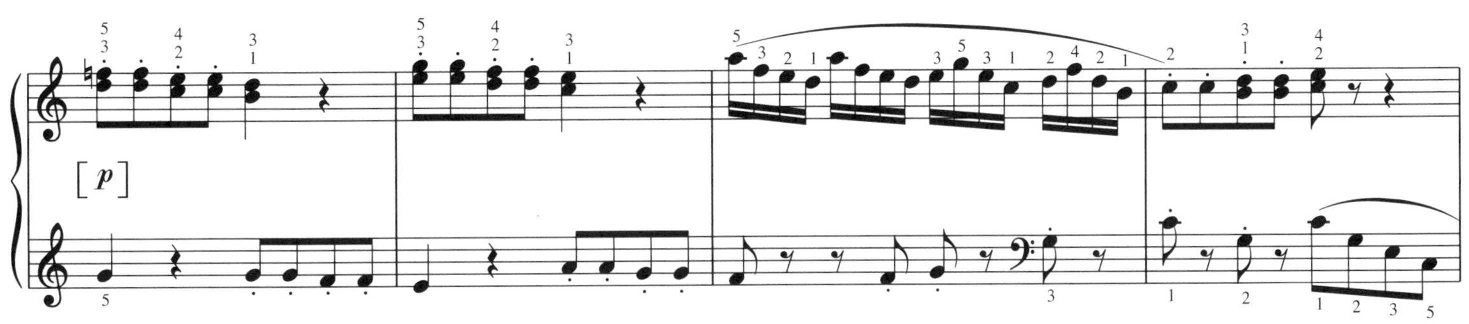

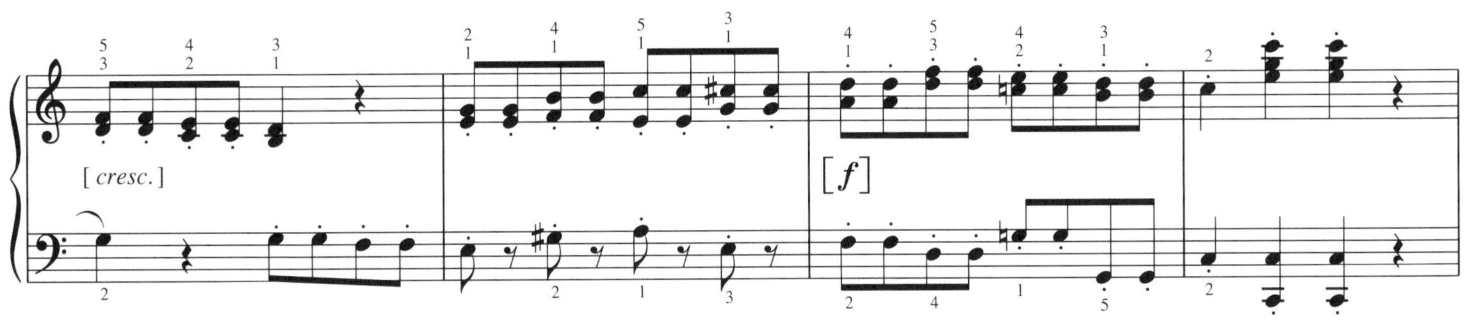

[cresc.]
[f]
[p]
[cresc.]
[f]
[p]
[cresc.]
[f]
[p]
[cresc.]
[f]
dimin.
[pp]
[f]

[p]
[cresc.
f
ff]
[p]
[cresc.
f]
tr

[p]
[cresc.]
tr
[f]
[p
cresc.
f]
II
Un poco adagio
[p]
[sf p]
[cresc.]
[f]
[dimin.]
[p]

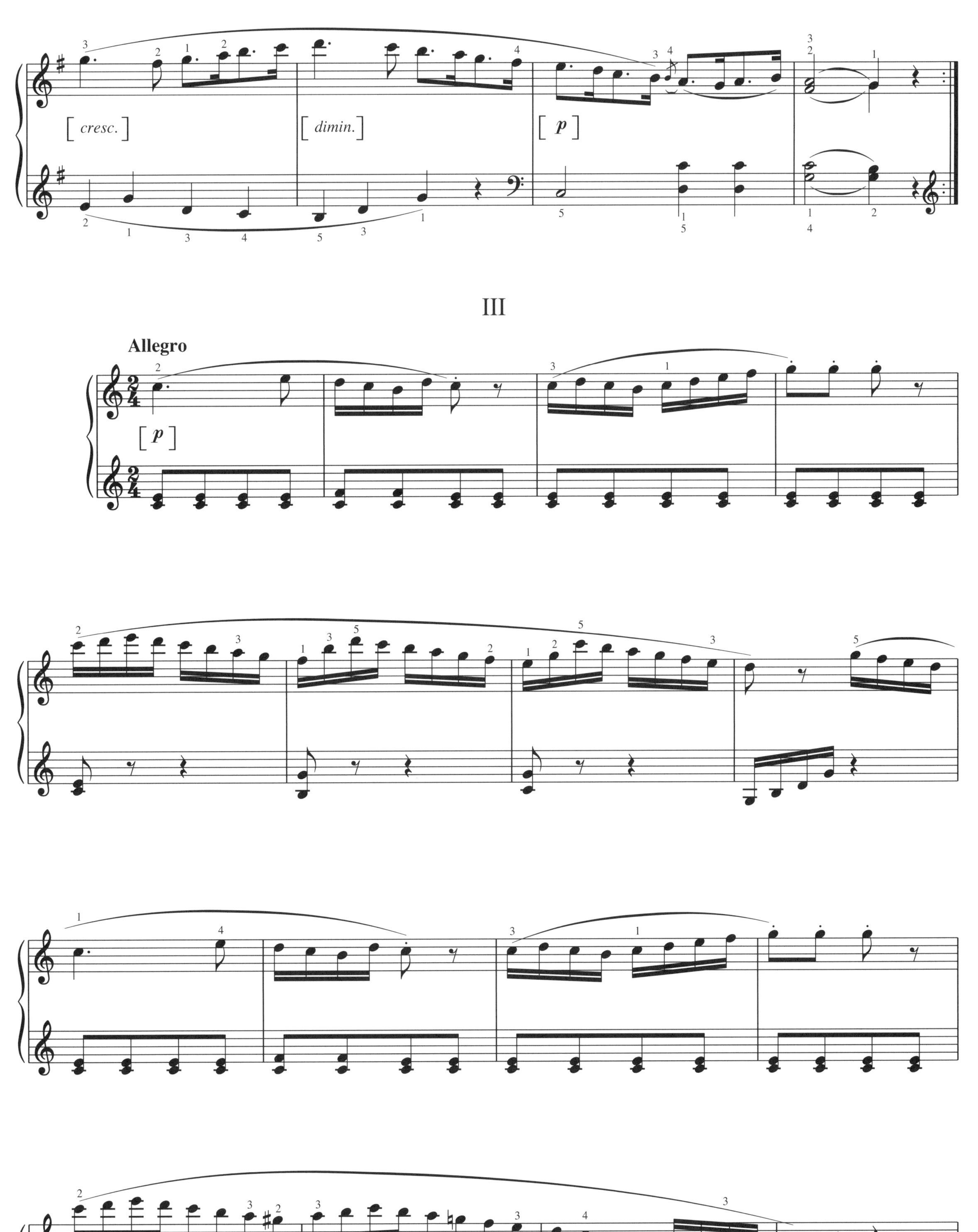
[cresc.]
[dimin.]
[p]
III
Allegro
[p]

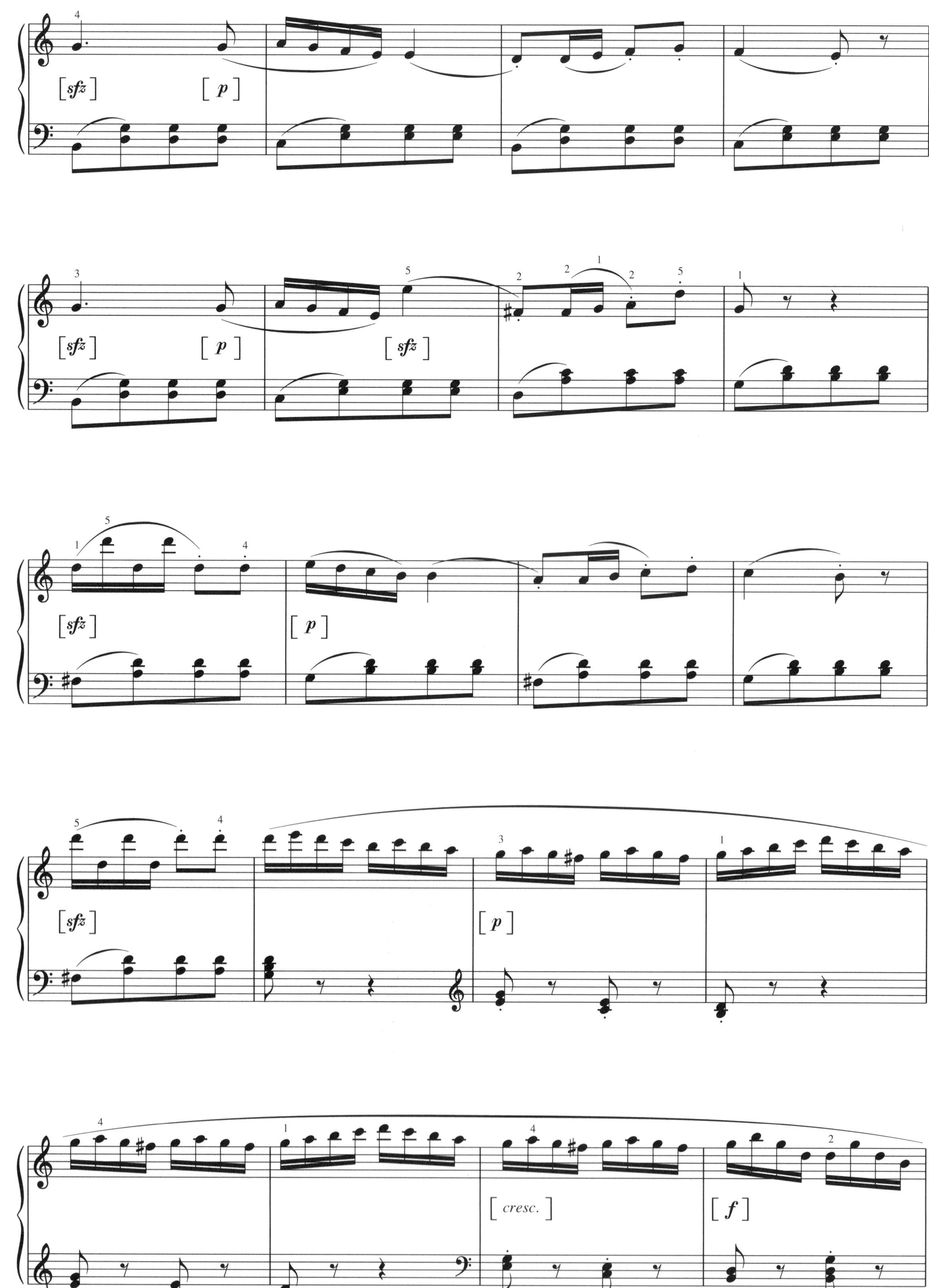
[sfz]
[p]
[sfz]
[p]
[sfz]
[sfz]
[p]
[sfz]
[p]
[cresc.]
[f]

[dimin.]
[p]
[pp]

[fz]
[p]
[fz]
[p]
[f]
[p]
[f]

Spanish Dance

from *An Introduction to the Art of Playing on the Pianoforte,* Op. 42

Muzio Clementi
1752–1832

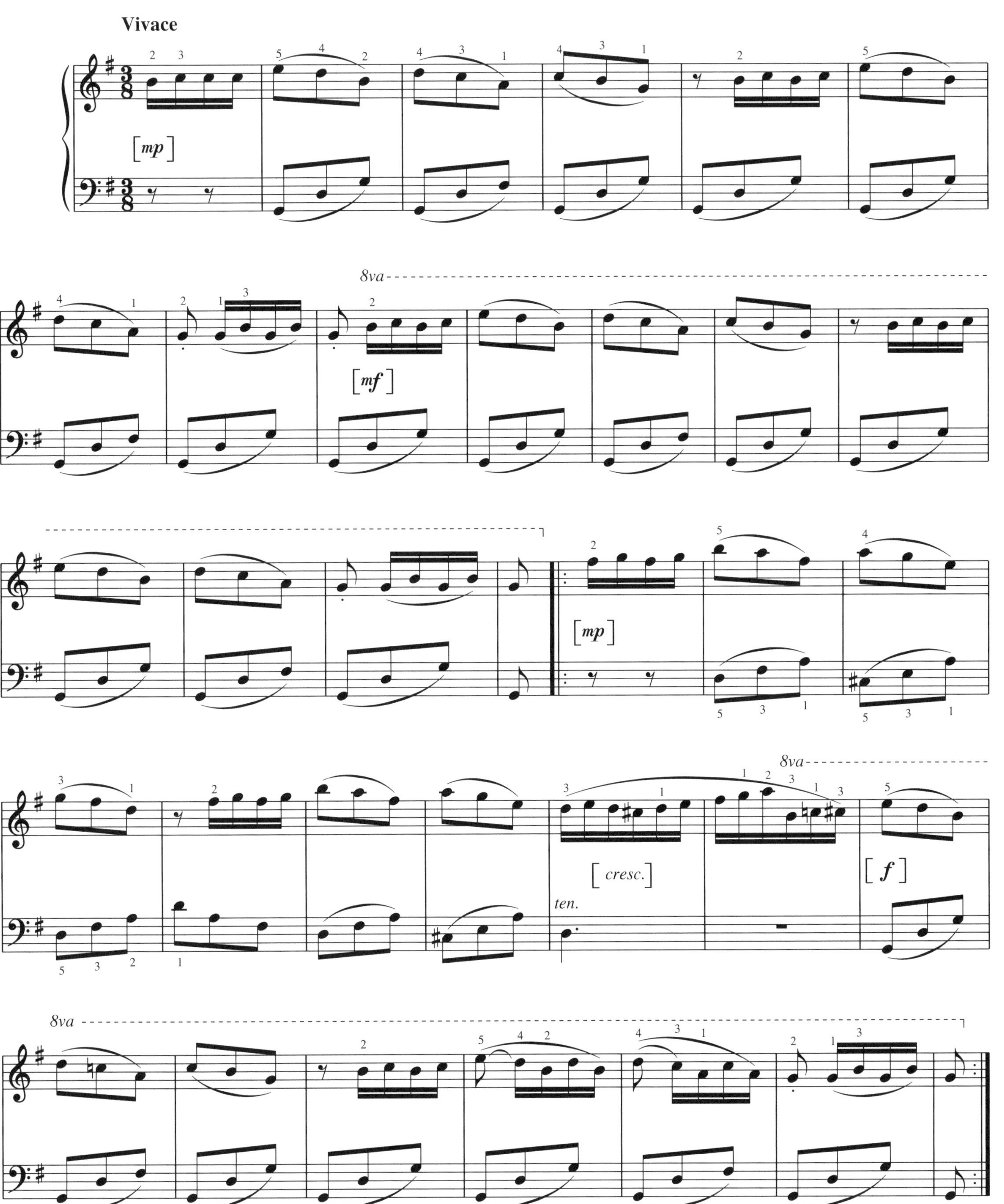

Gavotta in F Major

Arcangelo Corelli
1653–1713

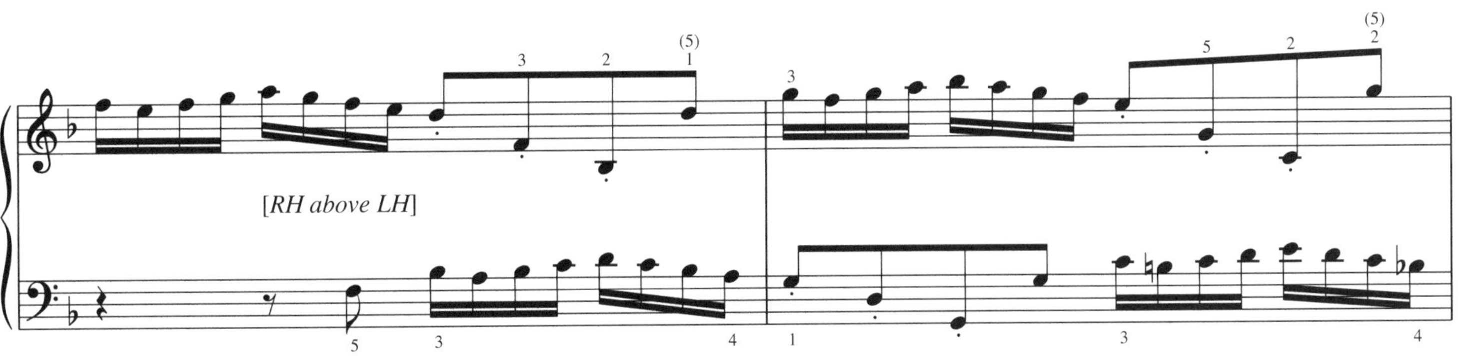
[RH above LH]

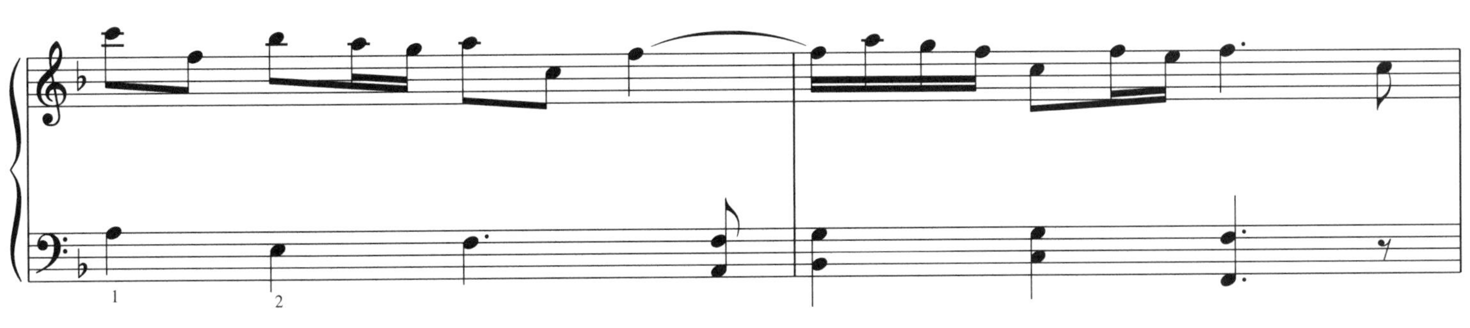

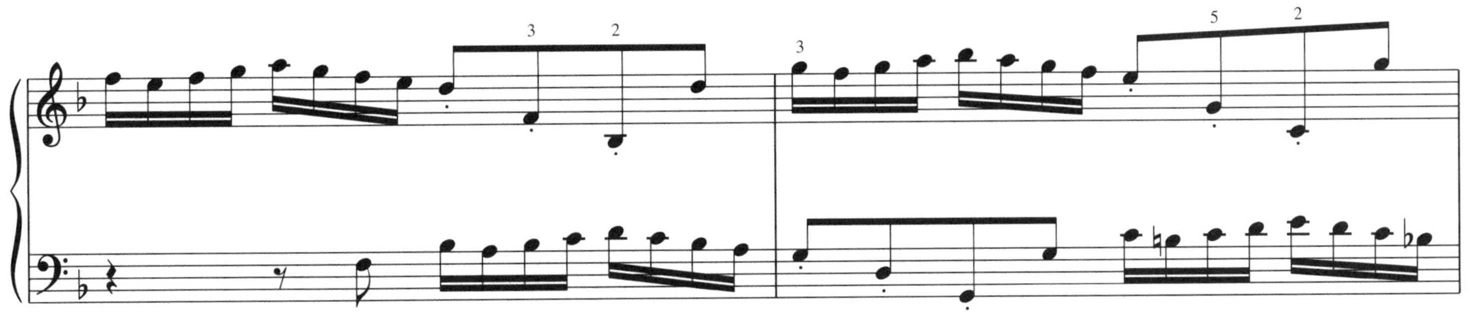

Benevolent Cuckoos Under Yellow Dominos

from *French Follies, or Costumes at a Masked Ball*

François Couperin
1668–1733

The Little Trifle

François Couperin
1668–1733

3
2 3 4 1 2 3
1
323
1 2
4
23
2
1
3 4
3232
1 3 1
4 1
4
1212
3
1 3 2 2
1
32
1 3
5
1 2
3 5

Cradle Song

François Couperin
1668–1733

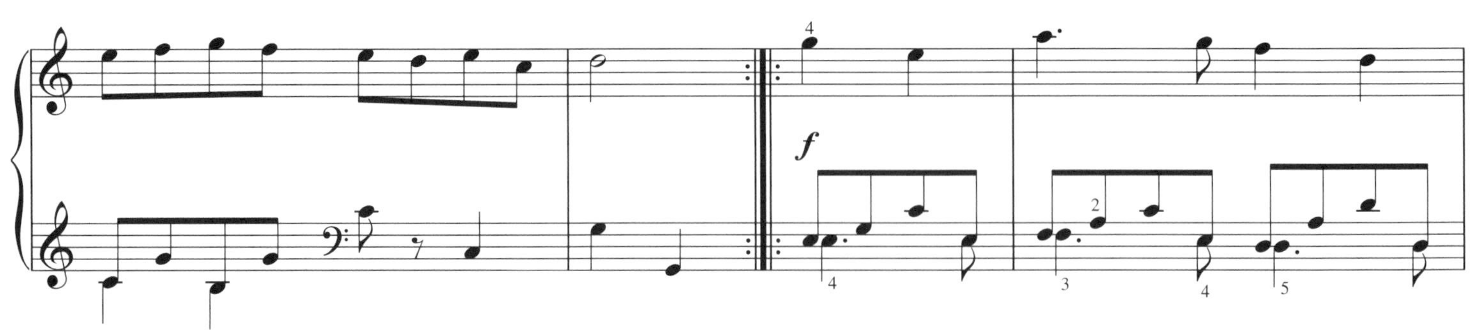

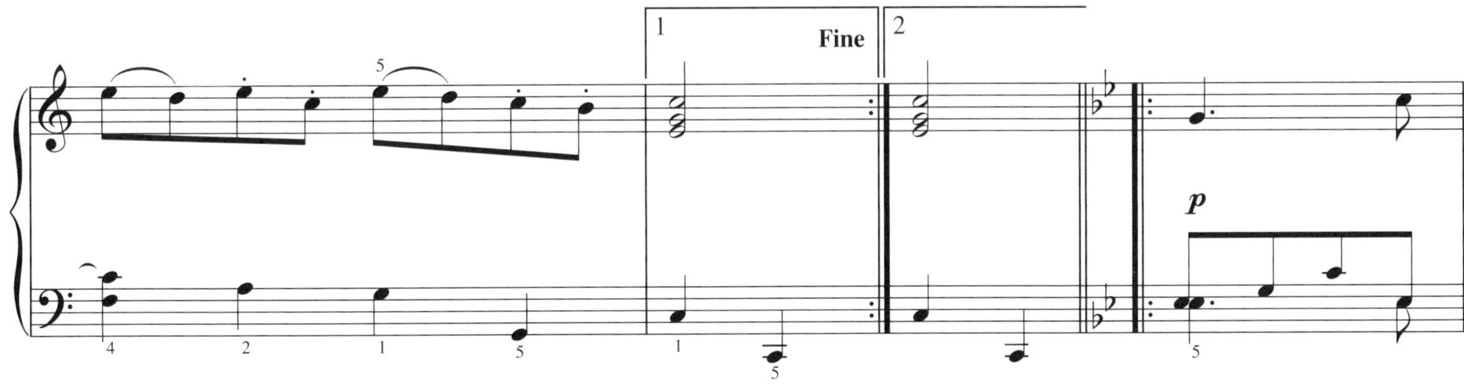
Fine

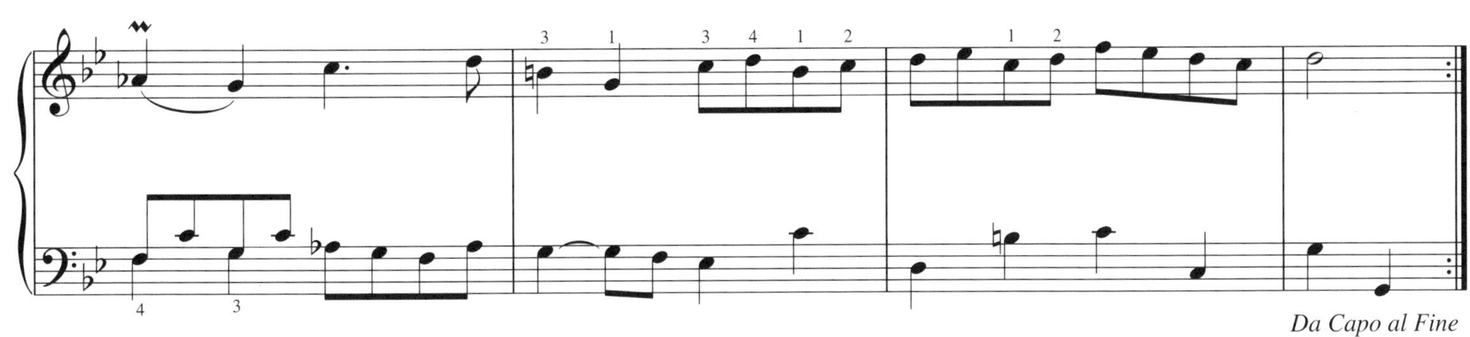
Da Capo al Fine

Lament

Jean-François Dandrieu
c. 1682–1738

[p] dolce
mf
[mf]

[p] dolce
[mf]
[dim.]
[poco rit.]

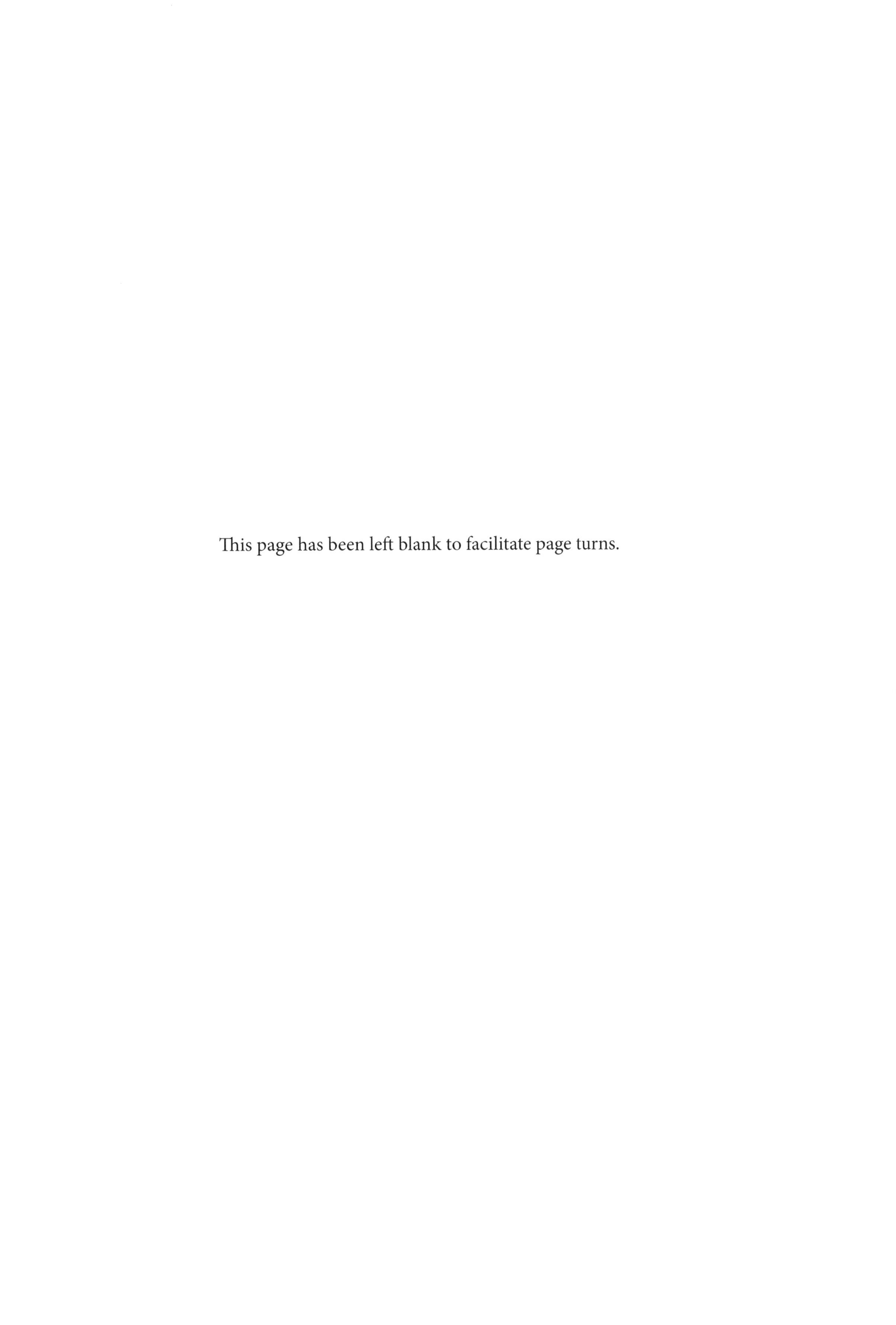

This page has been left blank to facilitate page turns.

The Cuckoo

Louis-Claude Daquin
1694–1772

D.C. al Coda
(with repeats)
CODA

Le petit nègre

Claude Debussy
1862–1918

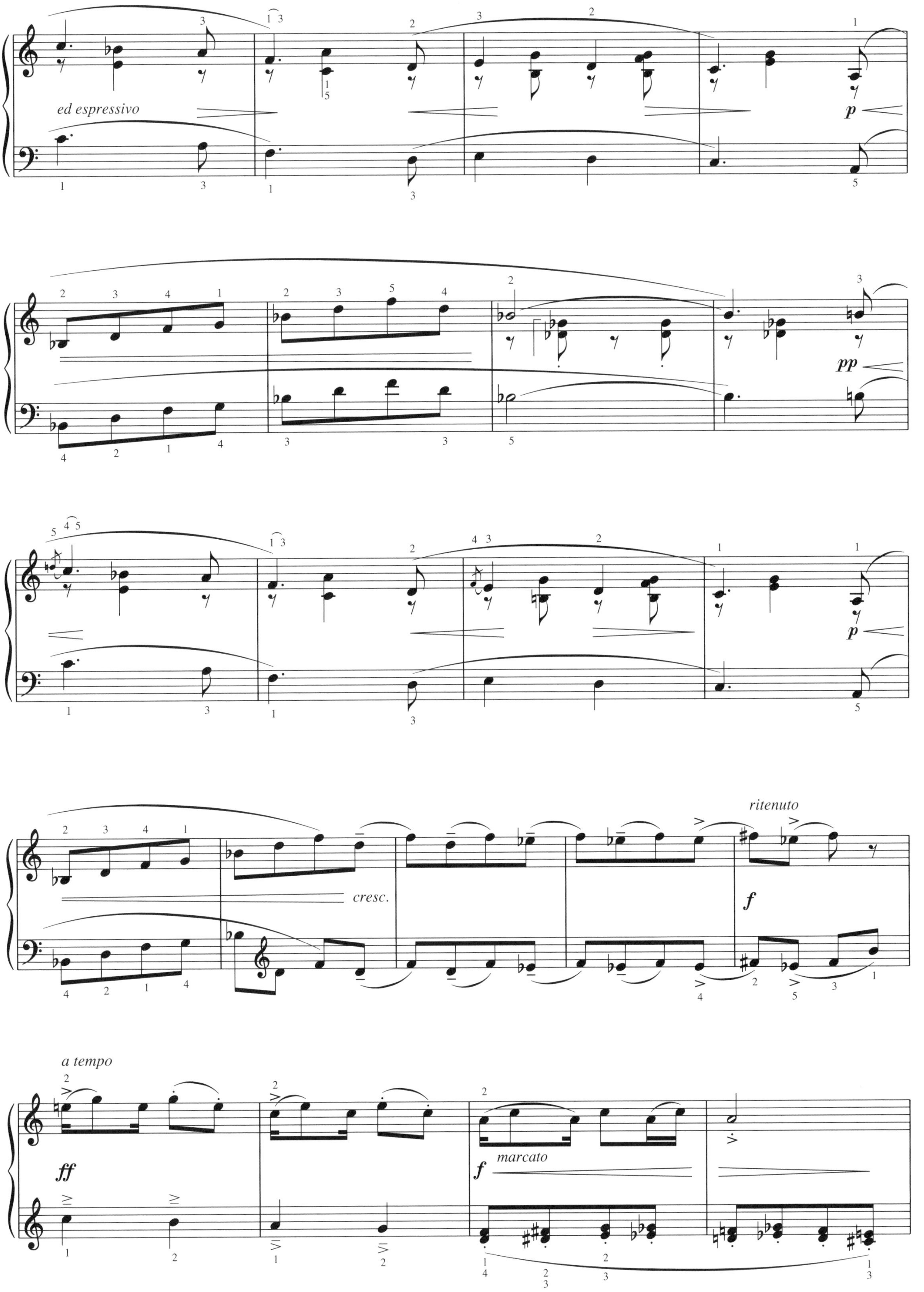
ed espressivo
p
pp
p
cresc.
ritenuto
f
a tempo
ff
f
marcato

mf e dim.
f
mf
dim.
cresc. molto
a tempo
ff
pp
dolce
ed espressivo
p
pp

p
cresc.
ritenuto
a tempo
f
ff
f
marcato
mf
e dim.
f
mf
dim.
cresc. molto
ff

Sonatina in G Major

Op. 151, No. 1

Anton Diabelli
1781–1858

I

Andante cantabile

dolce

p

p

legato

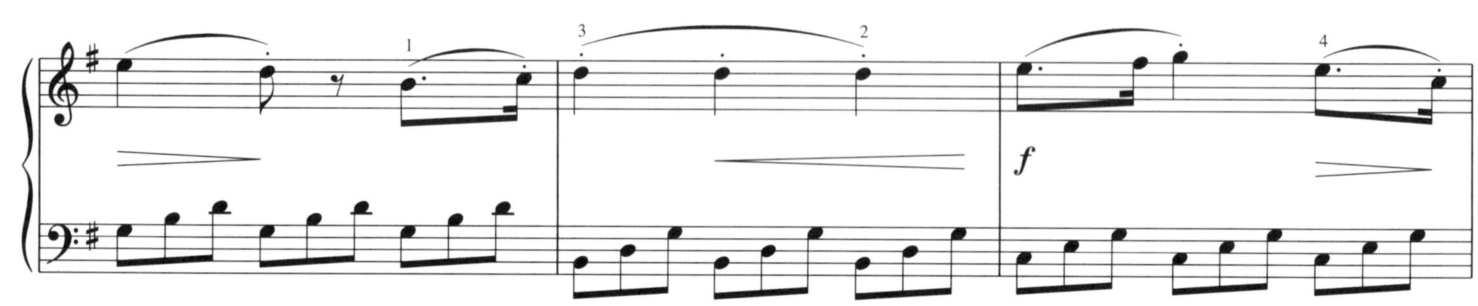

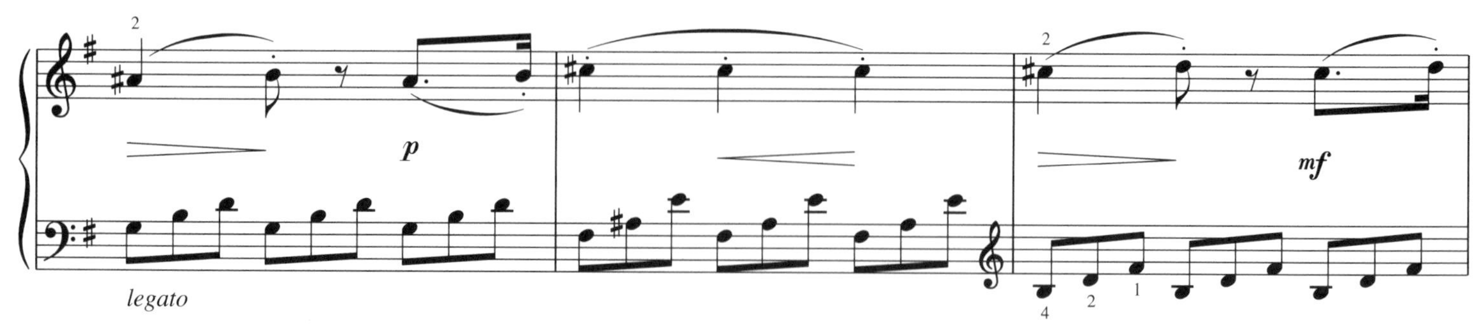

cresc.
f
p
dim.
legato

p
cresc.
sf
f
pp
sf
II
Scherzo
Allegro
p
legato
cresc.
f

sf
3
p
legato

sf
cresc.
3
1 4 2

sf
f

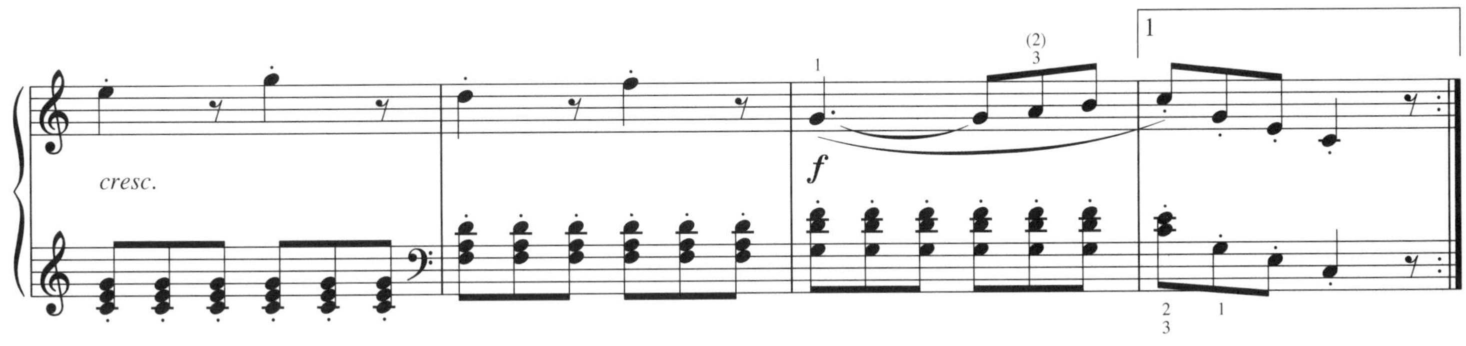
cresc.
1
(2)
3
f
1
2
3
1

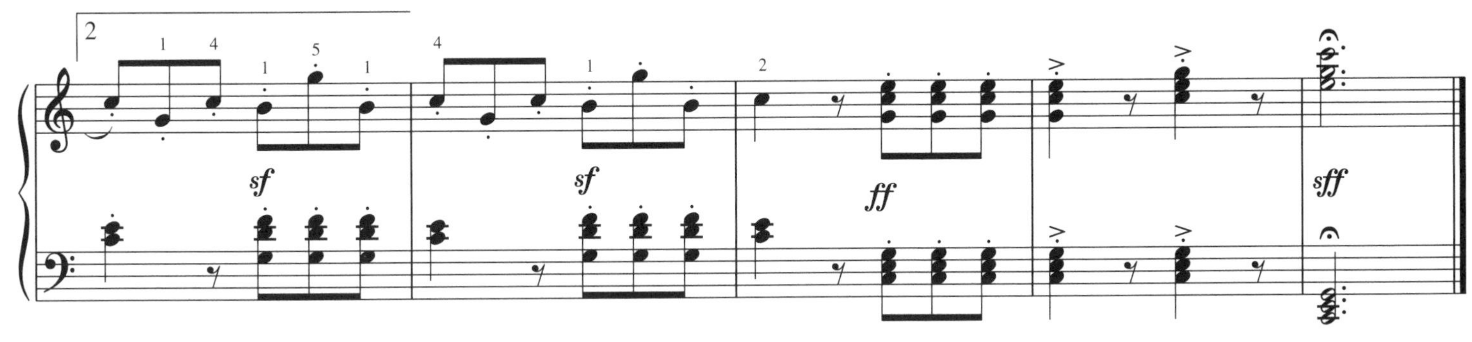
2
1 4
1 5 1
4
1
2
sf
ff
sff

III

Rondo

Allegretto

f
sf
sf
sf
dim.
p
cresc.
f
p
p
p
cresc.
f

p
p
p
mf
f
p
cresc.
f
p
cresc.

f
sf
sf
f
f
f
f
sf
sf
sf
dim.
p

cresc.
f
fp
dolce
legato
mf
cresc.
f
sf
sf
ff
sff
sff

Sonatina in C Major

William Duncombe
c. 1736–c. 1818

Sonatina in G Major

Op. 20, No. 1

Jan Ladislav Dussek
1760–1812

I

RONDO
Allegretto, tempo di minuetto
II
sim.
dolce

cresc.
cresc.
dolce

Spinning Song

Op. 14, No. 4

Albert Ellmenreich
1816–1905

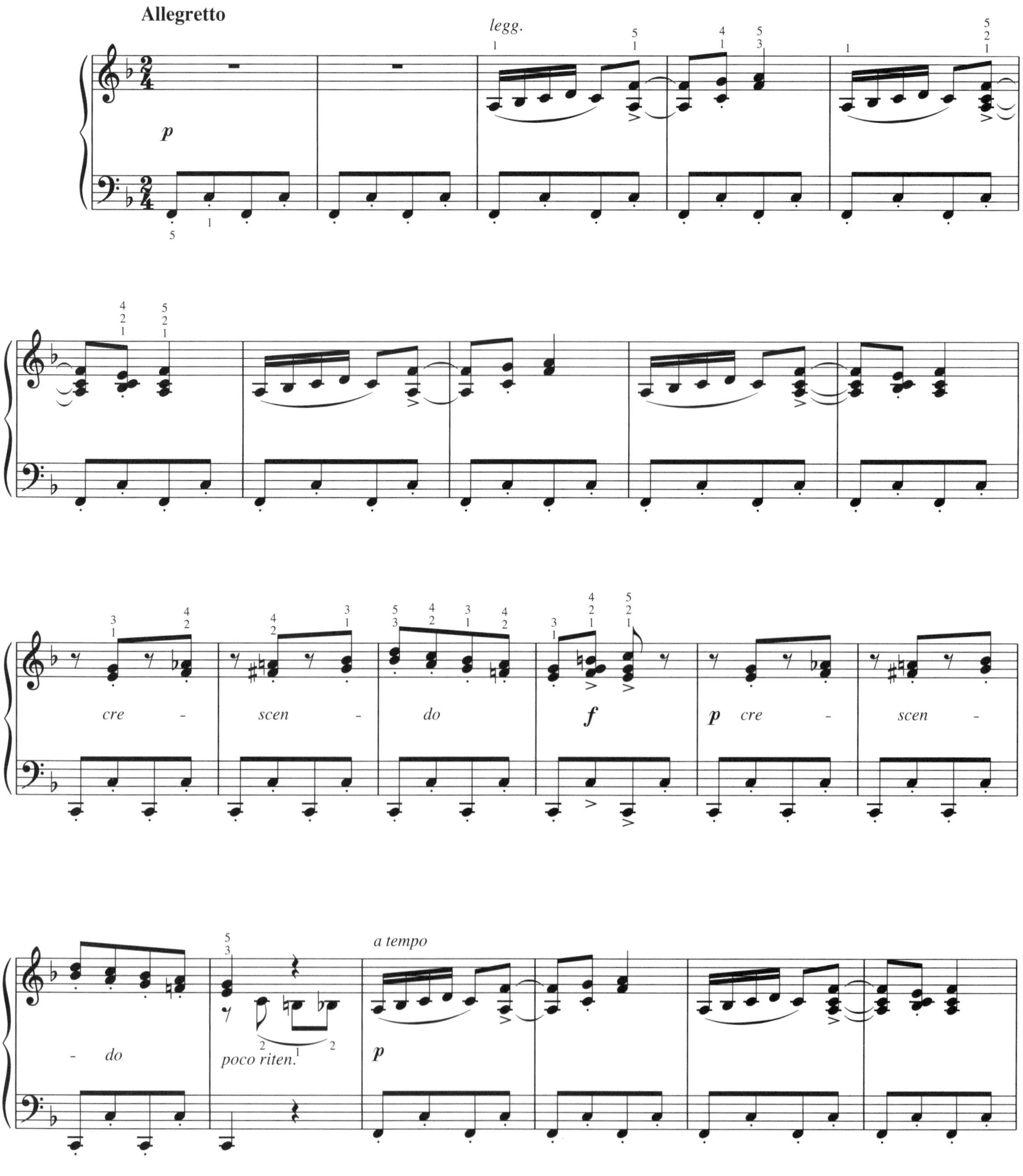
Allegretto
p
legg.
cre - scen - do
f
p cre - scen - do
poco riten.
a tempo
p

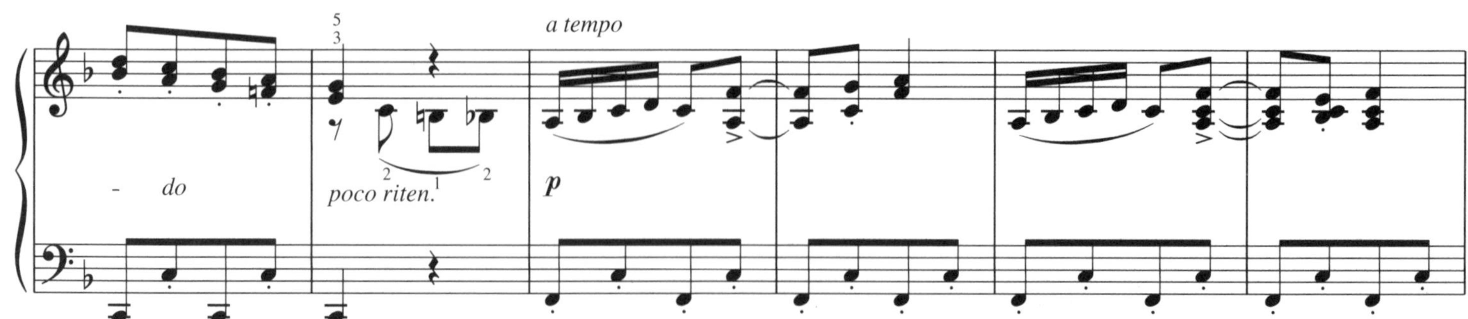

p

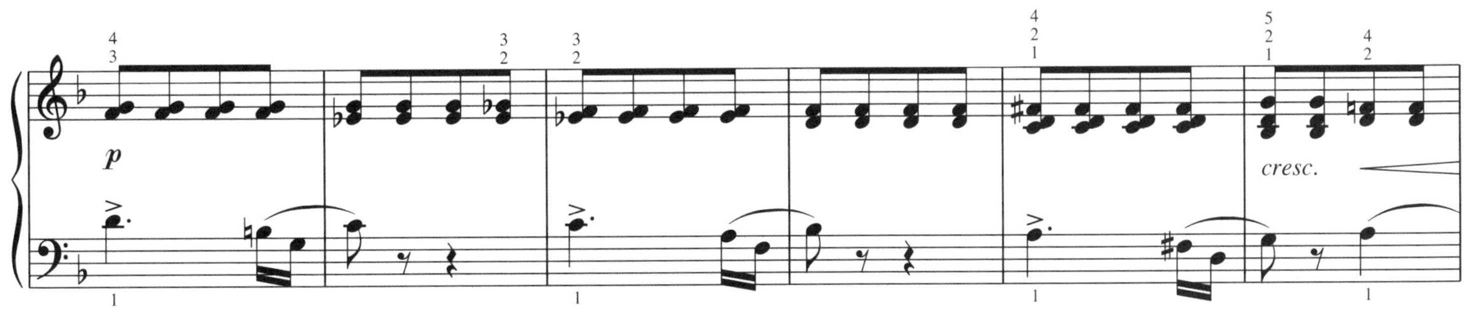
p
cresc.

p

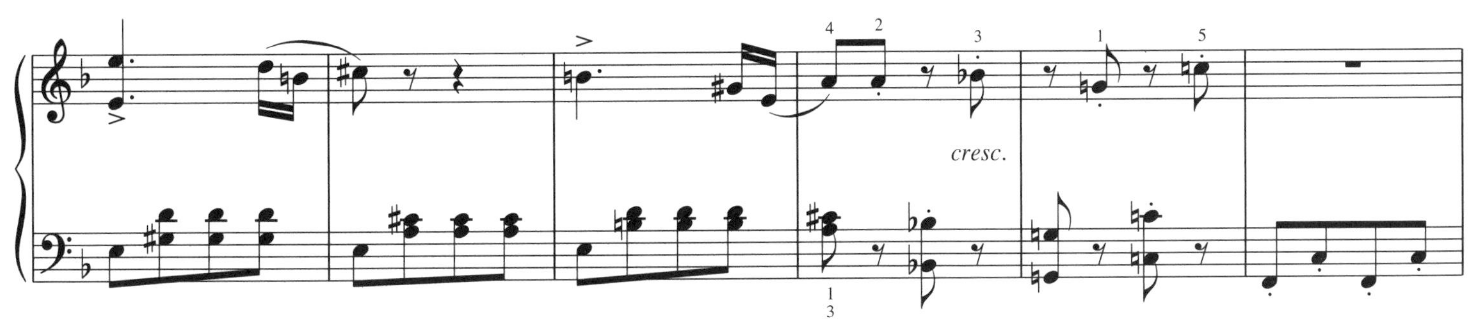
cresc.

legg.
cre
-
scen
-
do
f
p
cre
-
scen
-
do
poco rit.
a tempo
p
rit.

Gagliarda in G minor

Girolamo Frescobaldi
1583–1643

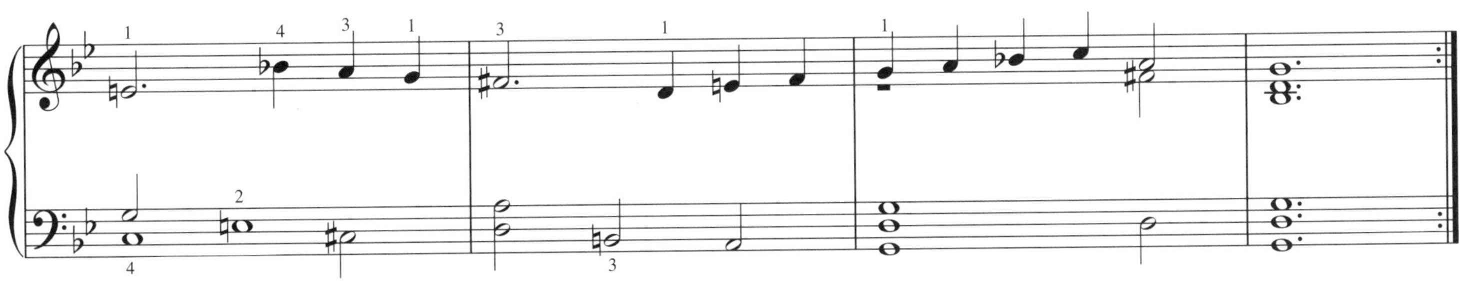

Waltz in A minor

from *Lyric Pieces,* Op. 12, No. 2

Edvard Grieg
1843–1907

Allegro moderato

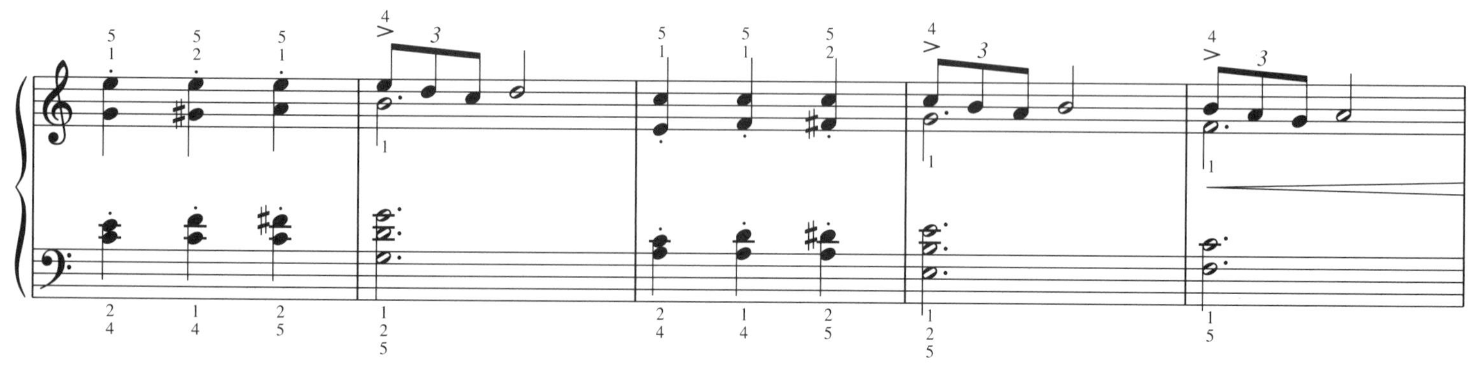

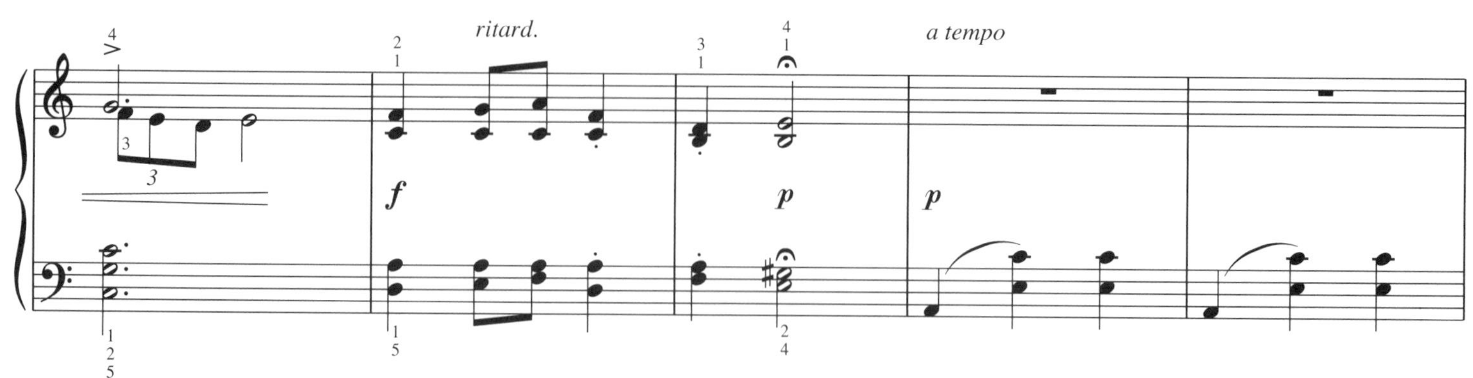

ritard.
f
p
L.H.
R.H.
p
ritard
a tempo

ritard
f
pp
ritard.
f
p
CODA
a tempo
p
dolce
pp

Watchman's Song

from *Lyric Pieces,* Op. 12, No. 3

Edvard Grieg
1843–1907

Molto andante e semplice

INTERMEZZO

Spirit of the Night

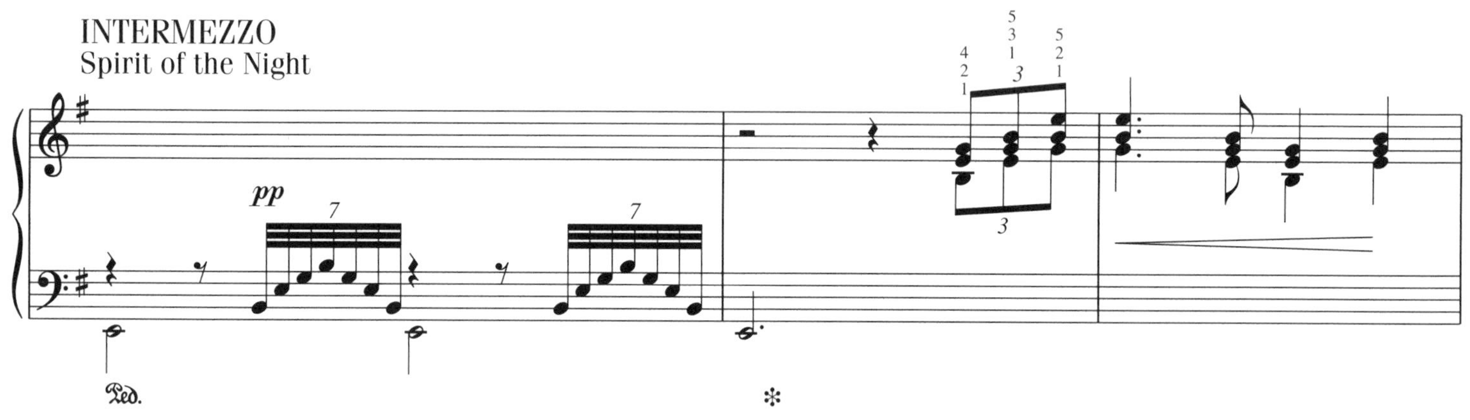

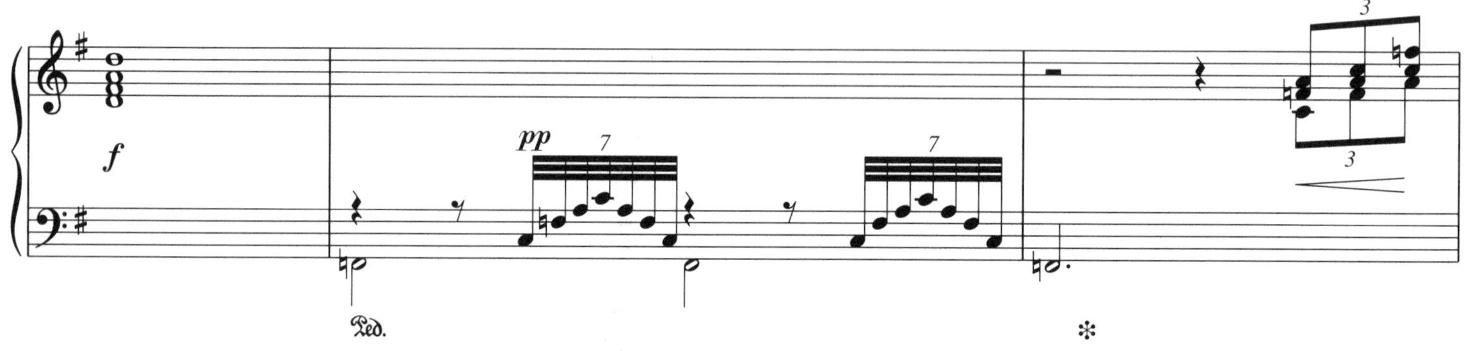

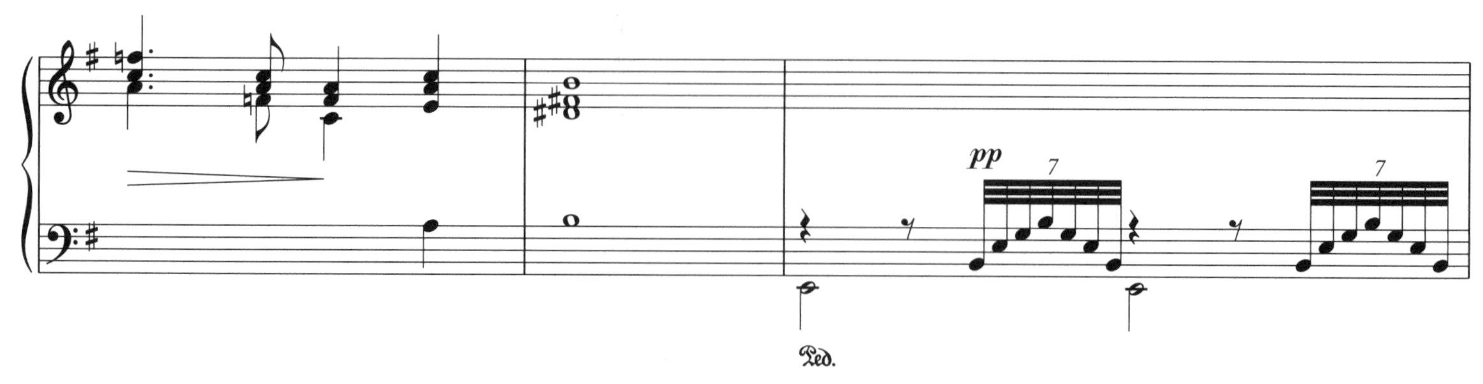

pp
f
p
rit.

Folksong

from *Lyric Pieces,* Op. 38, No. 2

Edvard Grieg
1843–1907

sempre cresc.
dim. poco a poco
rit.
a tempo
cresc.
dim. e rit.

Sailor's Song

from *Lyric Pieces,* Op. 68, No. 1

Edvard Grieg
1843–1907

p
cresc.
poco ritard.
a tempo
ma ben tem.
ff
poco a poco ritard.
Ped.

p
cresc.
poco ritard.
a tempo
ma ben ten.
ff
poco a poco ritard.
Ped.

Morning Prayer

from *Albumleaves for the Young,* Op. 101, No. 2

Cornelius Gurlitt
1820–1901

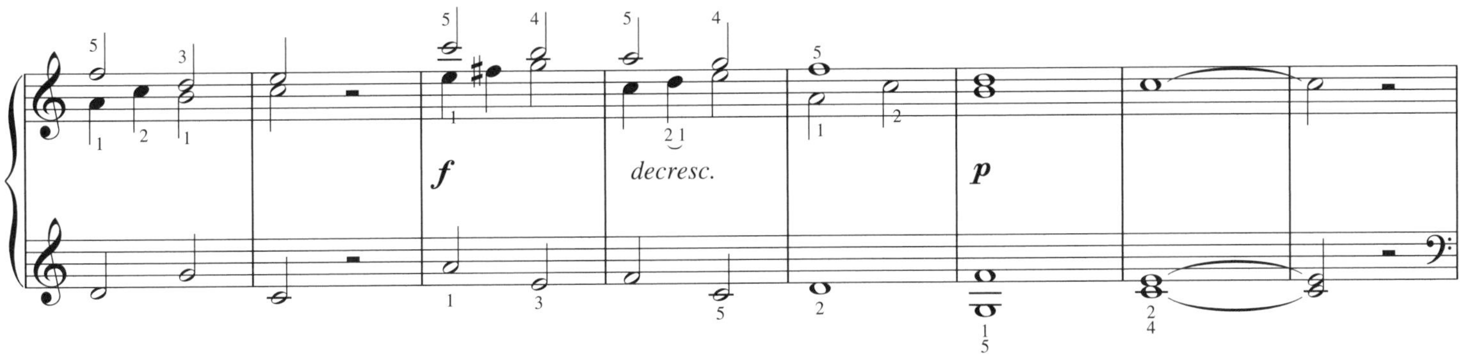

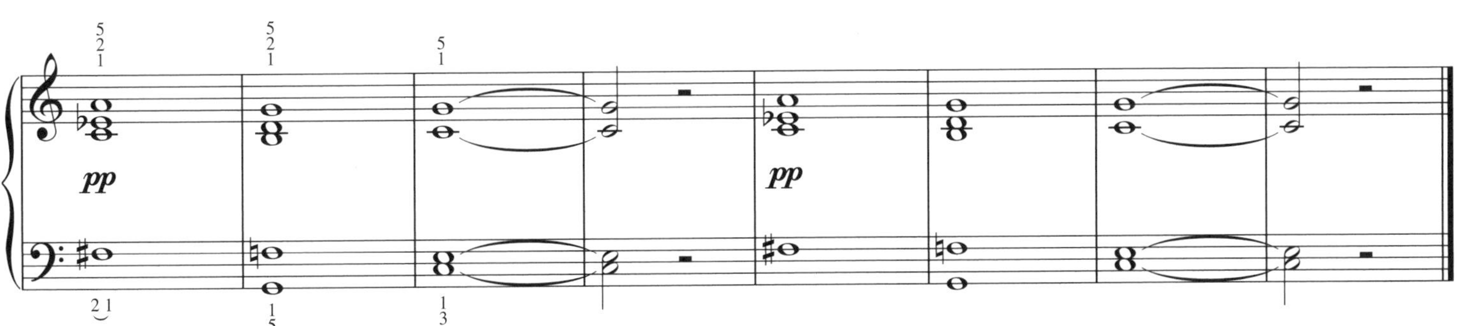

March in D Major

from *Albumleaves for the Young,* Op. 101, No. 1

Cornelius Gurlitt
1820–1901

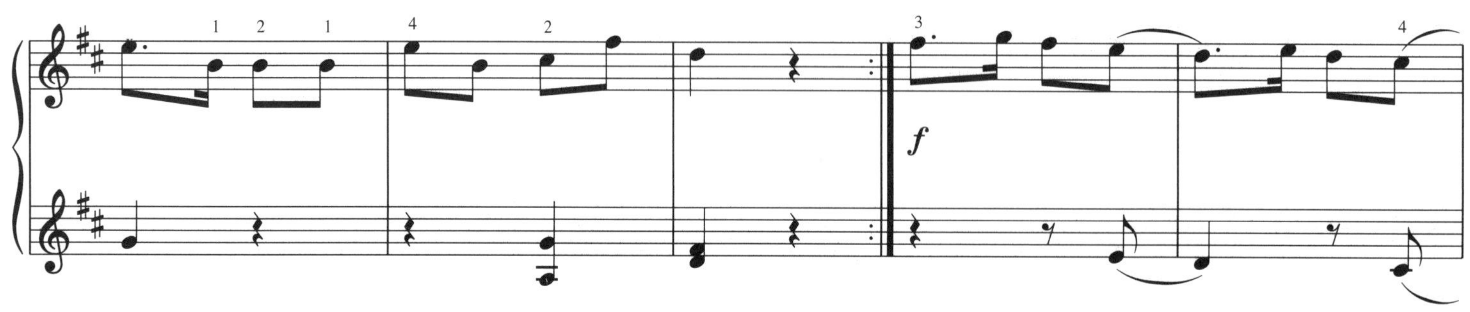

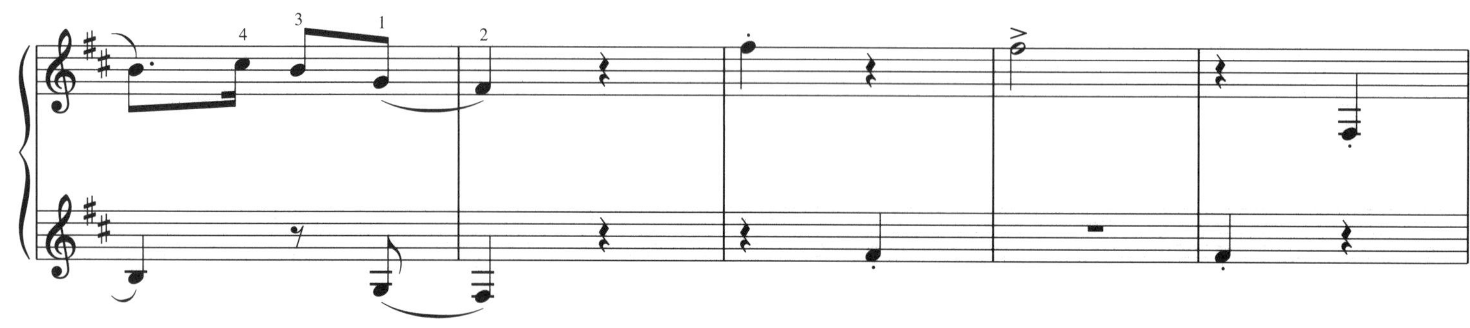

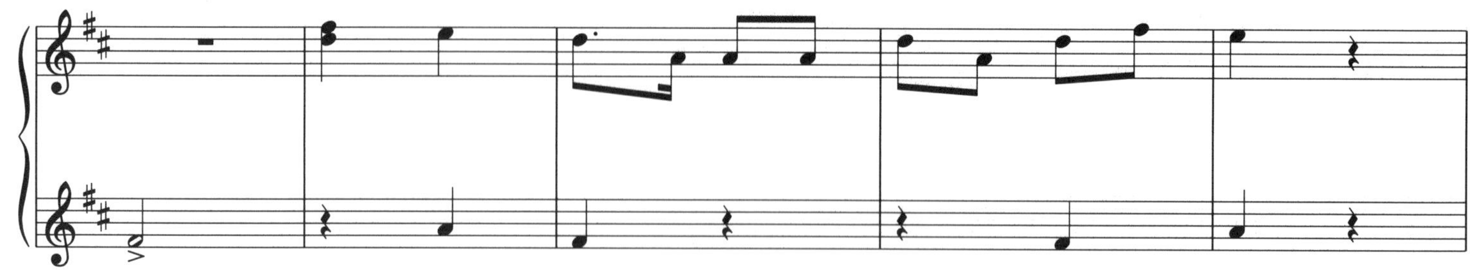

f

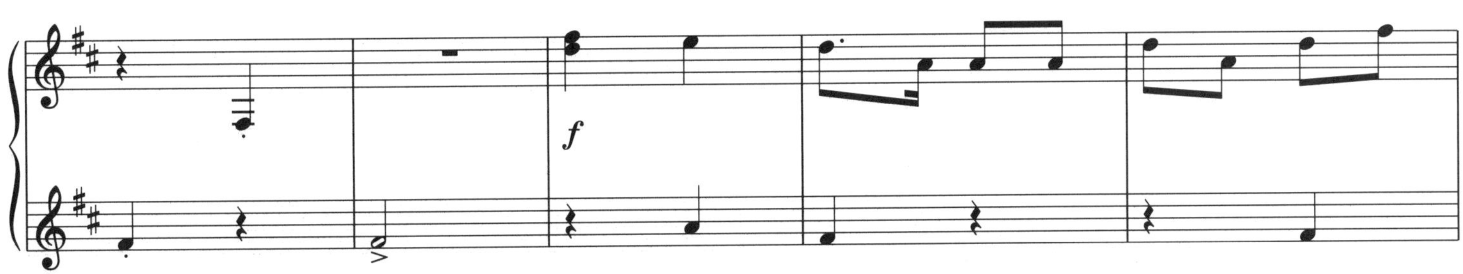
f

A Sunshiny Morning

from *Albumleaves for the Young,* Op. 101, No. 3

Cornelius Gurlitt
1820–1901

Northern Strains

from *Albumleaves for the Young,* Op. 101, No. 4

Cornelius Gurlitt
1820–1901

By the Spring

from *Albumleaves for the Young,* Op. 101, No. 5

Cornelius Gurlitt
1820–1901

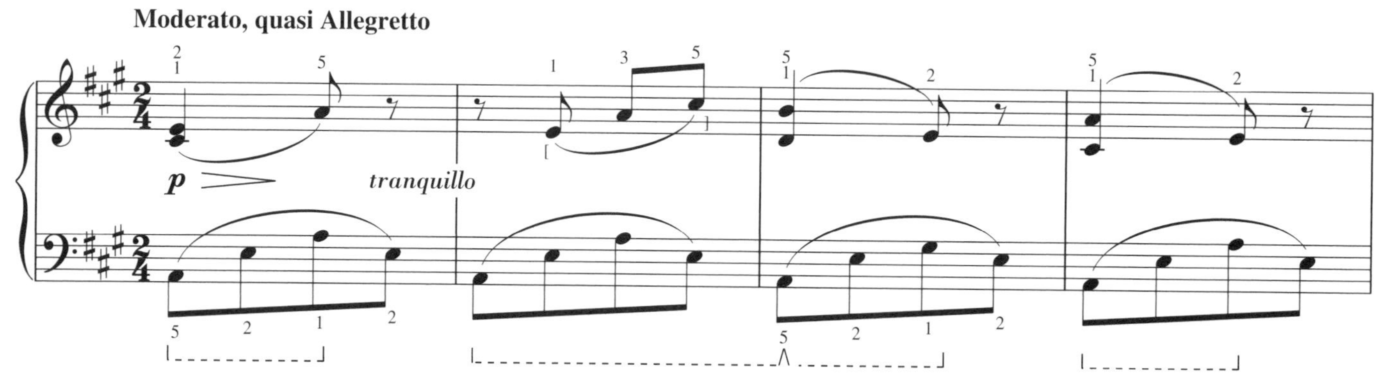

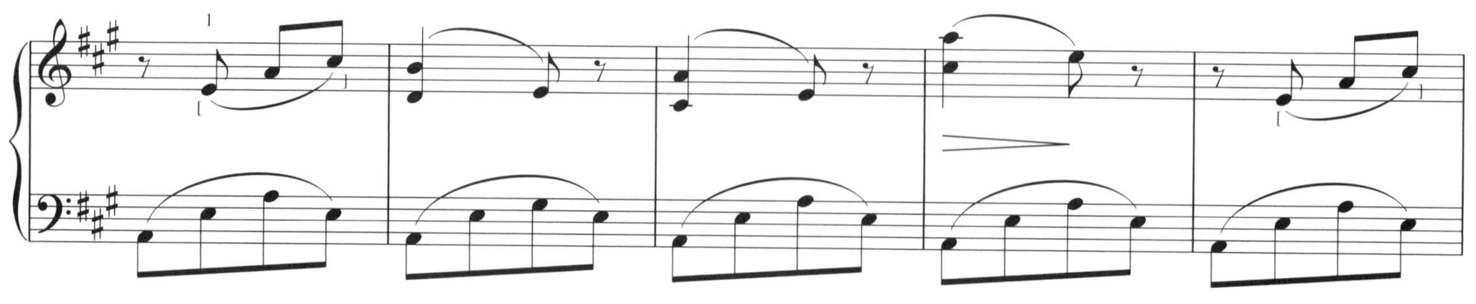

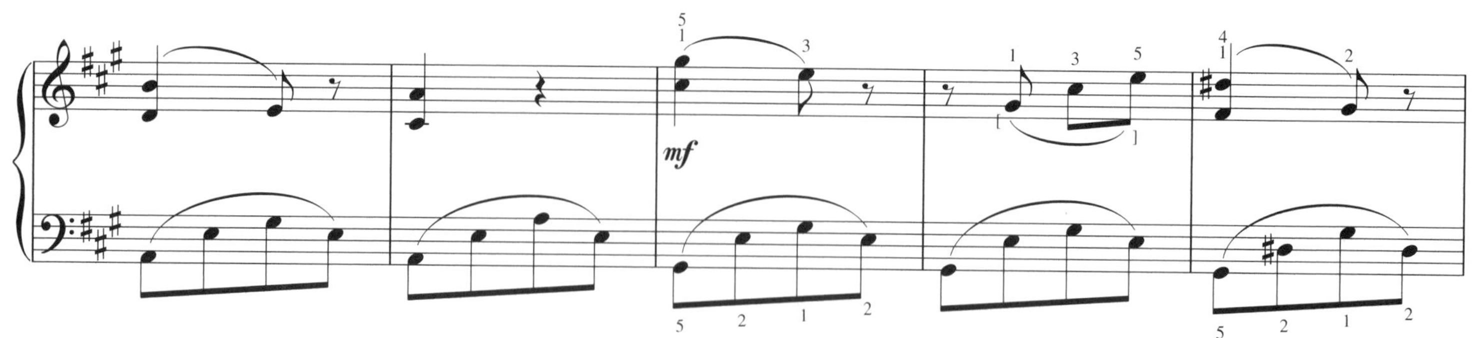

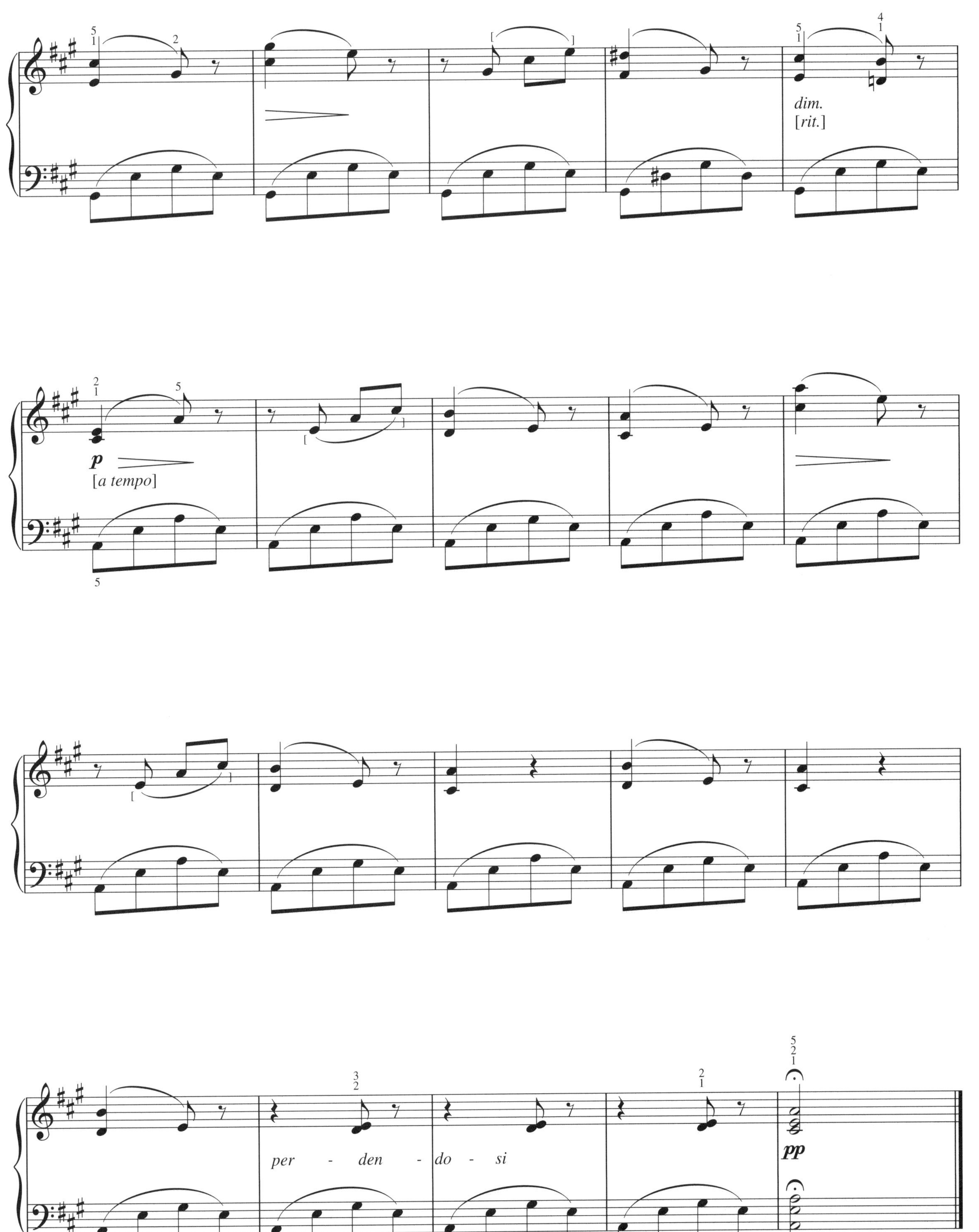
dim.
[rit.]
p
[a tempo]
per - den - do - si
pp

Lullaby

from *Albumleaves for the Young,* Op. 101, No. 6

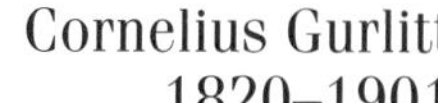

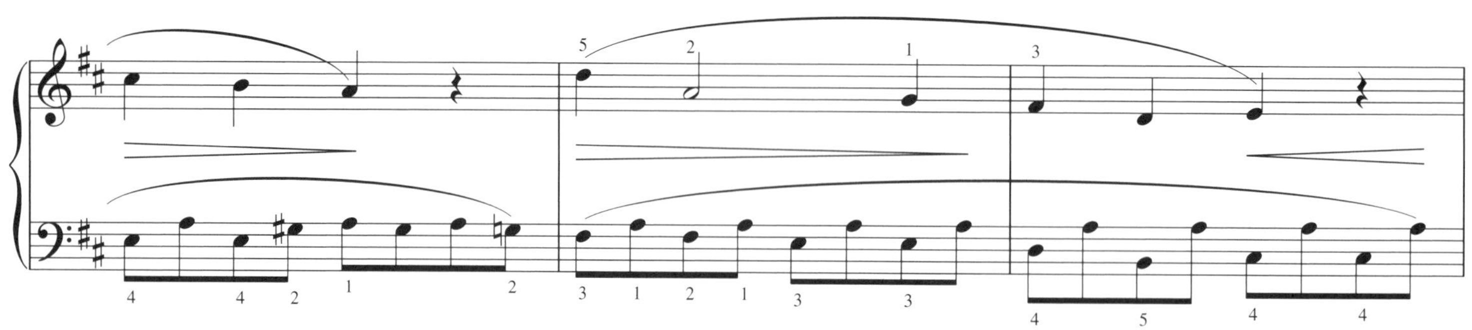

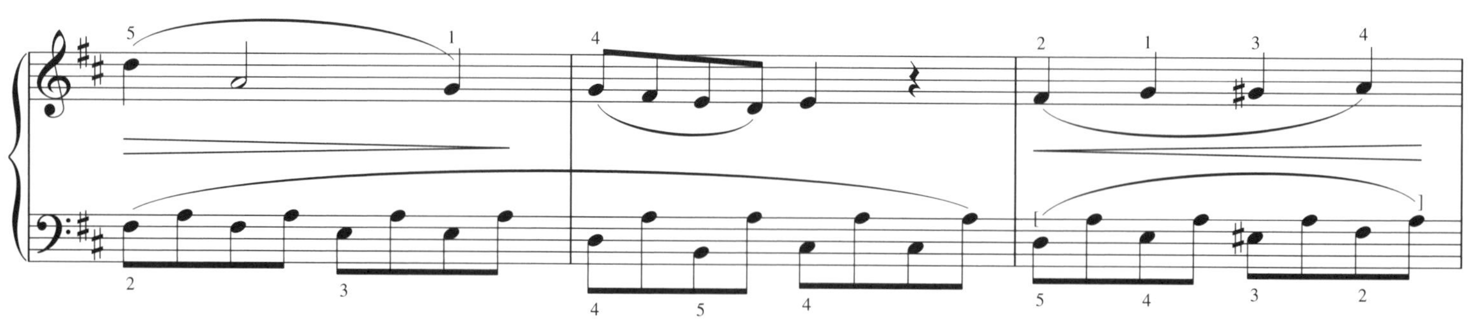

*Bring out the melody.

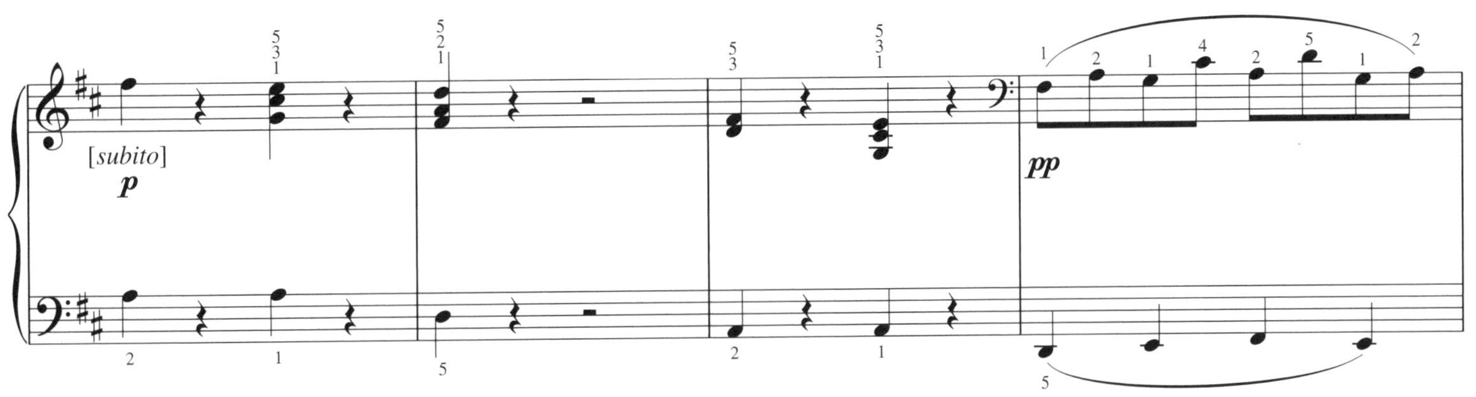
[subito]
p
pp

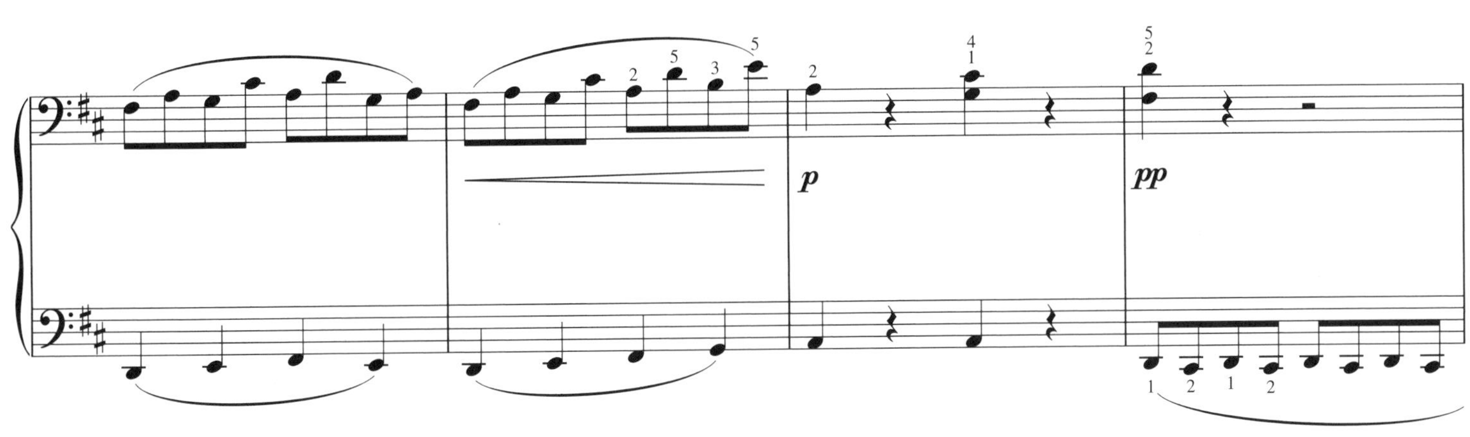
p
pp

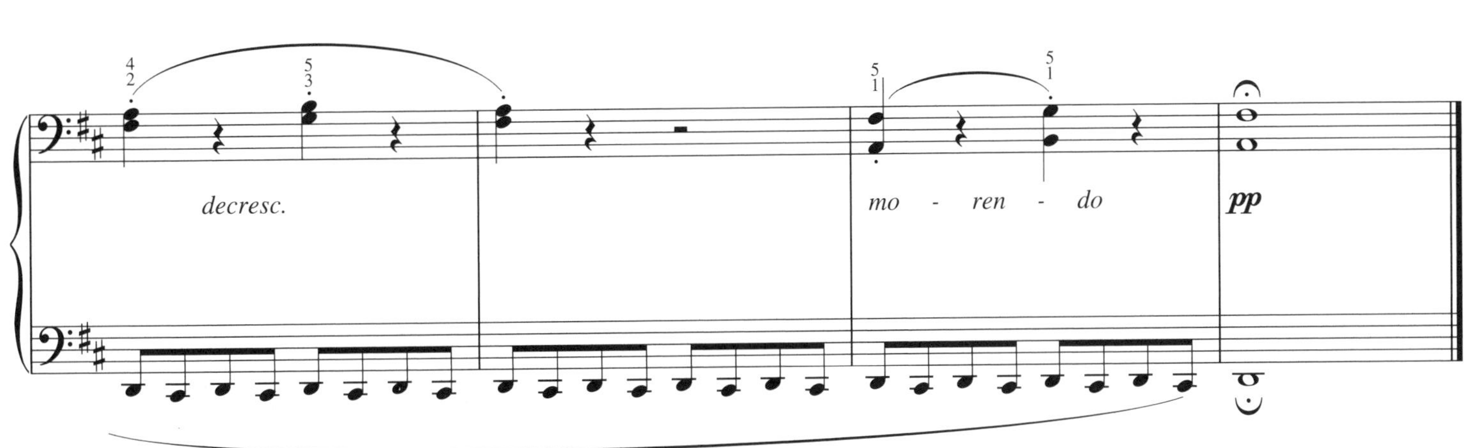
decresc.
mo - ren - do
pp

Lament

from *Albumleaves for the Young,* Op. 101, No. 7

Cornelius Gurlitt
1820–1901

Waltz in C Major

from *Albumleaves for the Young,* Op. 101, No. 11

Cornelius Gurlitt
1820–1901

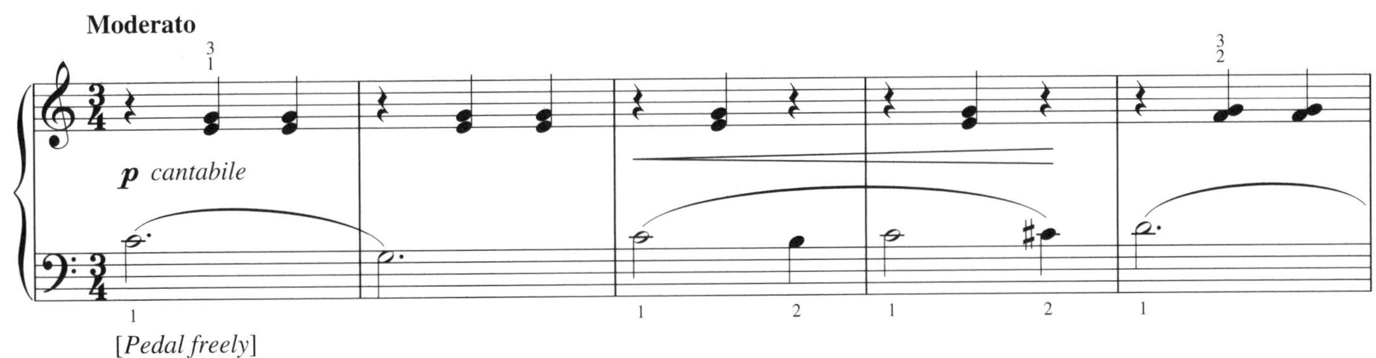

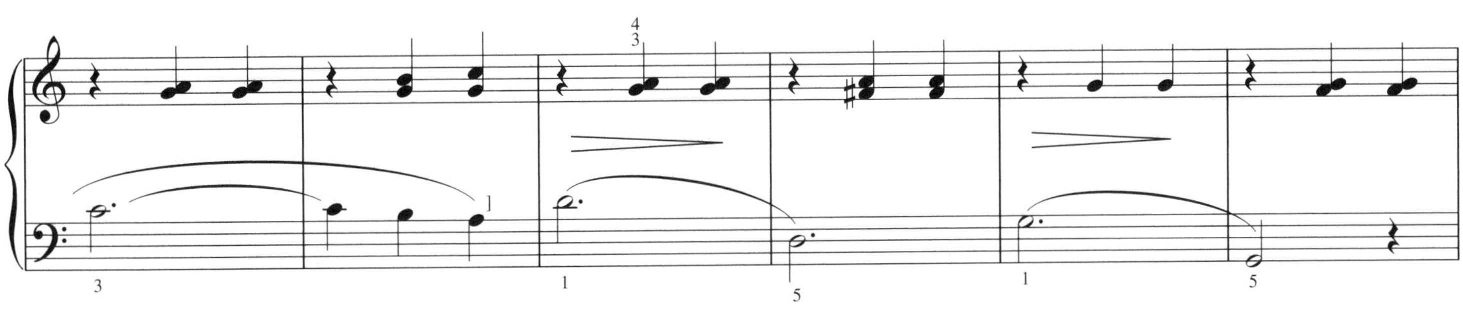

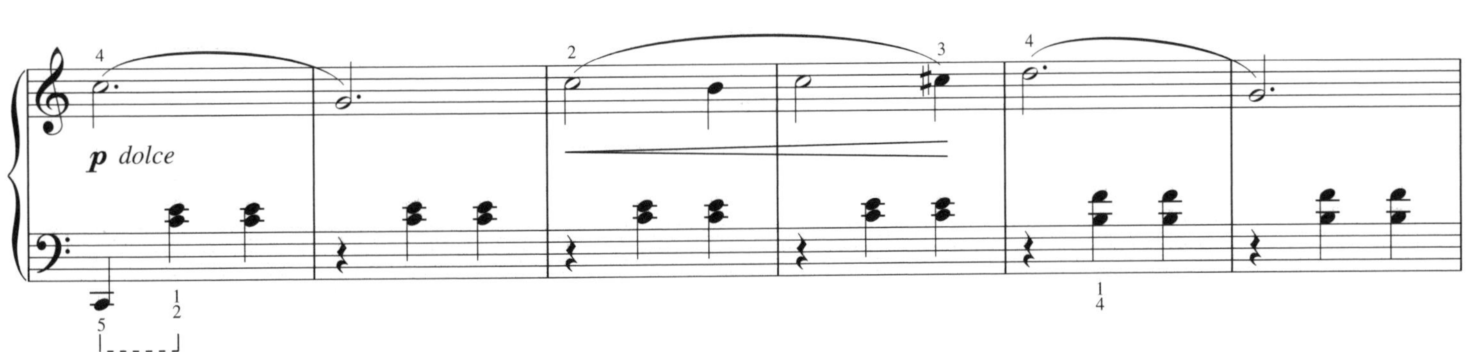

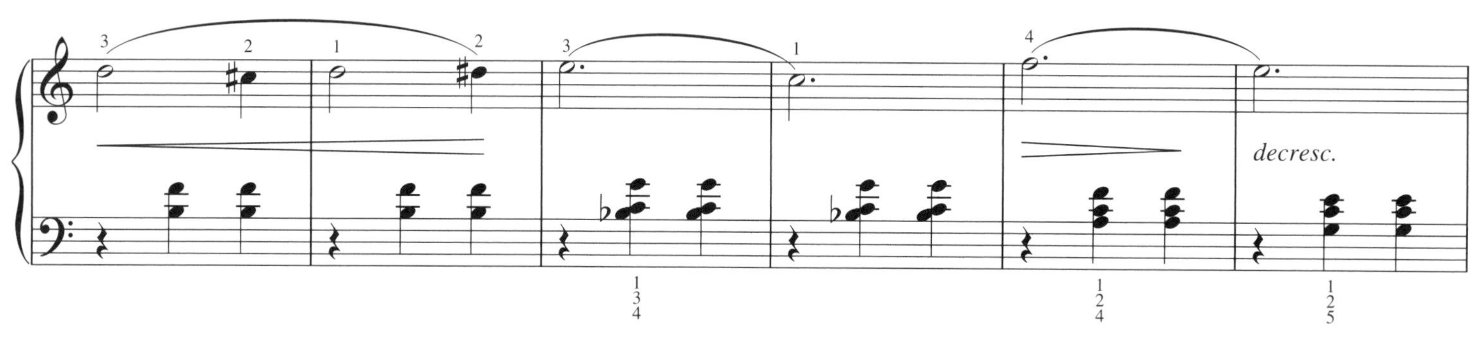
decresc.

Fine

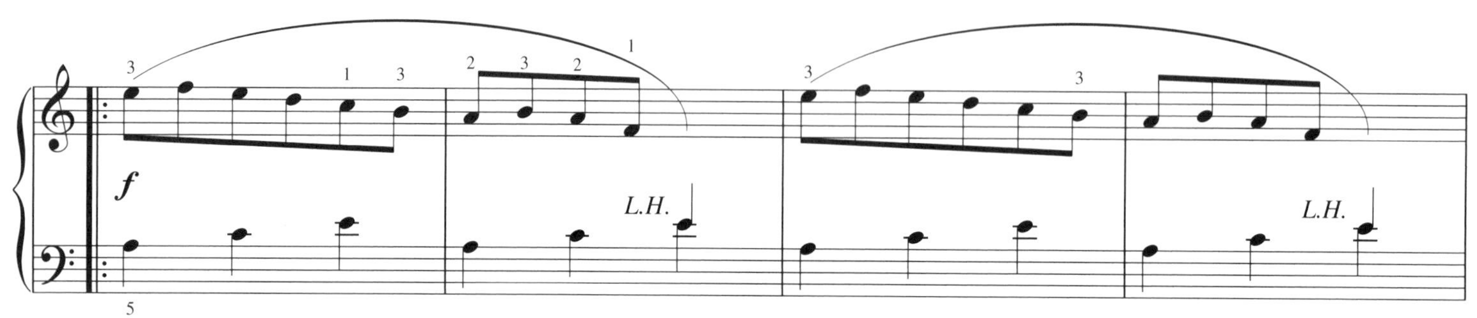
L.H.
L.H.

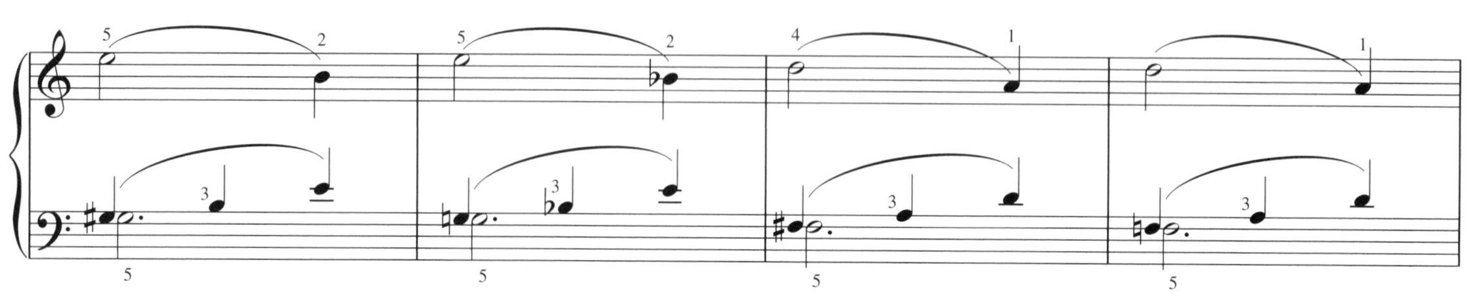

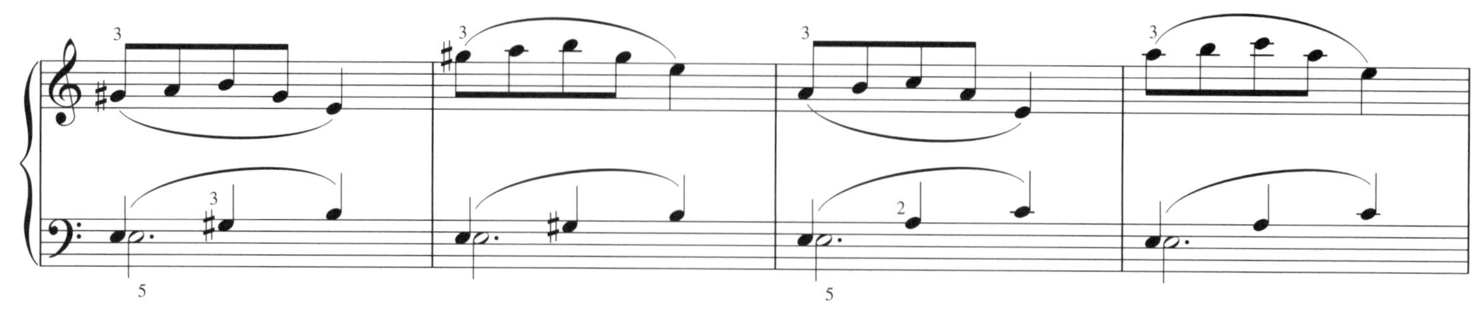

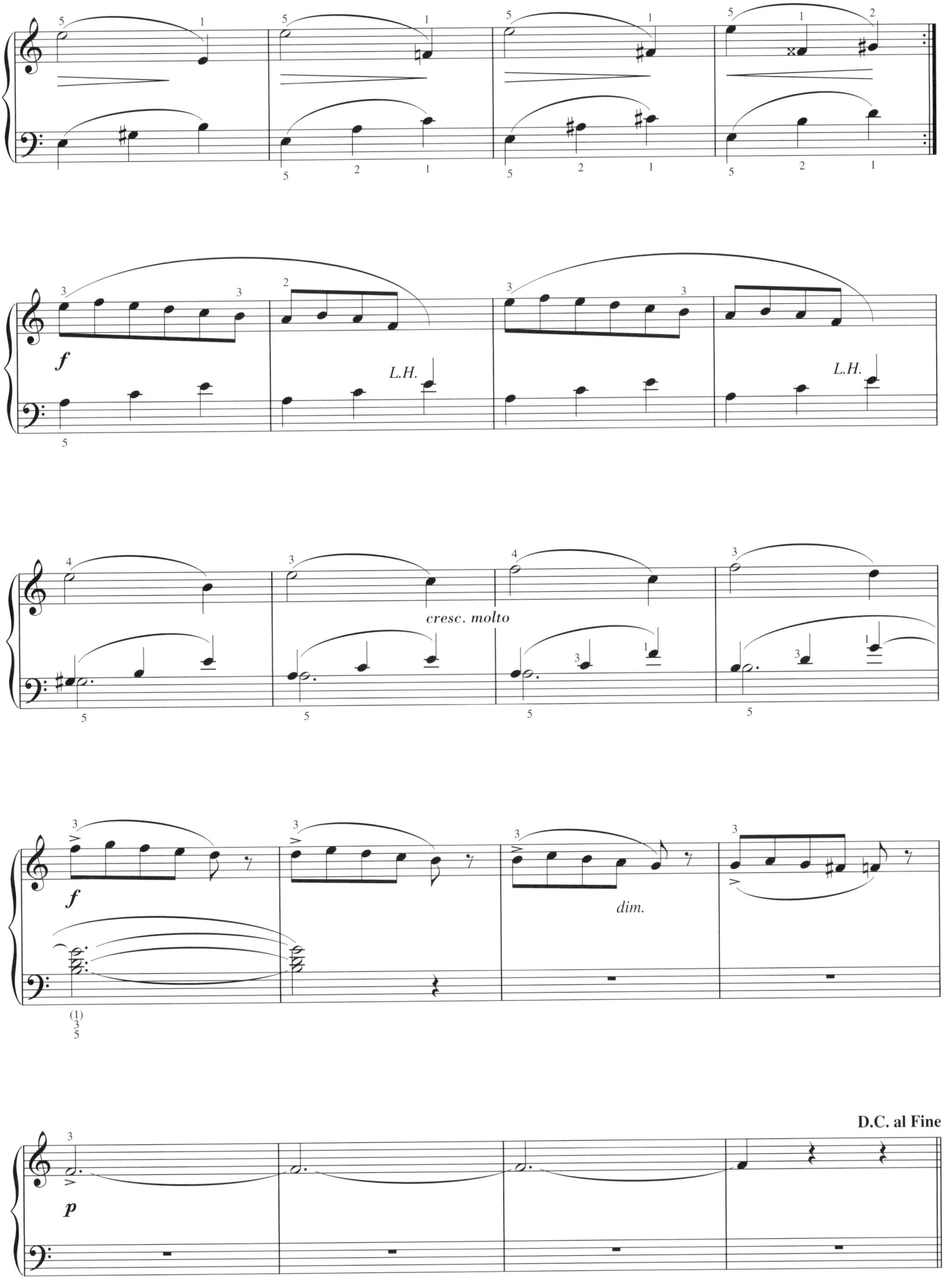

f

L.H.

L.H.

cresc. molto

f

dim.

D.C. al Fine

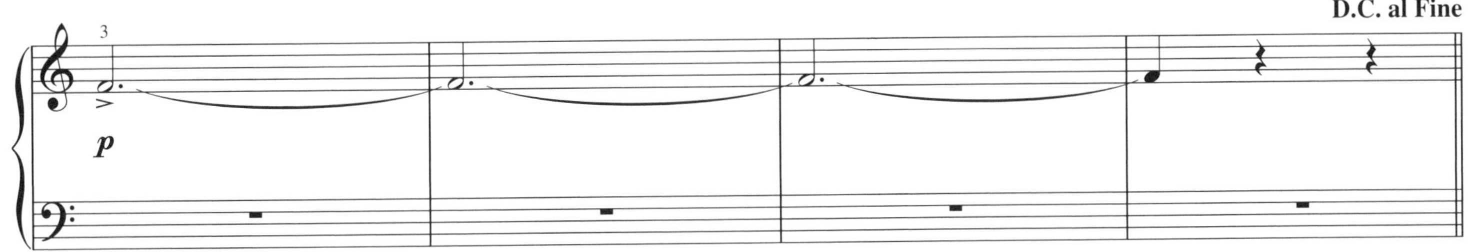

Grandfather's Birthday

from *Albumleaves for the Young,* Op. 101, No. 13

Cornelius Gurlitt
1820–1901

Valse Noble

from *Albumleaves for the Young,* Op. 101, No. 14

Cornelius Gurlitt
1820–1901

Courante in G Major

George Frideric Handel
1685–1759

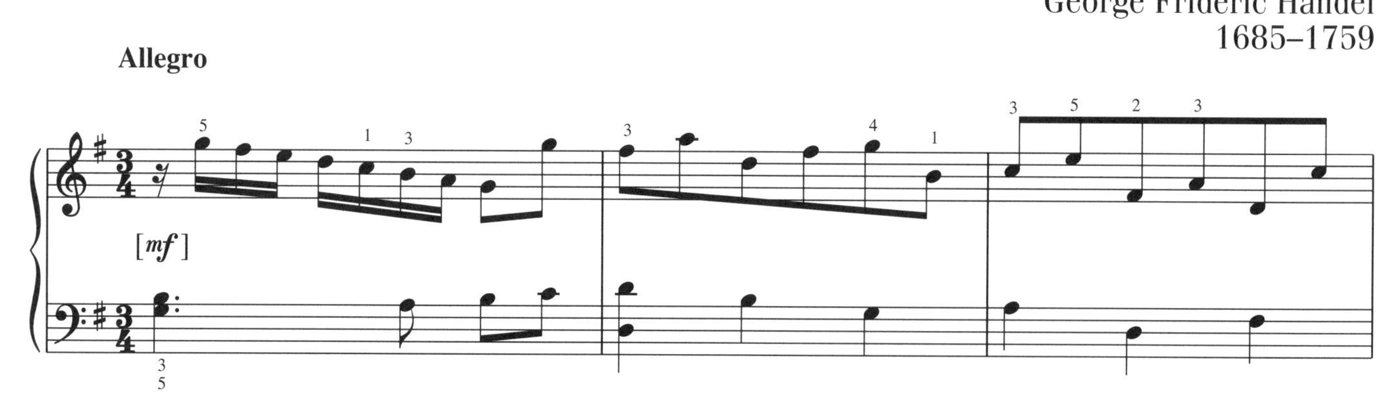

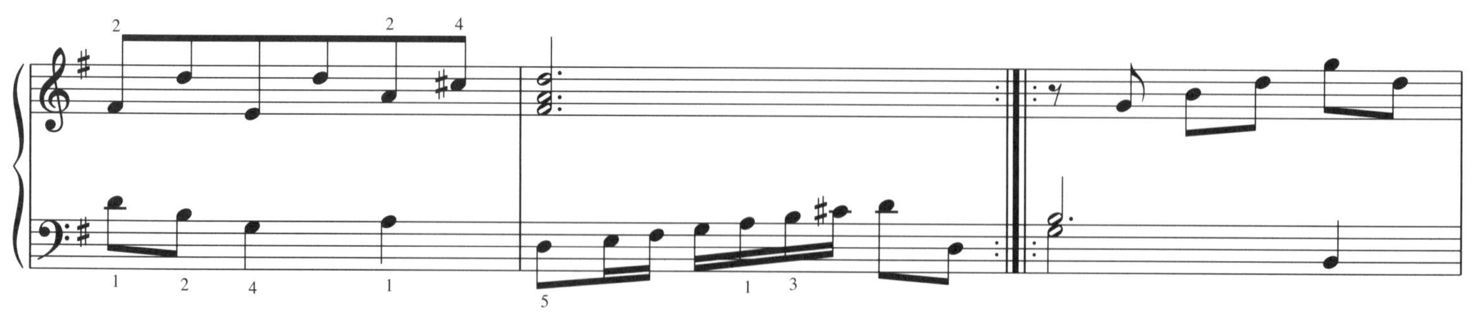

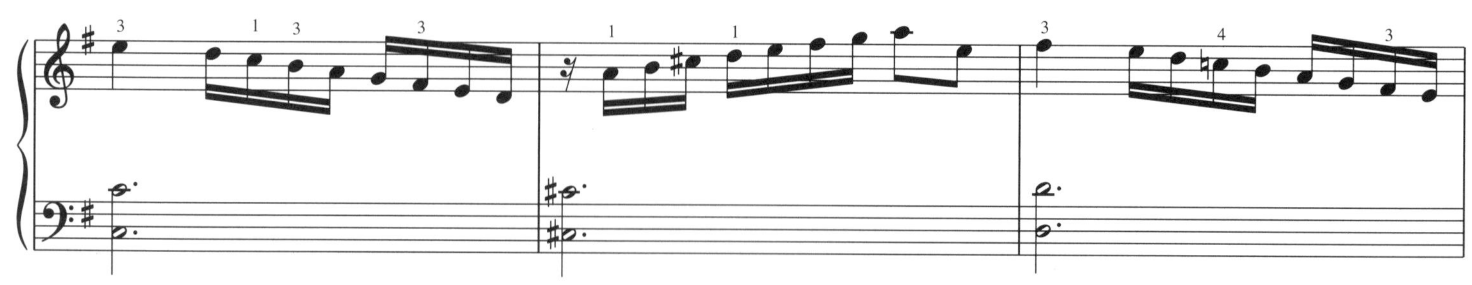

Minuet in F Major

George Frideric Handel
1685–1759

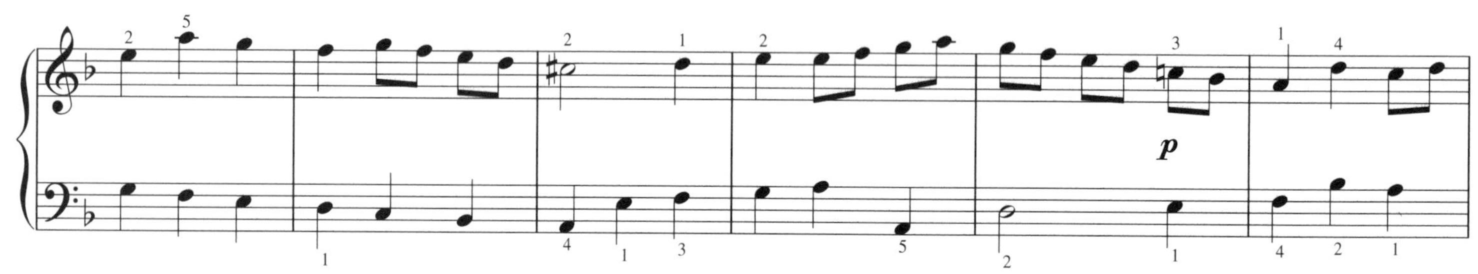

Rigaudon in G Major

George Frideric Handel
1685–1759

Sarabande

from Suite in D minor, HWV 437

George Frideric Handel
1685–1759

Var. 1

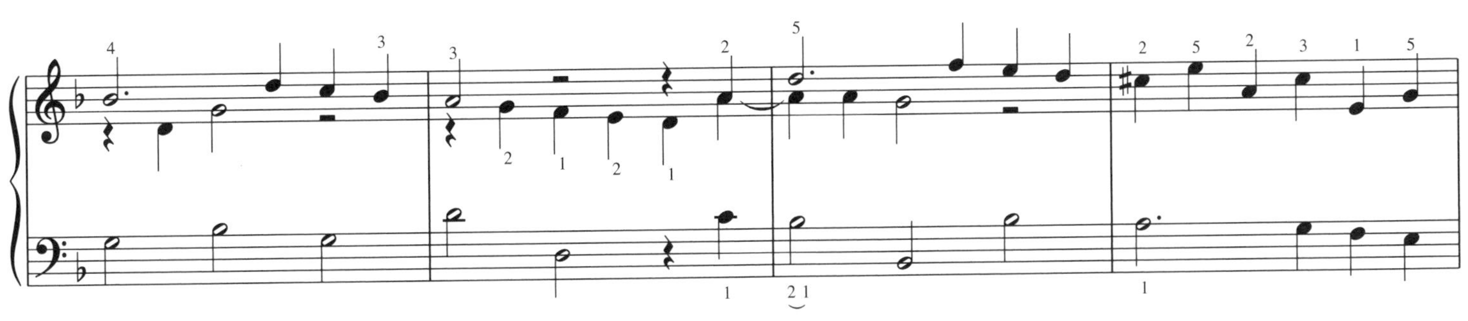

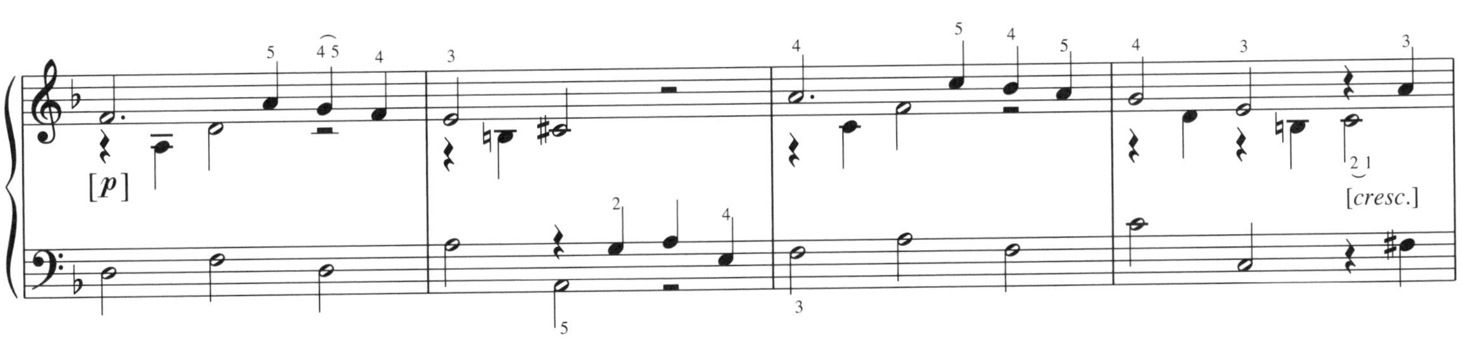

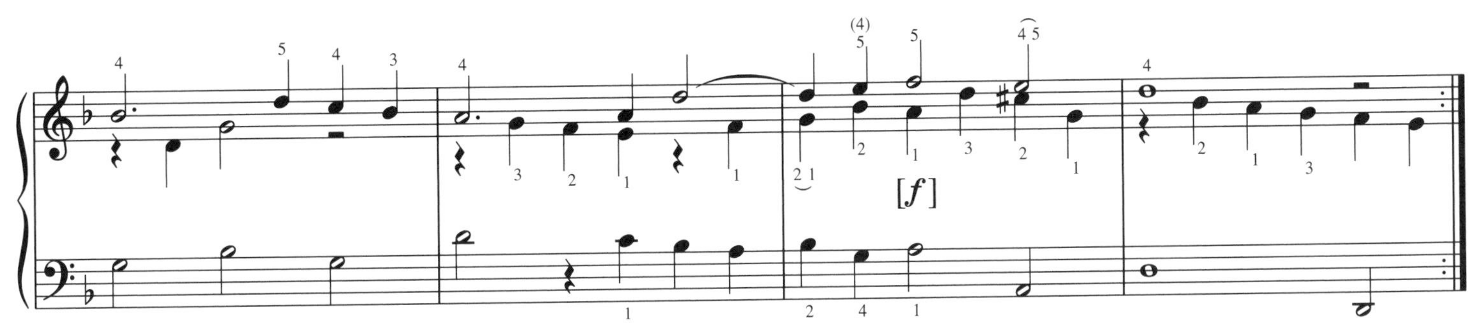

Var. 2

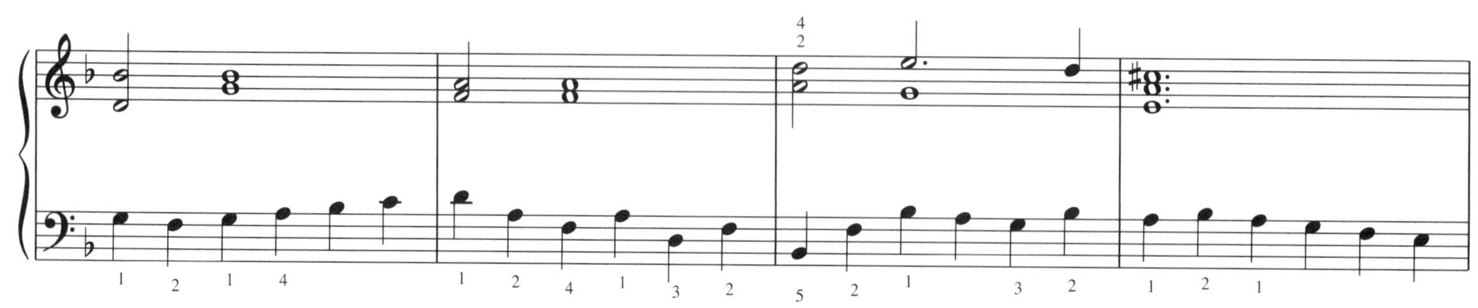

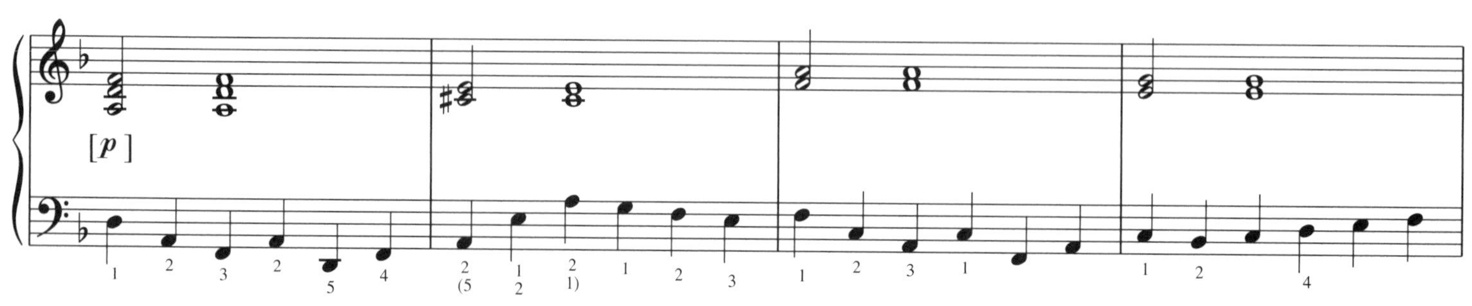

Country Dance in C Major

Franz Joseph Haydn
1732–1809

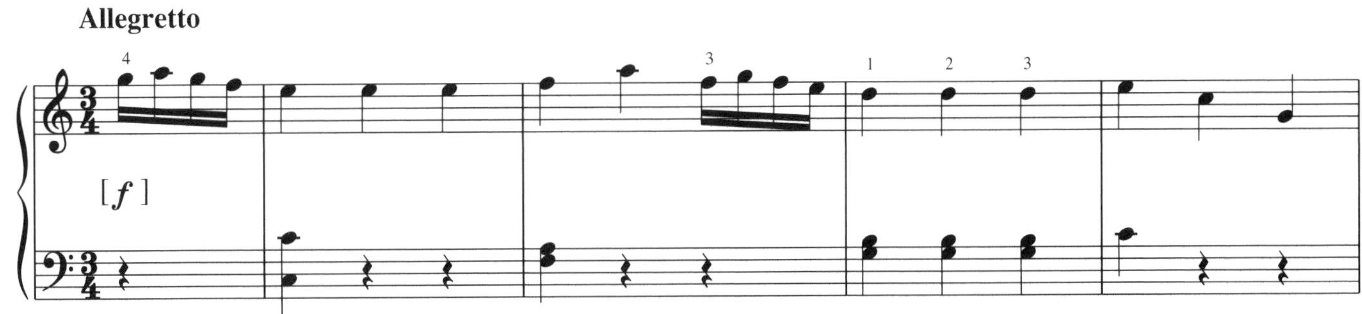

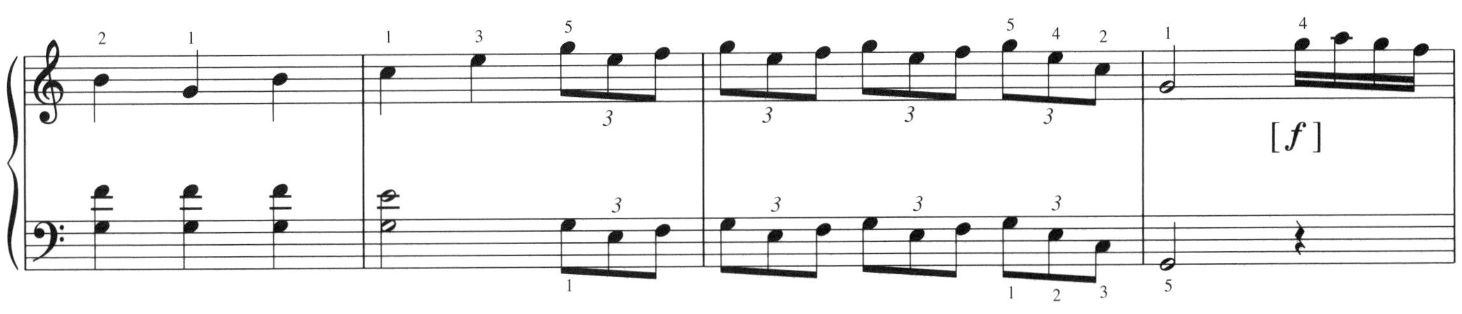

Allegro in F Major

Franz Joseph Haydn
1732–1809

poco rit.
p
a tempo
mf
mp
p
f
p
f
p
f

Dance in G Major

Franz Joseph Haydn
1732–1809

The Brook

from *25 Melodious Etudes,* Op. 45, No. 1

Stephen Heller
1813–1888

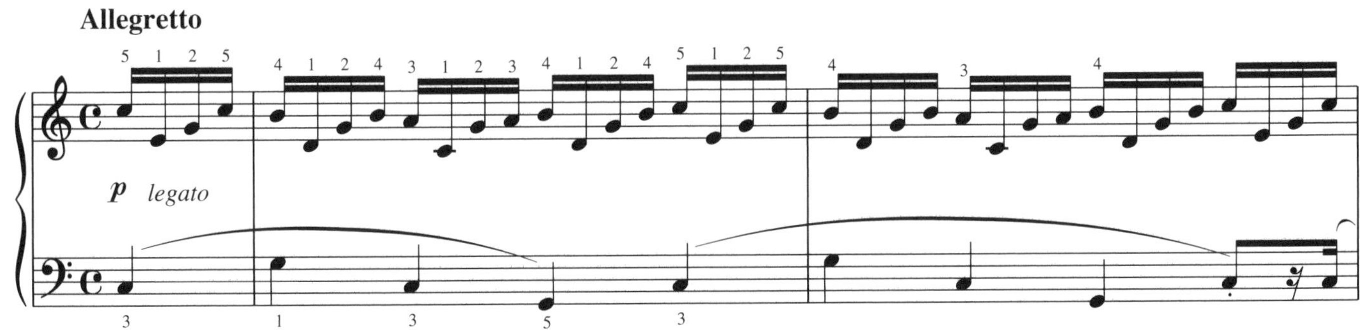

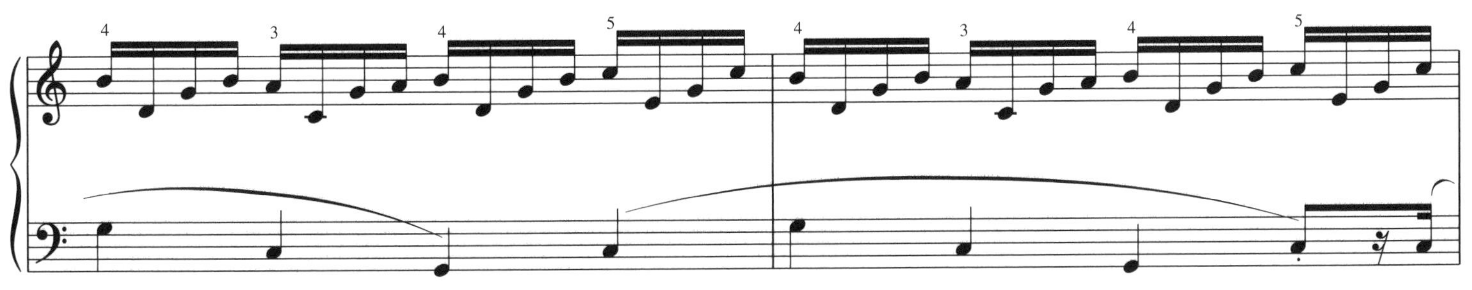

p

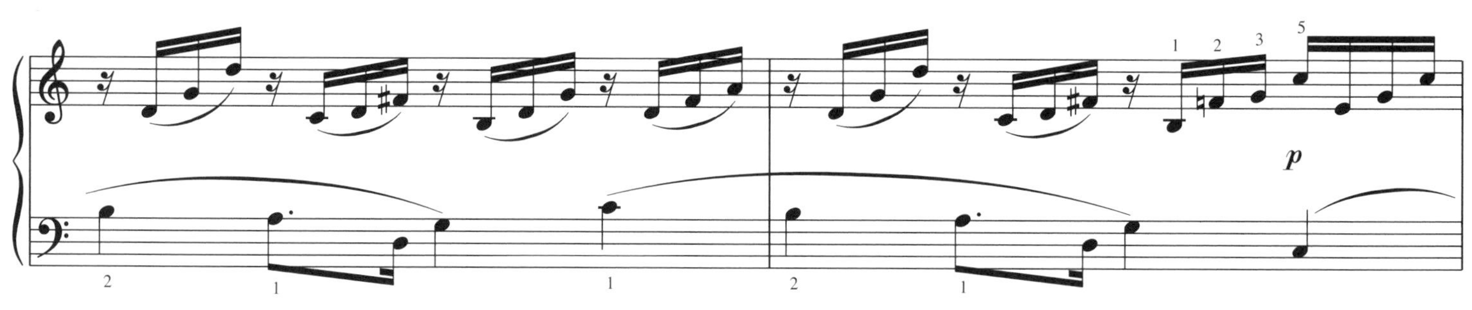
p

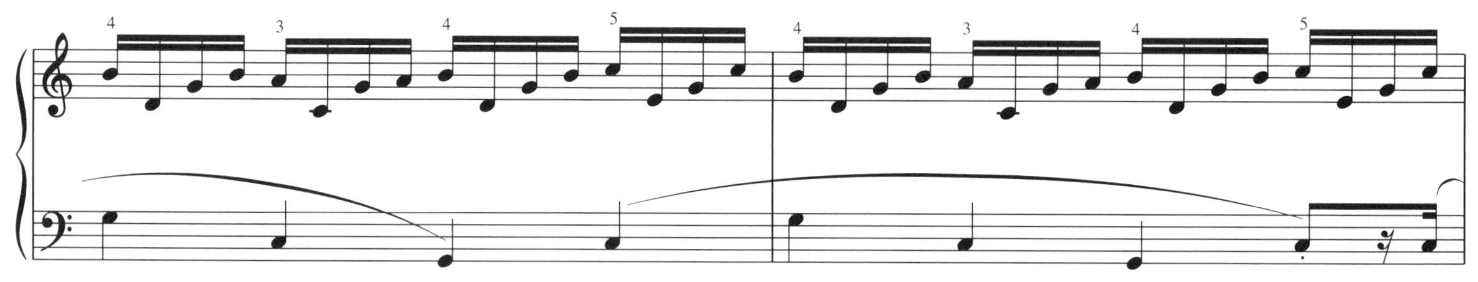

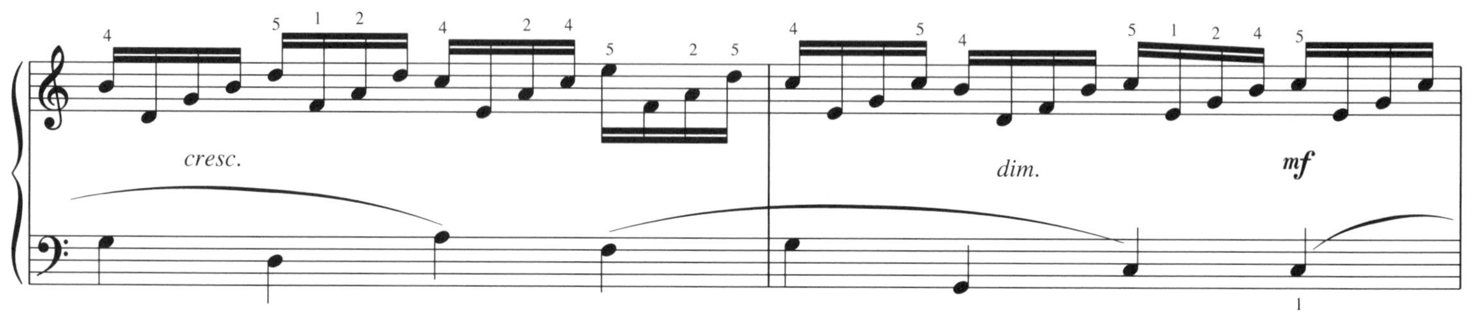
cresc.
dim.
mf

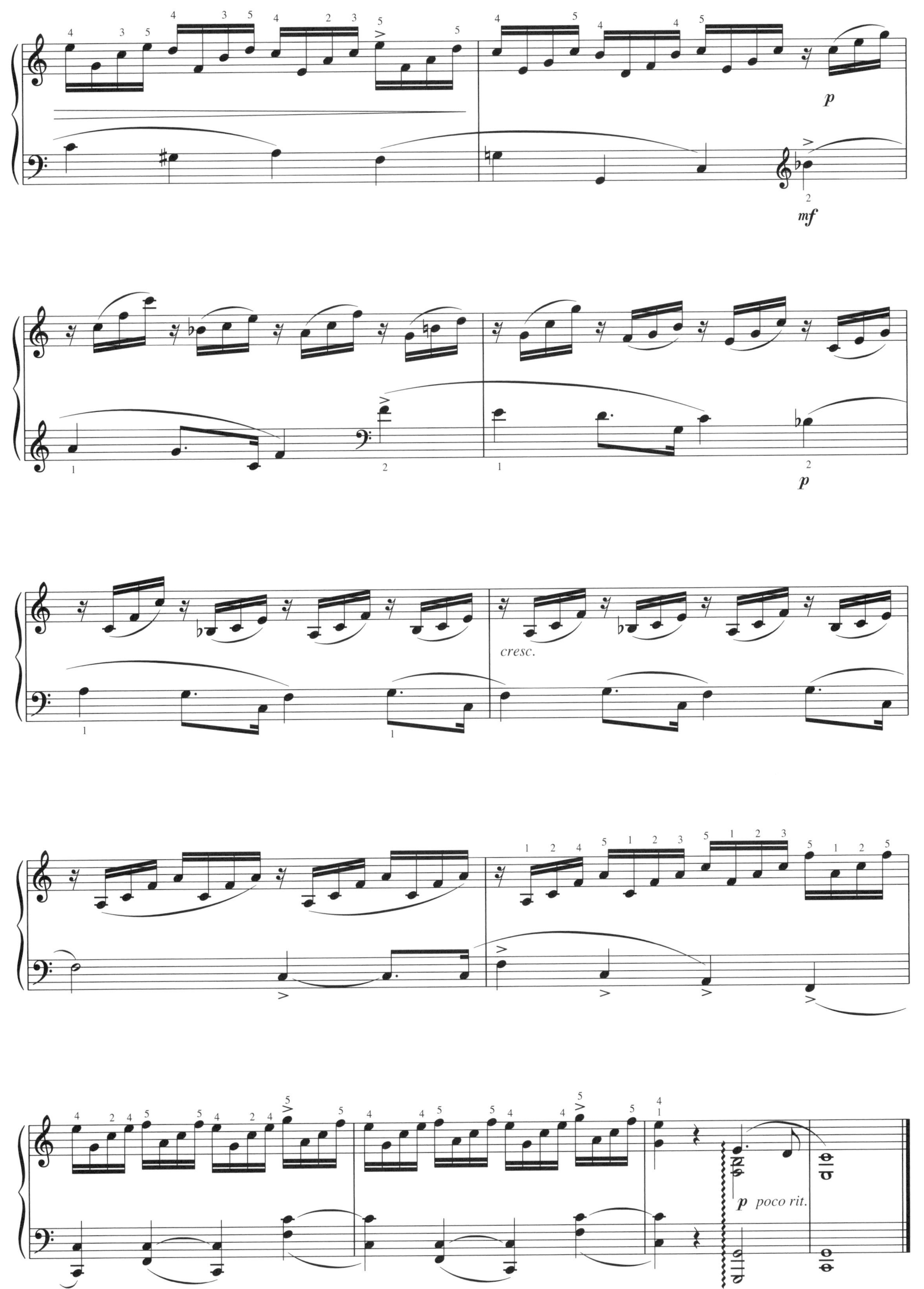
p
mf
p
cresc.
p poco rit.

Avalanche

from *25 Melodious Etudes,* Op. 45, No. 2

Stephen Heller
1813–1888

Allegro vivace

mf

Ped. * Ped. * Ped. *

Ped. *

poco meno mosso

p

a tempo

mf

Ped. * Ped. *

poco meno mosso
p
a tempo
mf
R.H.
L.H.
p
cresc.
Ped.
p
cresc.
p
Ped.
mf
R.H.
p
cresc.
L.H.
mf
p
cresc.

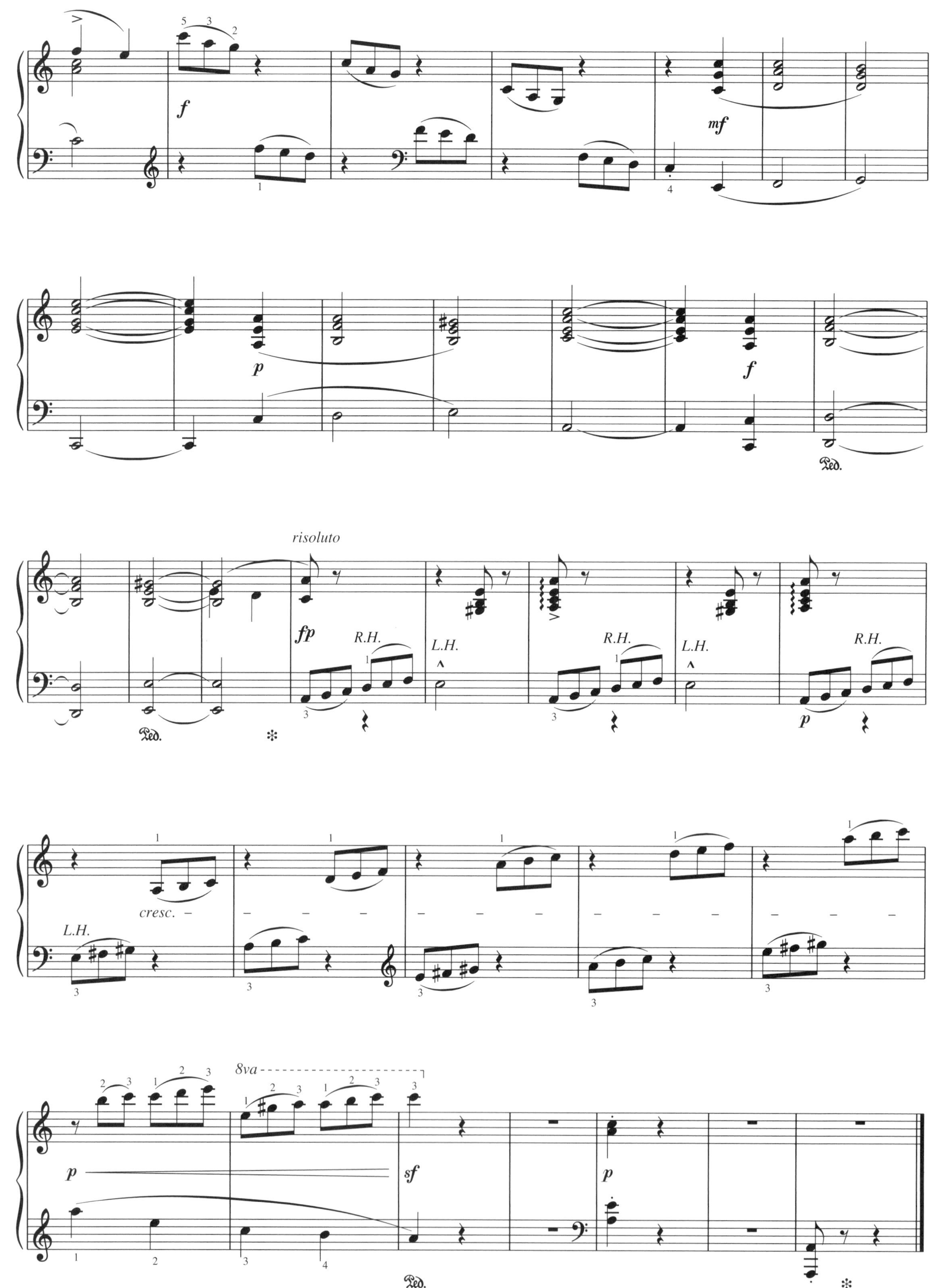
f
mf
p
f
Ped.
risoluto
fp
R.H.
L.H.
R.H.
L.H.
R.H.
p
Ped.
L.H.
cresc.
8va
p
sf
p
Ped.

Etude in C Major

from *25 Studies,* Op. 47, No. 19

Stephen Heller
1813–1888

Con moto (♩ = 192)
semplice e con grazia
p
legatiss.
p
p
pp

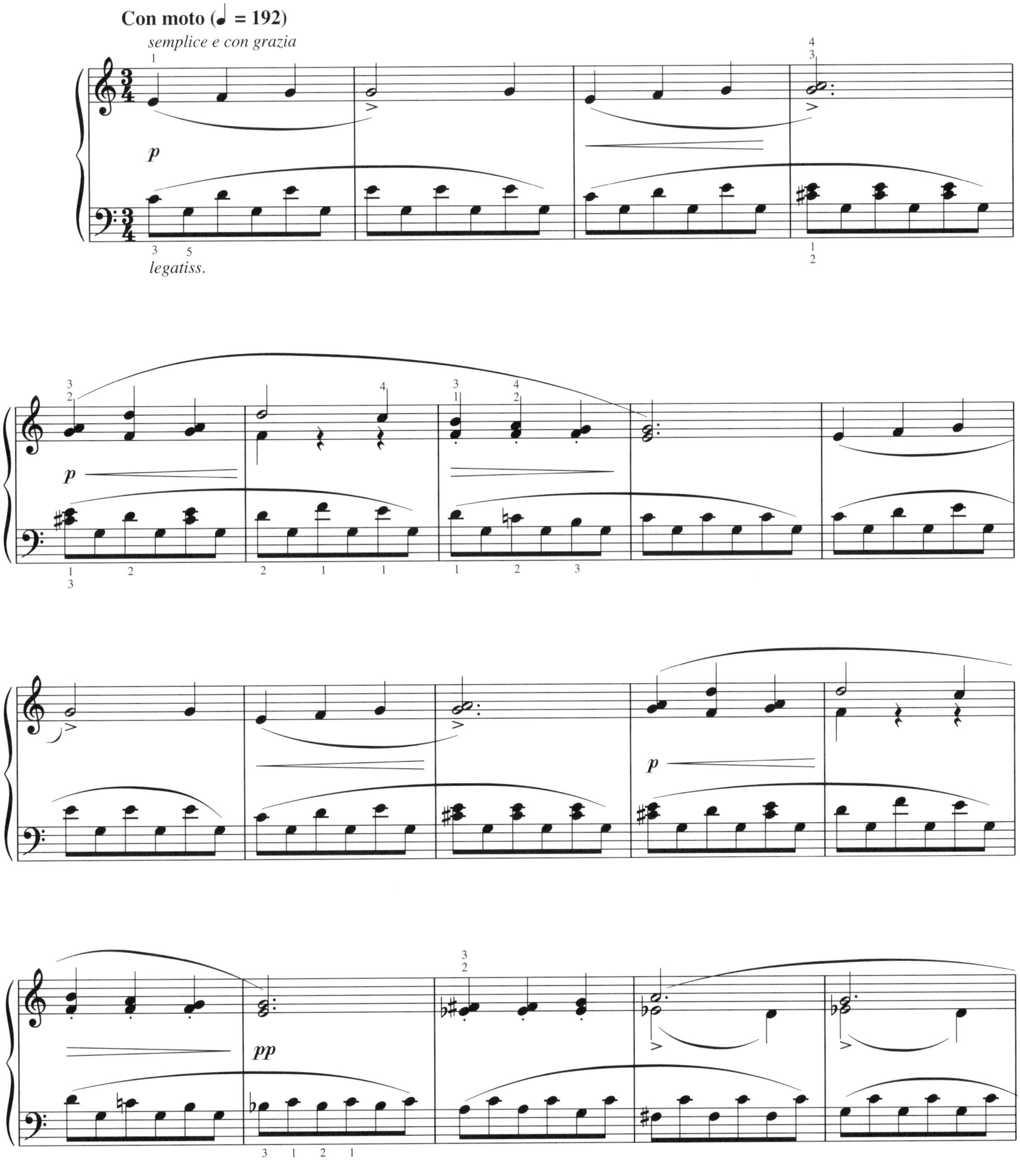

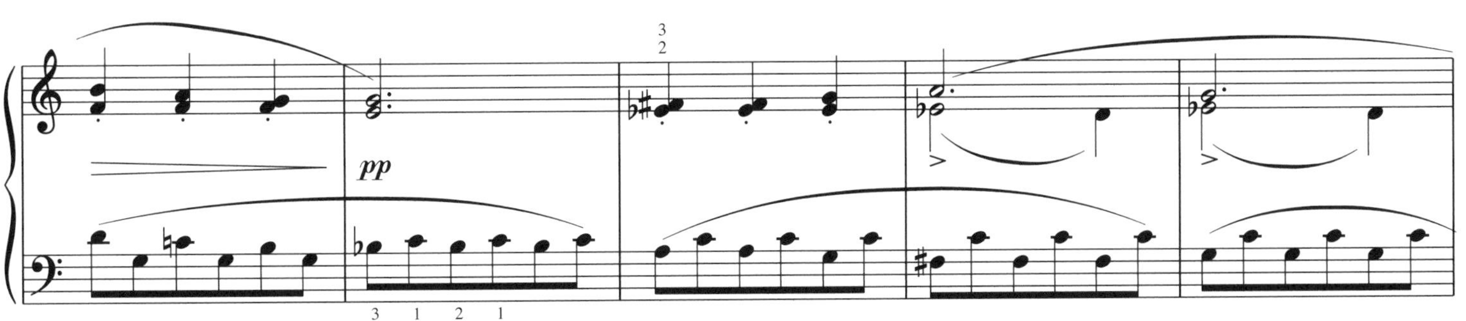

p
p
p
pp
a tempo
sf
pp

Over Hill and Dale

from *25 Melodious Etudes,* Op. 45, No. 24

Stephen Heller
1813–1888

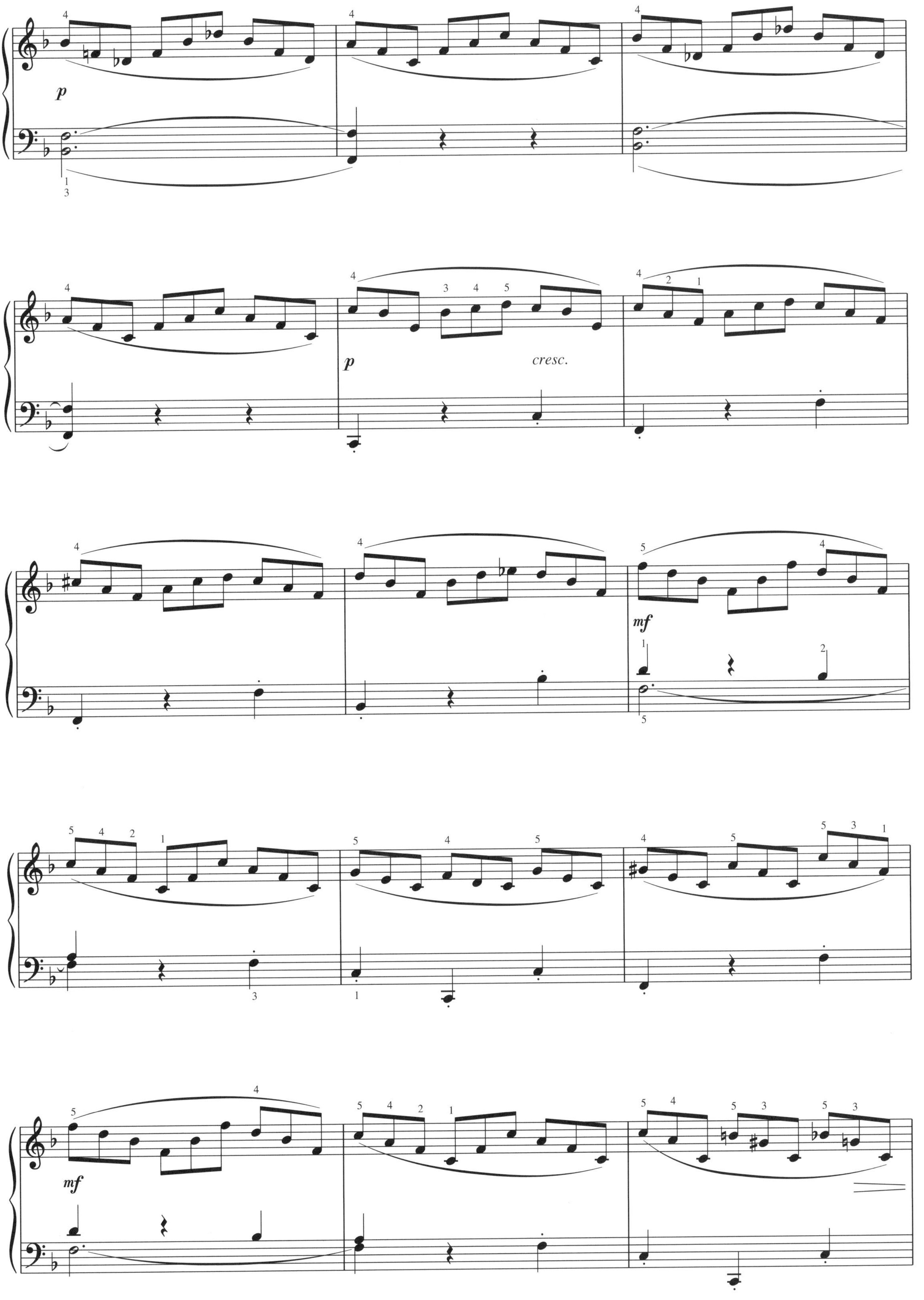
p
cresc.
mf

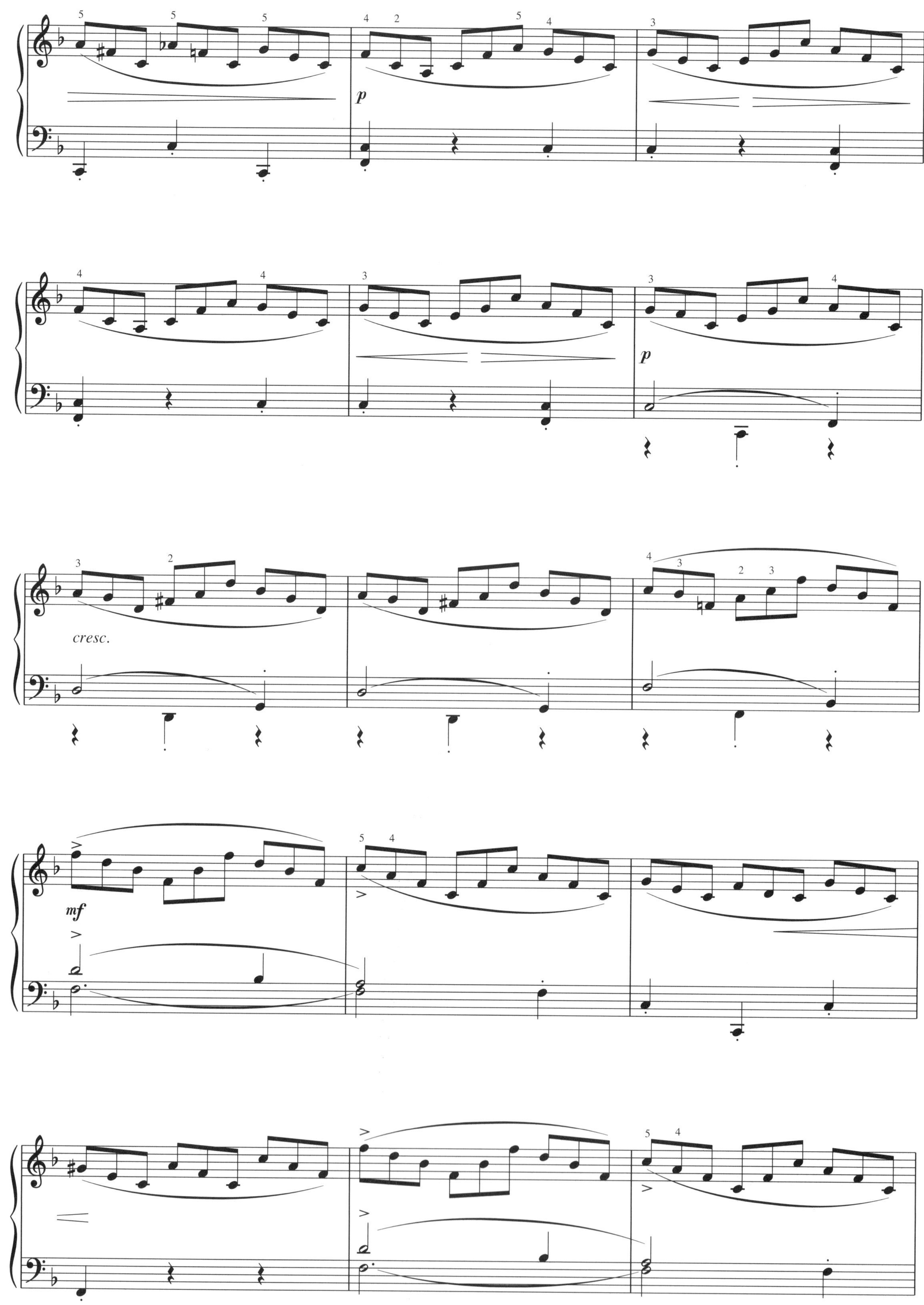
p
p
cresc.
mf

cresc.
f
p

Prelude in C minor

from *32 Preludes,* Op. 119, No. 25

Stephen Heller
1813–1888

dim.
f
sf
sf
R.H.
L.H.
poco rall.
mp
sf
sf
f
sf
sf

The Chimes

Johann Philipp Kirnberger
1721–1783

Alternativo

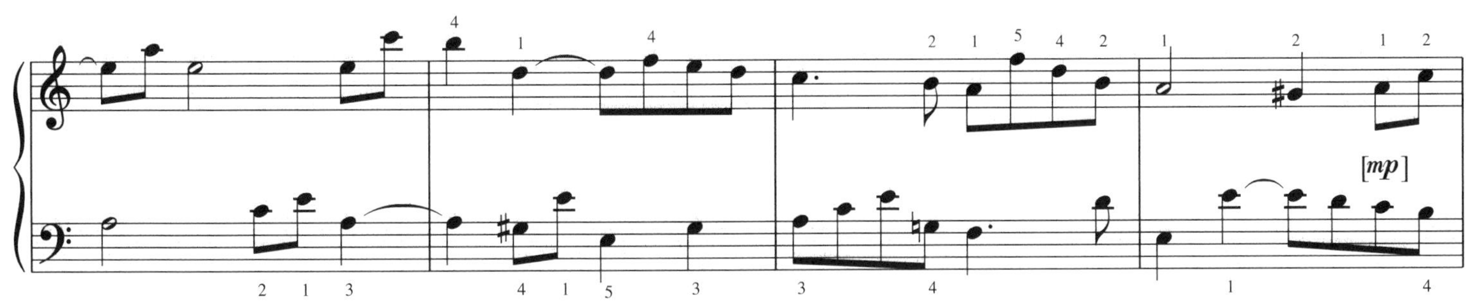

D. C. al Fine

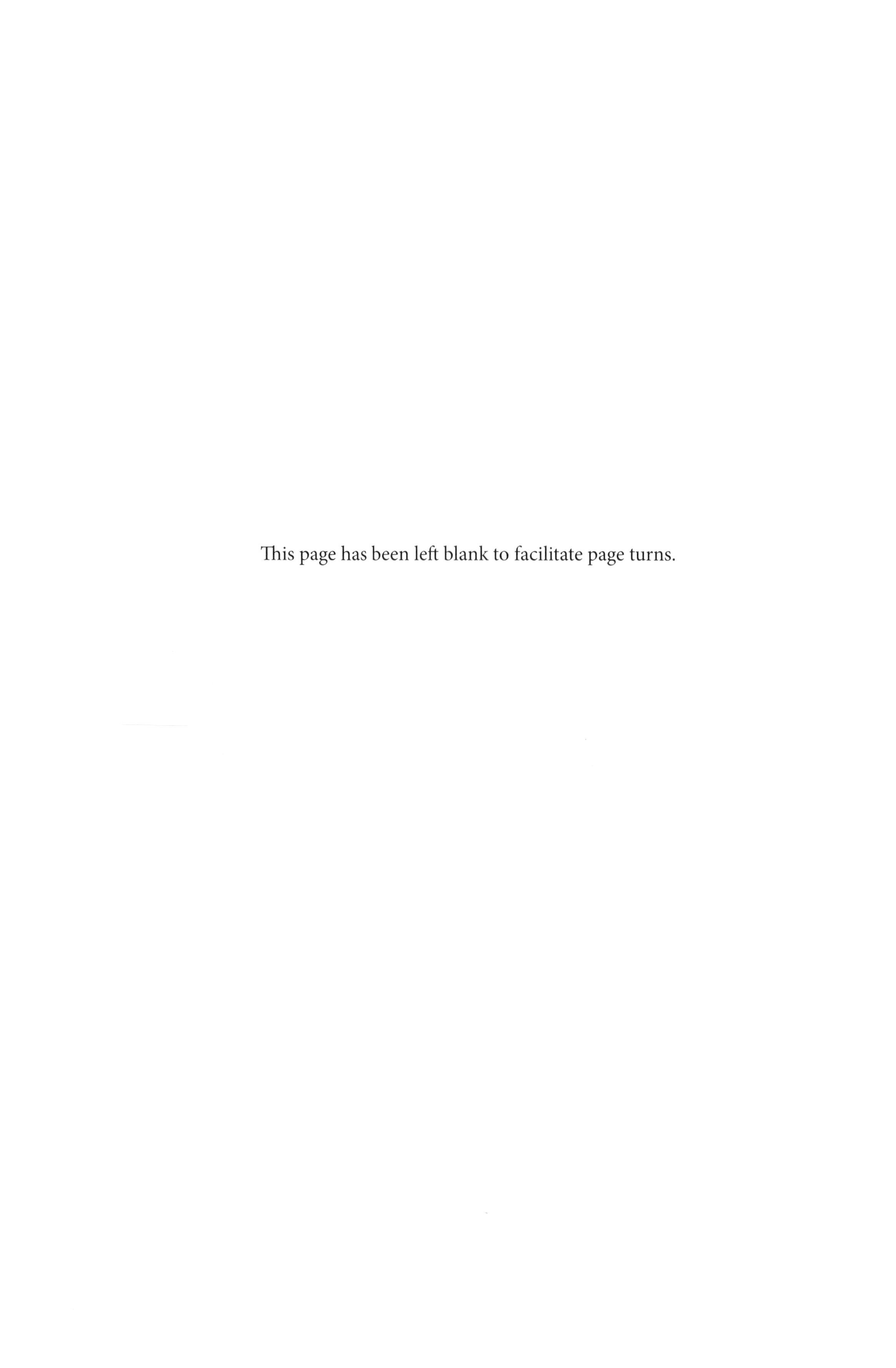

This page has been left blank to facilitate page turns.

Sonatina in C Major

Op. 55, No. 1

I

Friedrich Kuhlau
1786–1832

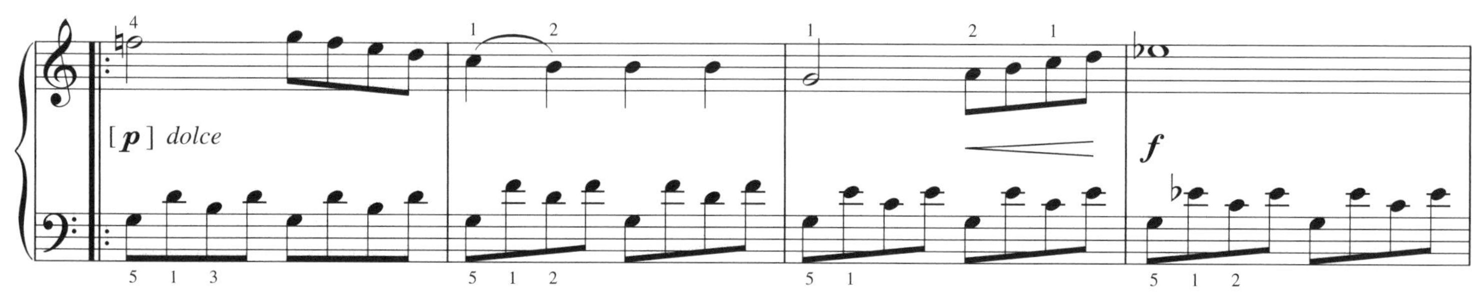
[p] dolce
f

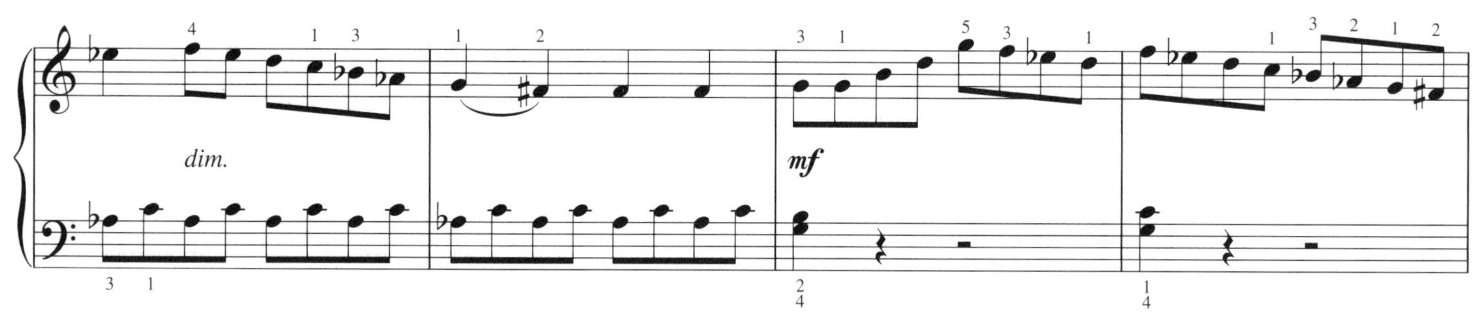
dim.
mf

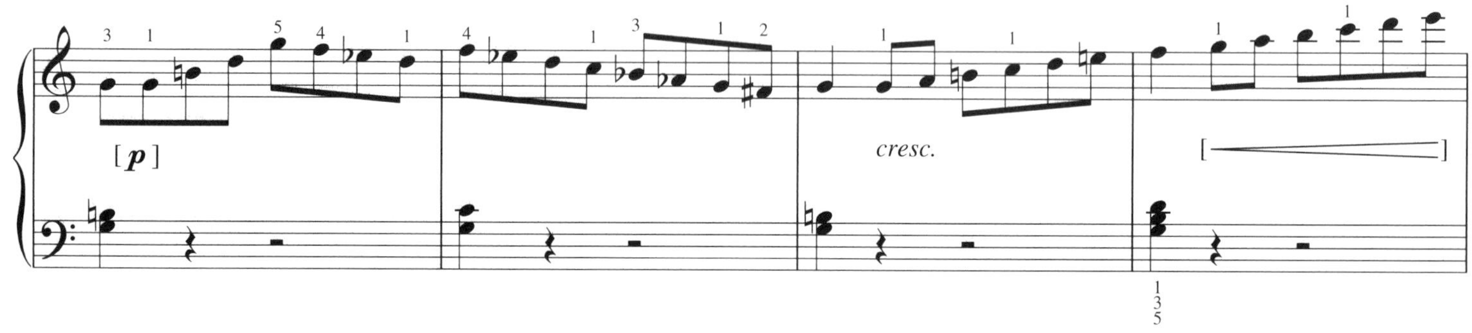
[p]
cresc.

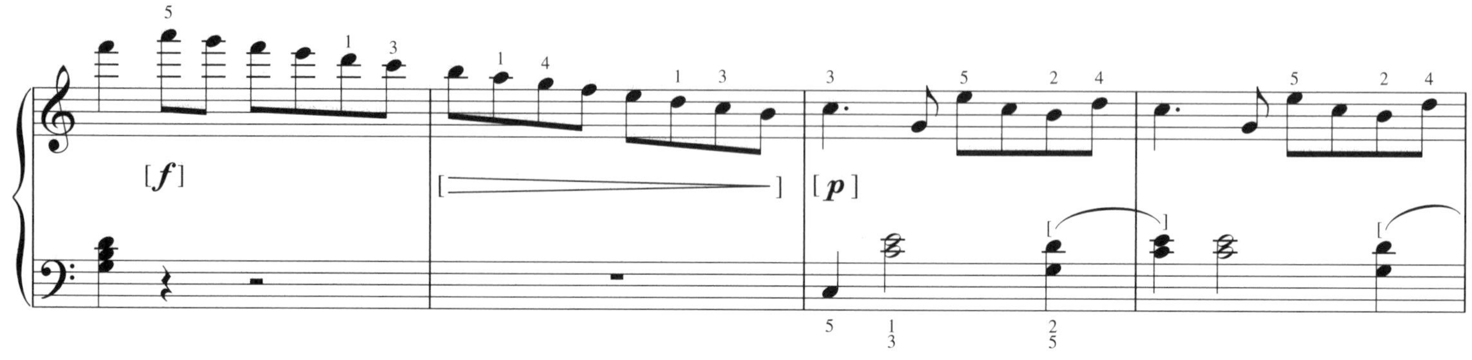
[f]
[p]

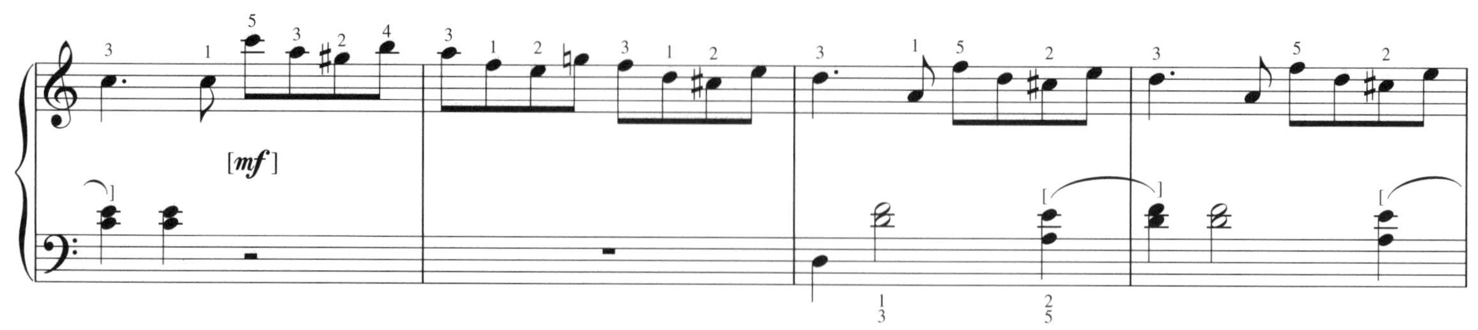
[mf]

cresc.
[f]
f
[p]
[mf]
dolce
cresc.
rf
rf
f

II

Vivace [♩. = ca. 69]

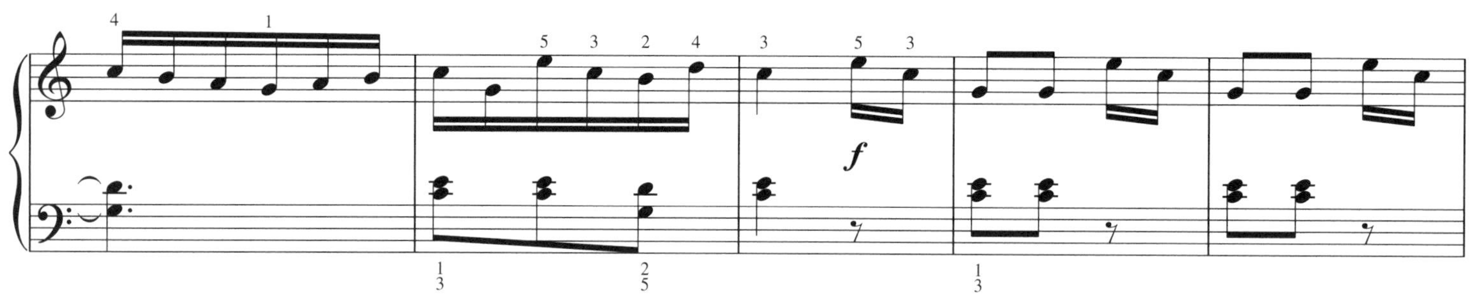

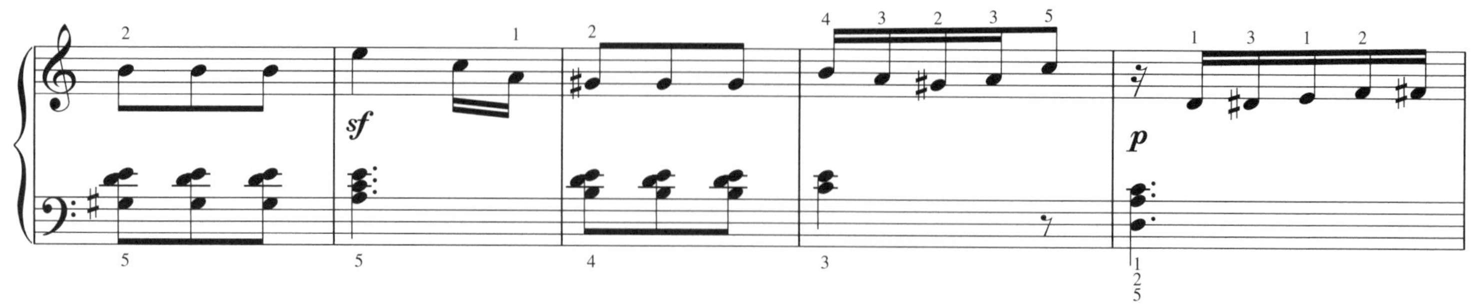

cresc.
f
8va
dim.
f
p

espressivo
poco rit.
pp
poco cresc.
p
sf

cresc.
sf
f
p
cresc.
8va
f
8
f
p
f
p
ff

Sonatina in C Major

Op. 55, No. 3

I

Friedrich Kuhlau
1786–1832

Allegro con spirito [♩ = ca. 126]

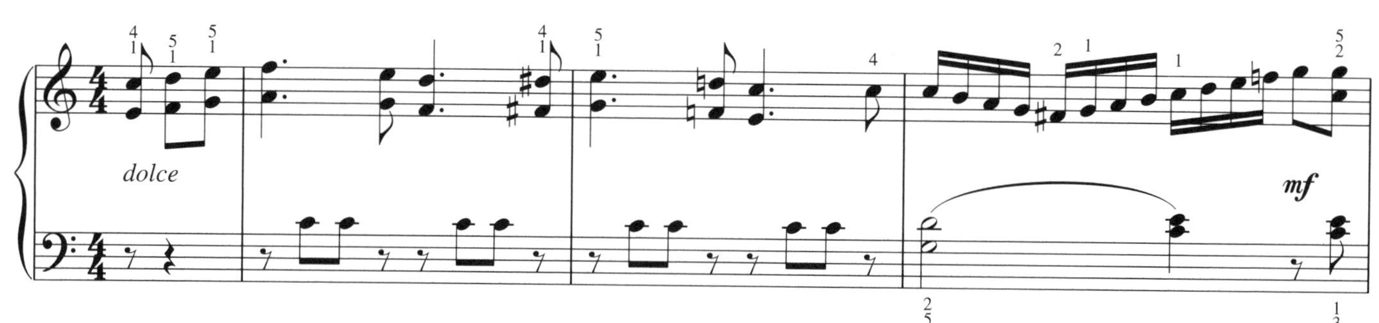

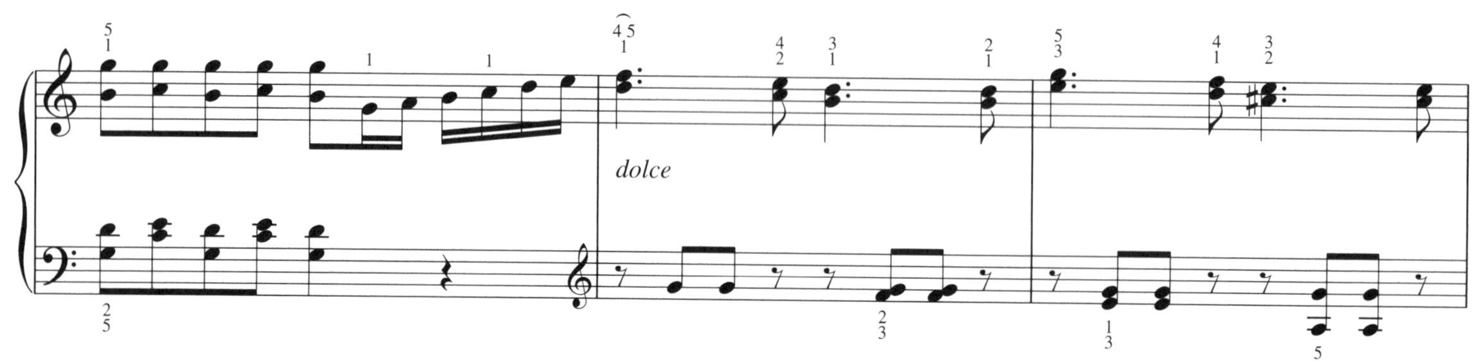

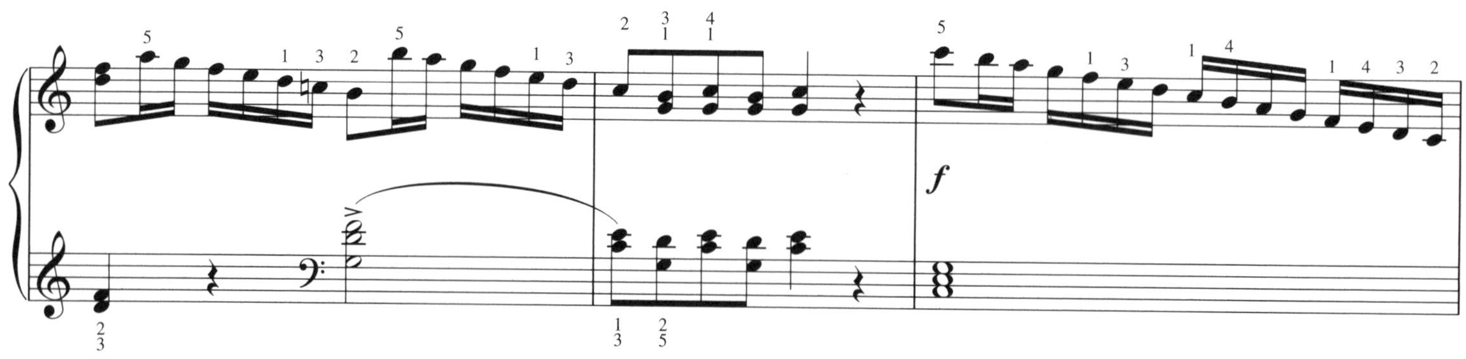

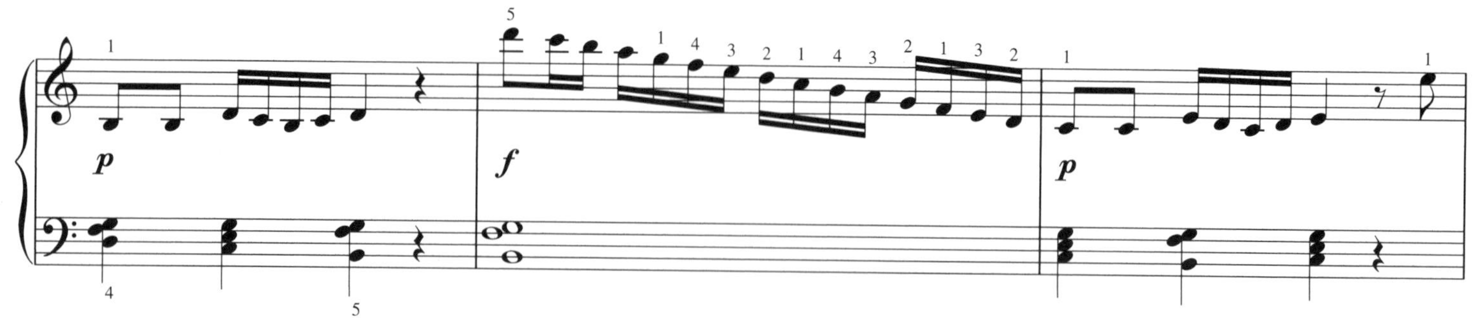

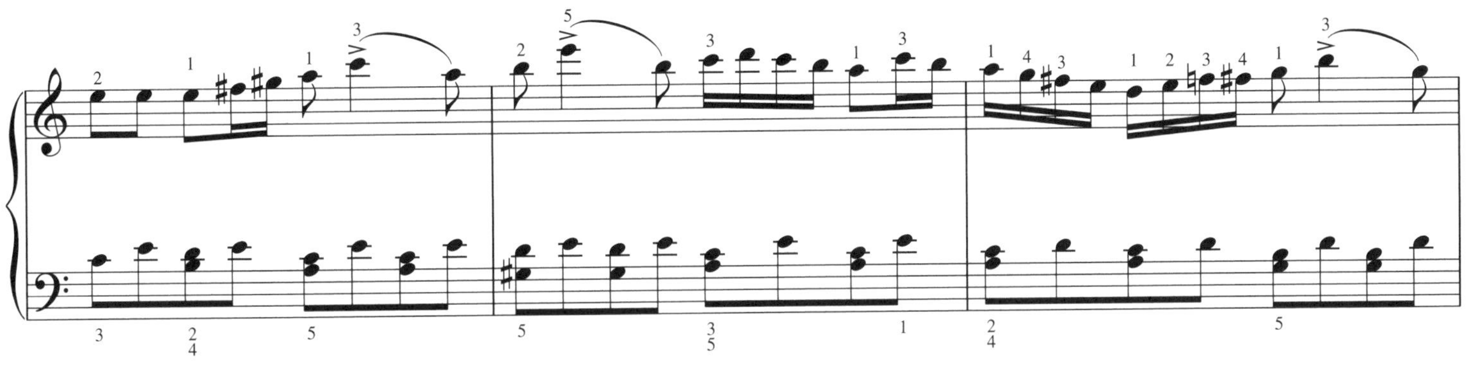

f

p

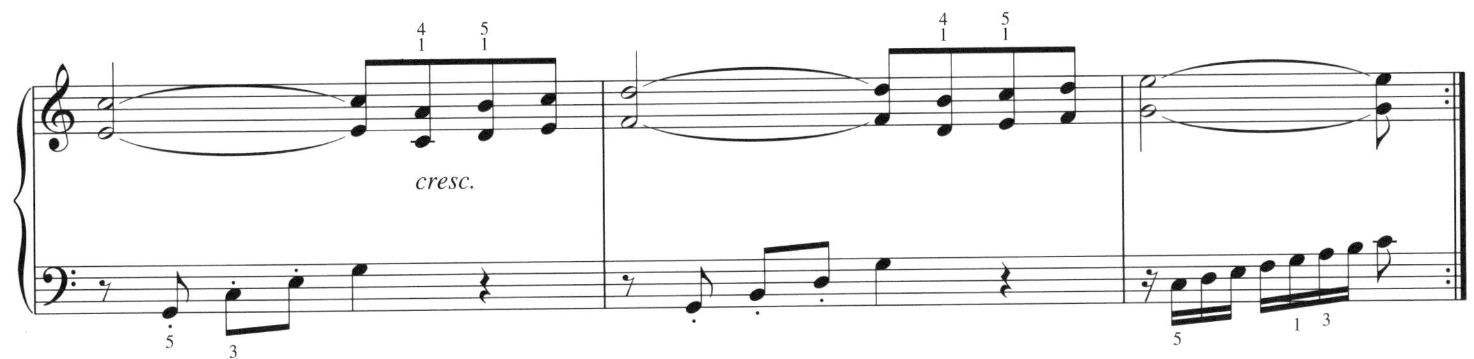
cresc.

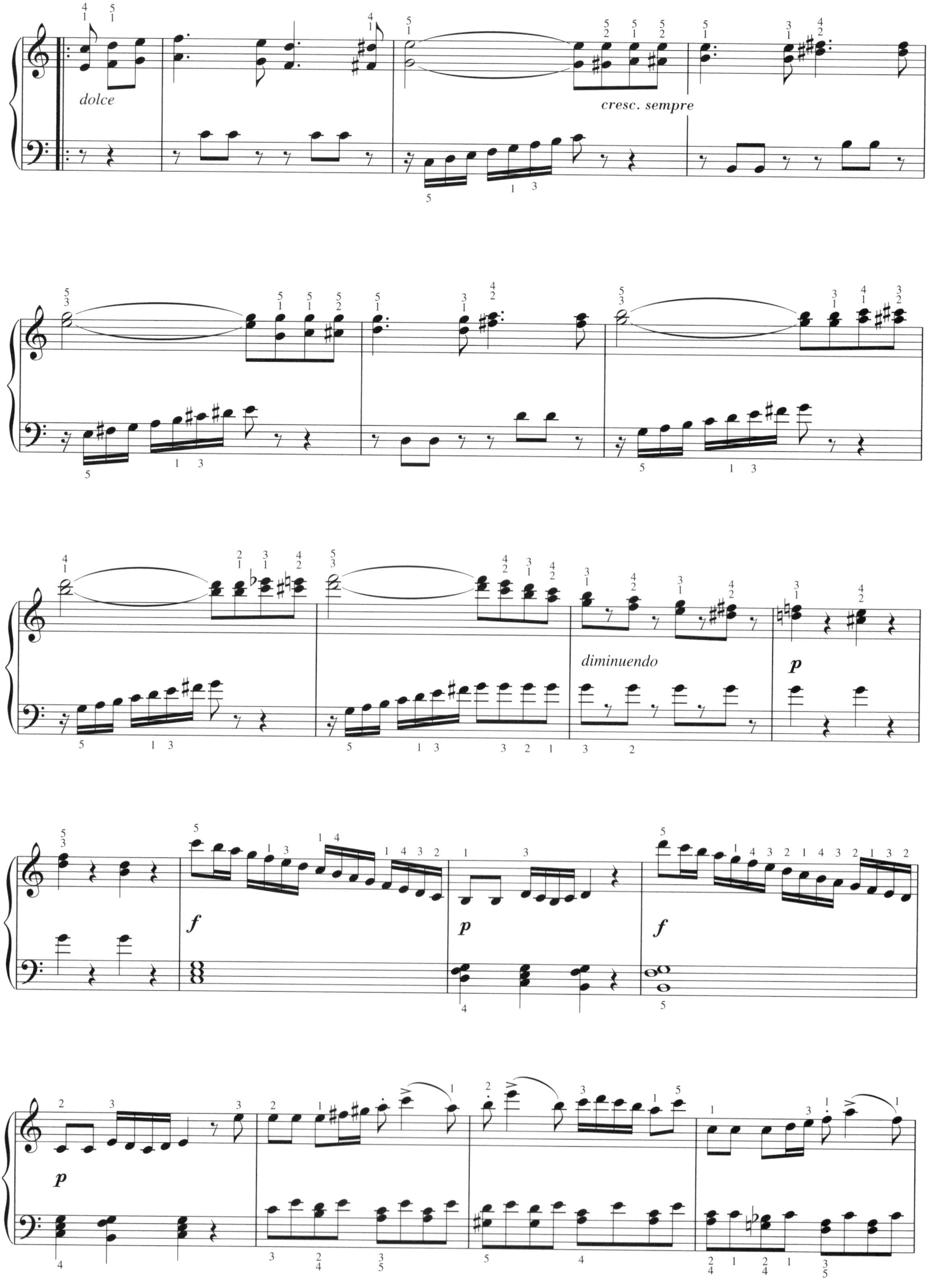

dolce

cresc. sempre

diminuendo

p

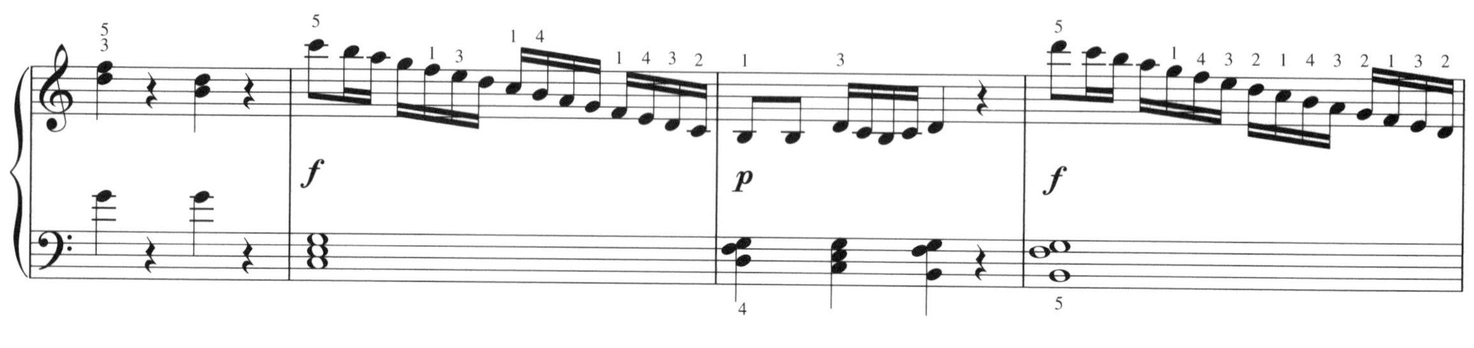

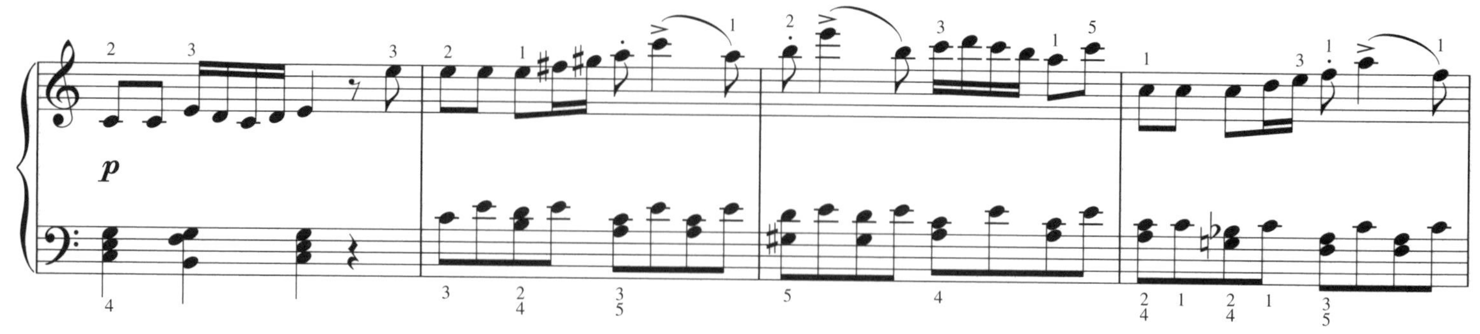

II

smorz.
p
mf

cresc.
f
p
mf
p
f
dim.
p

mf
p

cresc.
p
mf
f

Minuet in D Major

Jean Baptiste Loeillet
1680–1730

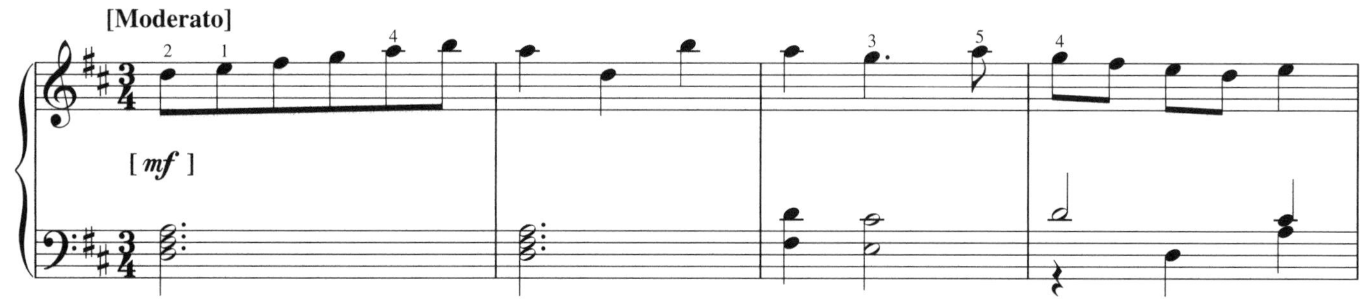

TRIO

To A Wild Rose

from *Woodland Sketches,* Op. 51, No. 1

Edward MacDowell
1860–1908

still increase
diminish
rit.
slightly marked

Minuet in G minor

Louis Marchand
1669–1732

Minuet in G Major

K. 1

Wolfgang Amadeus Mozart
1756–1791

Andante in C Major

K. 1a

Wolfgang Amadeus Mozart
1756–1791

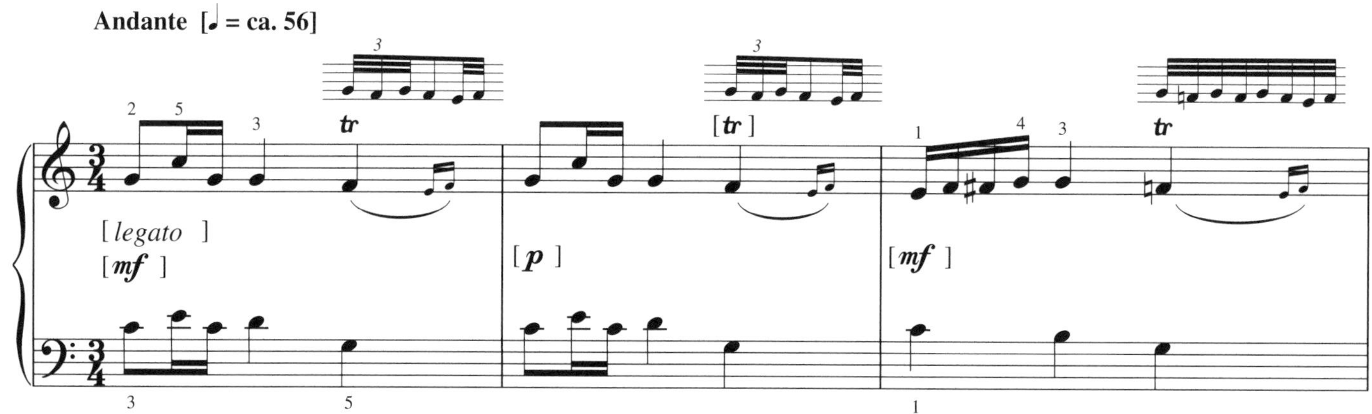

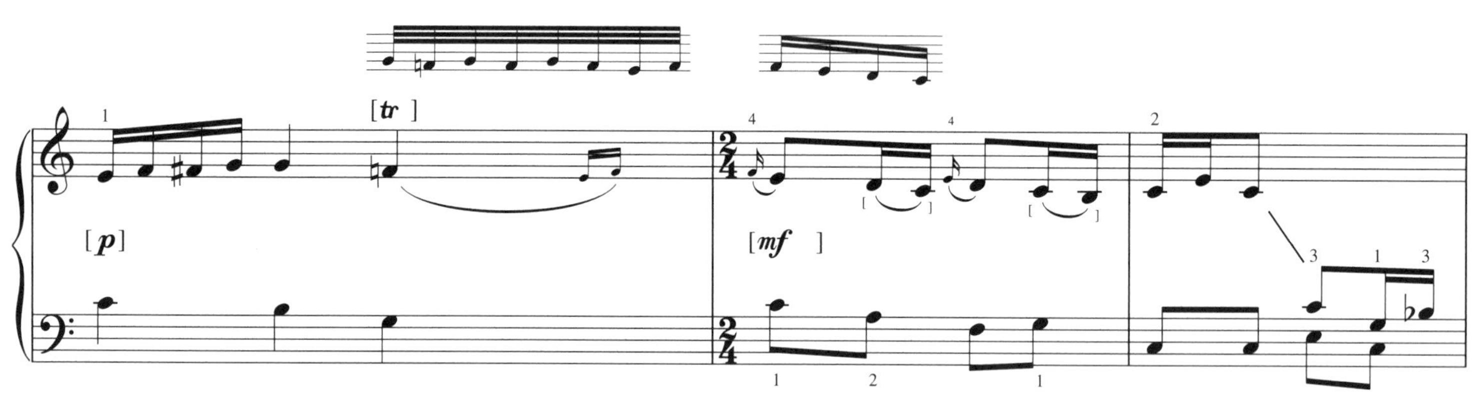

Minuet in F Major

K. 1d

Wolfgang Amadeus Mozart
1756–1791

Minuet in F Major

K. 2

Wolfgang Amadeus Mozart
1756–1791

Minuet in D Major

K. 7

Wolfgang Amadeus Mozart
1756–1791

Minuet in F Major

K. 5

Wolfgang Amadeus Mozart
1756–1791

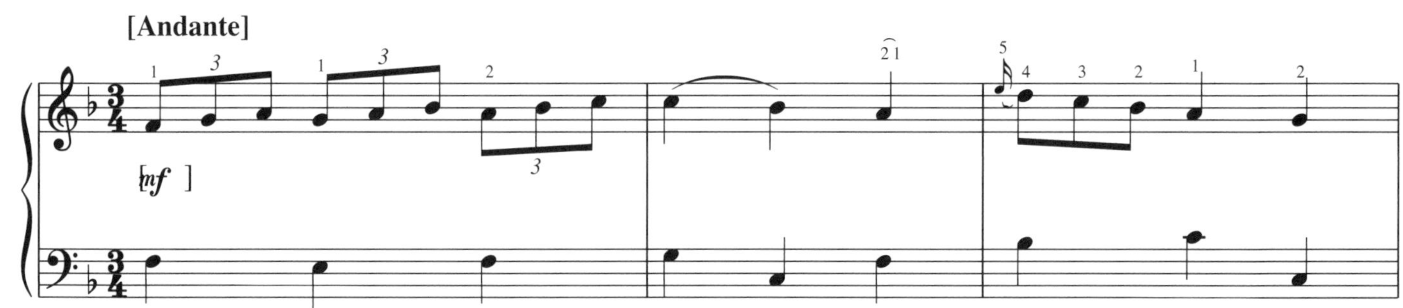

Minuet in C Major

K. 6

Wolfgang Amadeus Mozart
1756–1791

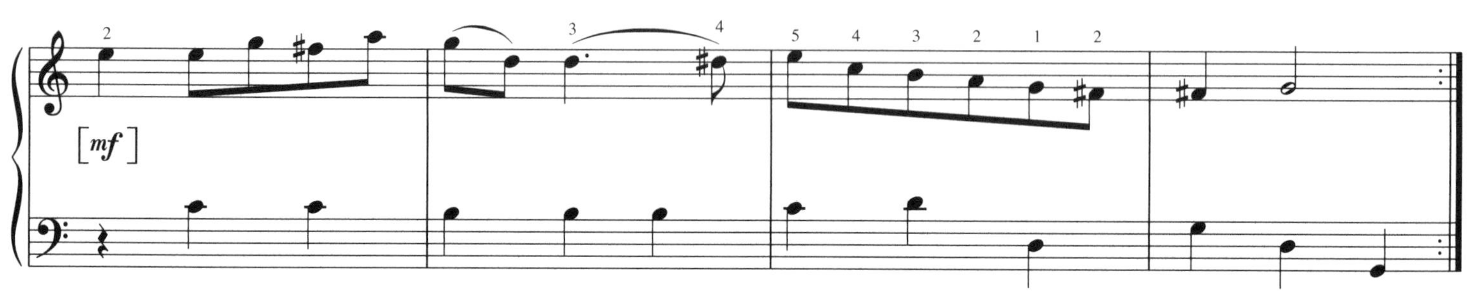

Minuet in F Major
K. 6 (II)

Wolfgang Amadeus Mozart
1756–1791

Minuet in G Major

K. 15c

Wolfgang Amadeus Mozart
1756–1791

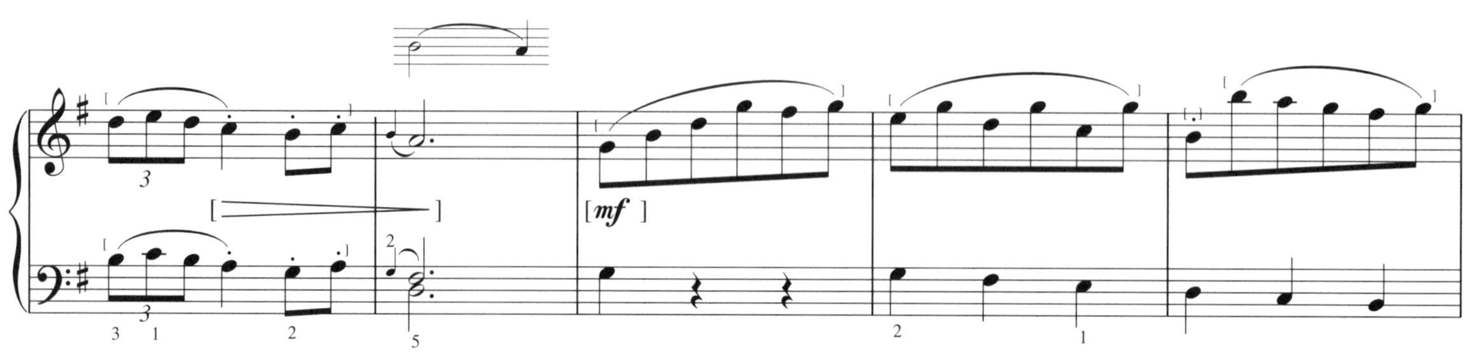

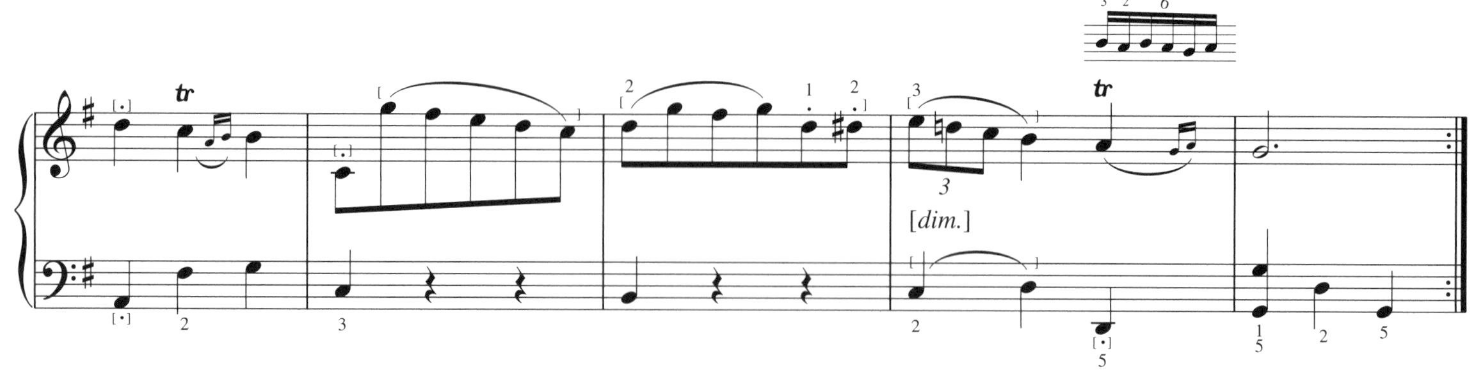

Contradance in G Major

K. 15e

Wolfgang Amadeus Mozart
1756–1791

Minuet in G Major

K. 15y

Wolfgang Amadeus Mozart
1756–1791

Andante in E-flat Major

K. 15mm

Wolfgang Amadeus Mozart
1756–1791

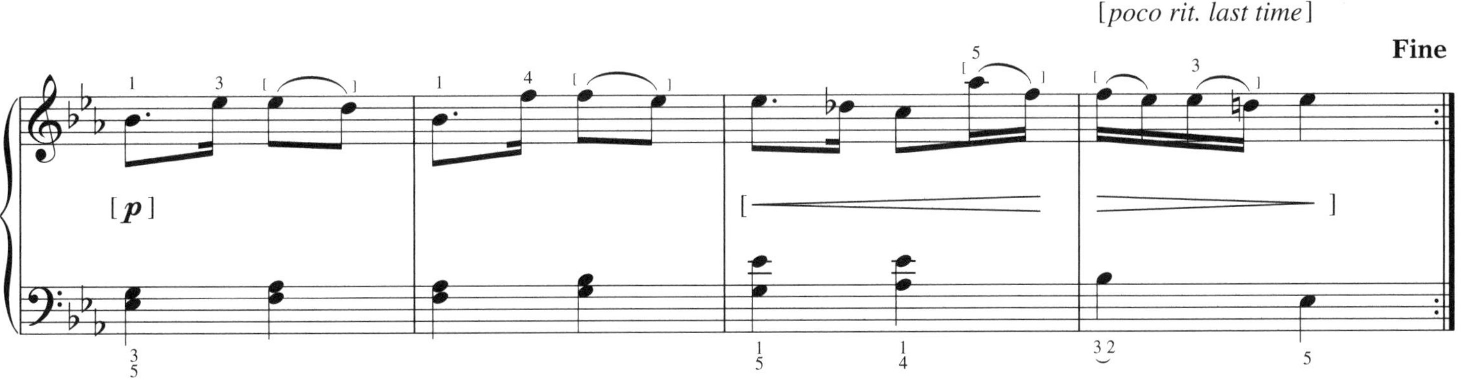

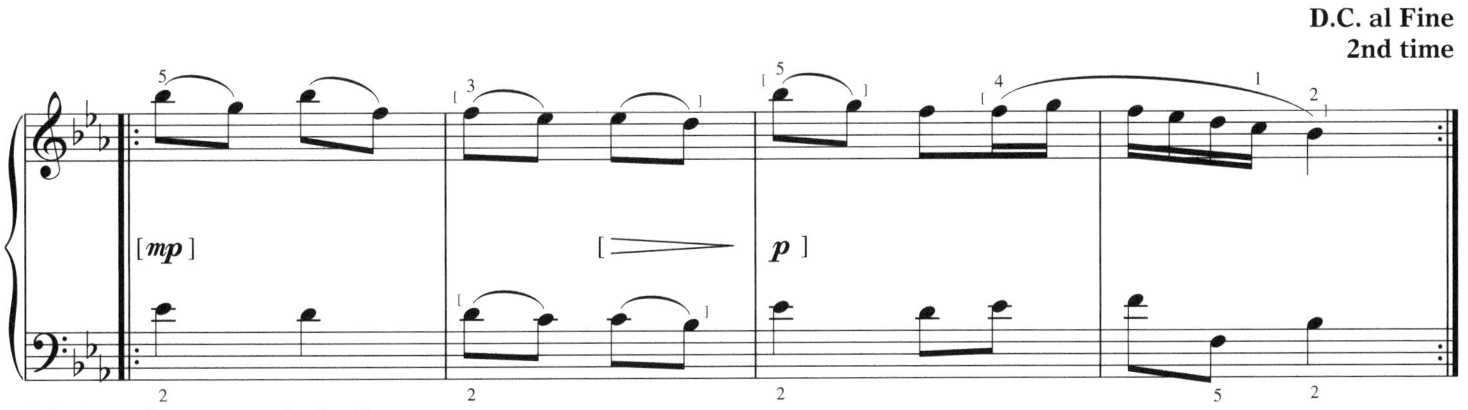

Eliminate the repeat on the Da Capo.

Minuet in B-flat Major

K. 15pp

Wolfgang Amadeus Mozart
1756–1791

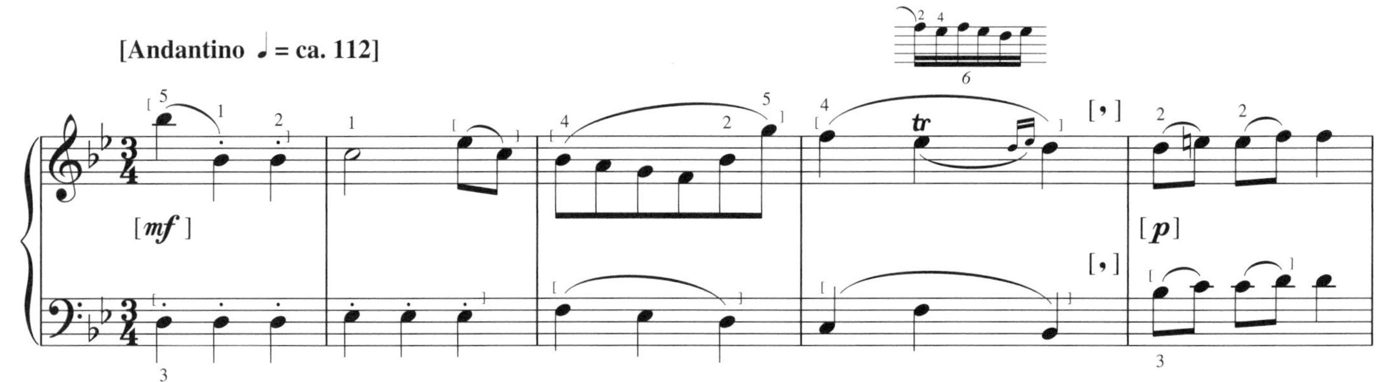

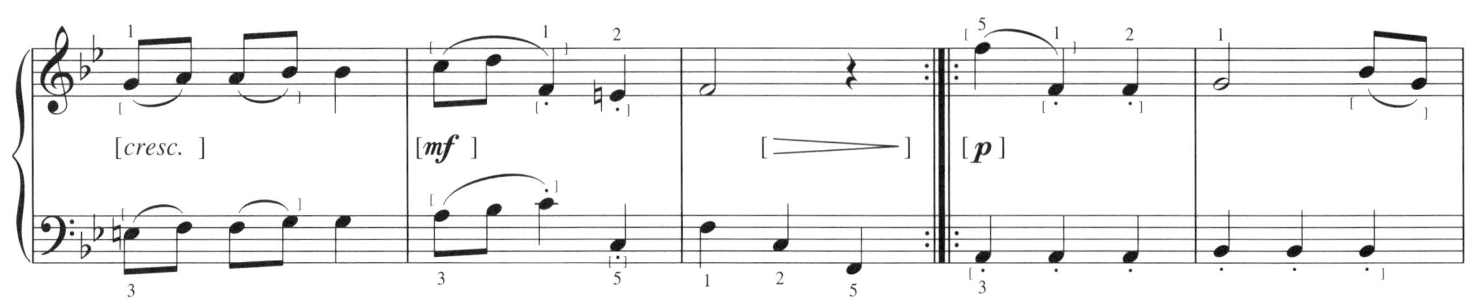

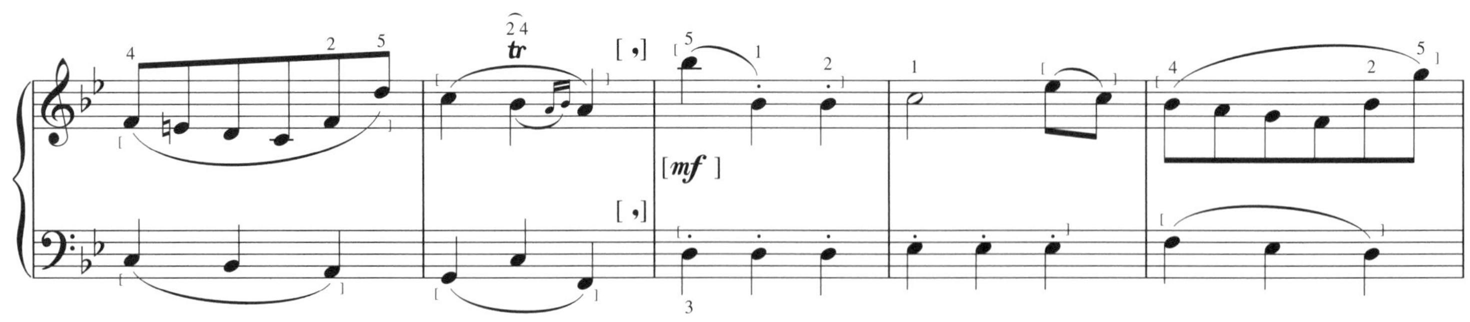

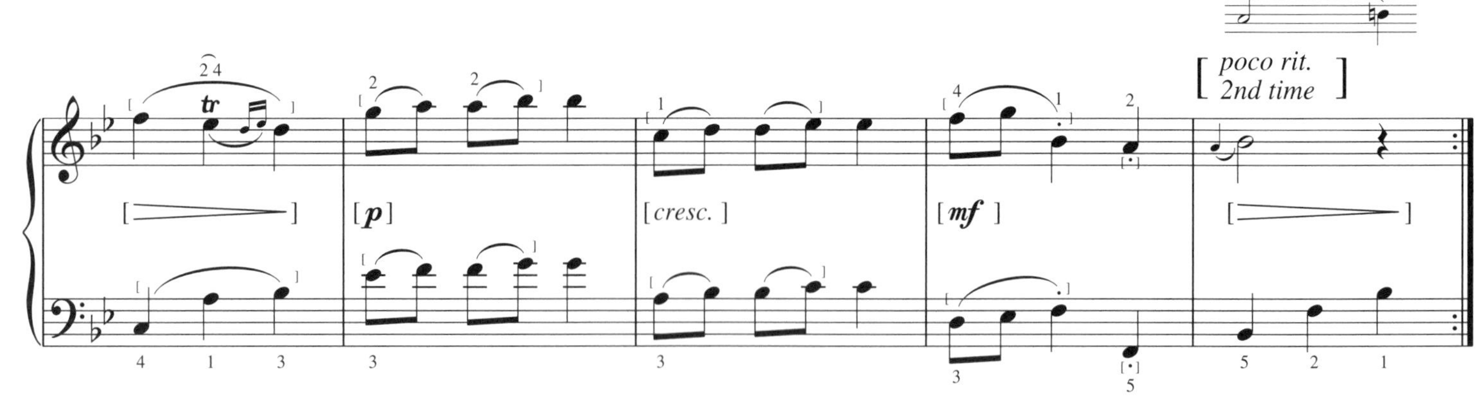

Minuet in E-flat Major
K. 15qq

Wolfgang Amadeus Mozart
1756–1791

Minuet in D Major

K. 94 (73h)

Wolfgang Amadeus Mozart
1756–1791

Air in A-flat Major

K. Anh. 109b, Nr. 8 (15ff)

Wolfgang Amadeus Mozart
1756–1791

Andantino in E-flat Major

Adaptation of an aria* by Christoph Willibald Gluck
K. 236 (588b)

Wolfgang Amadeus Mozart
1756–1791

* "Non vi turbate" from Gluck's *Alceste.*

Sarabande in B-flat Major

Johann Pachelbel
1653–1706

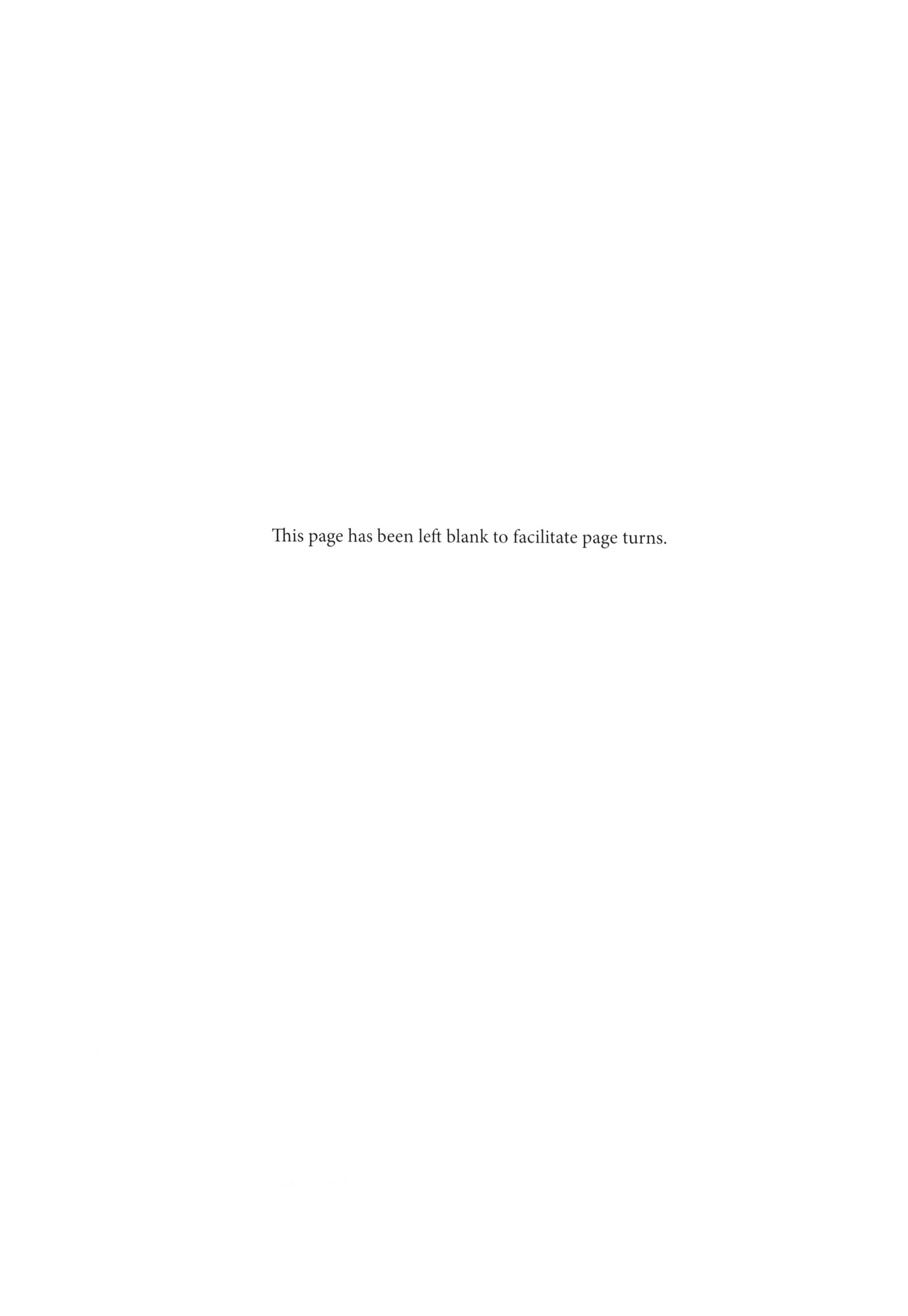

This page has been left blank to facilitate page turns.

Minuet in G Major

BWV Appendix 114

Christian Petzold
1677–1733

Minuet in G minor

BWV Appendix 115

Christian Petzold
1677–1733

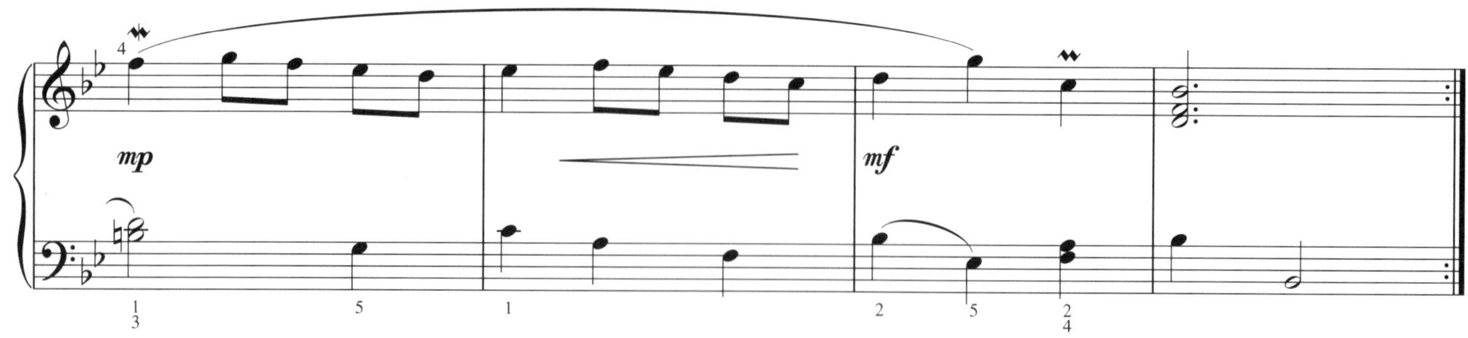

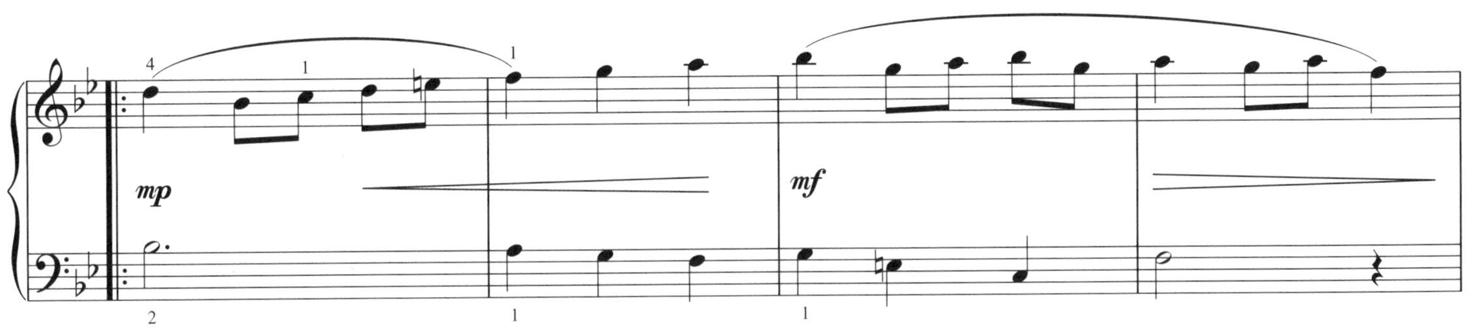
mp
mf

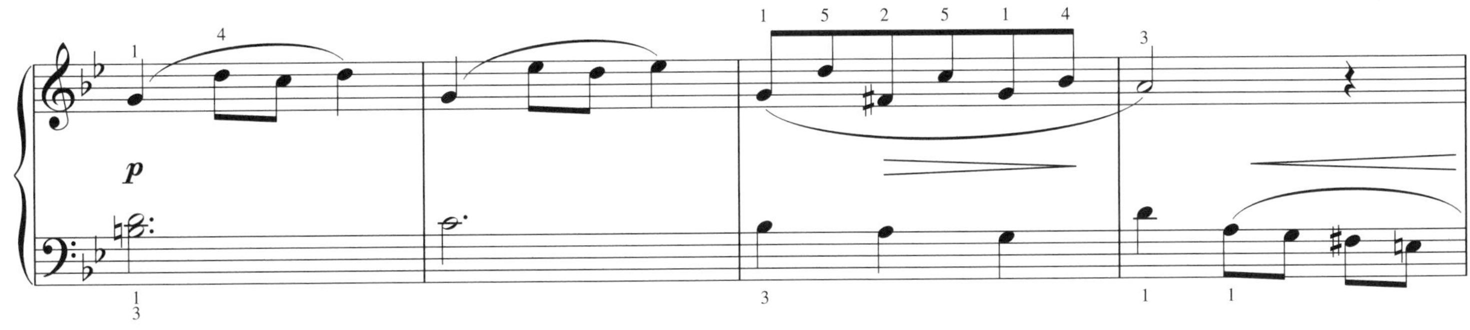
p

mf
f

Suite No. 1 in G Major

Henry Purcell
1659–1695

Courante

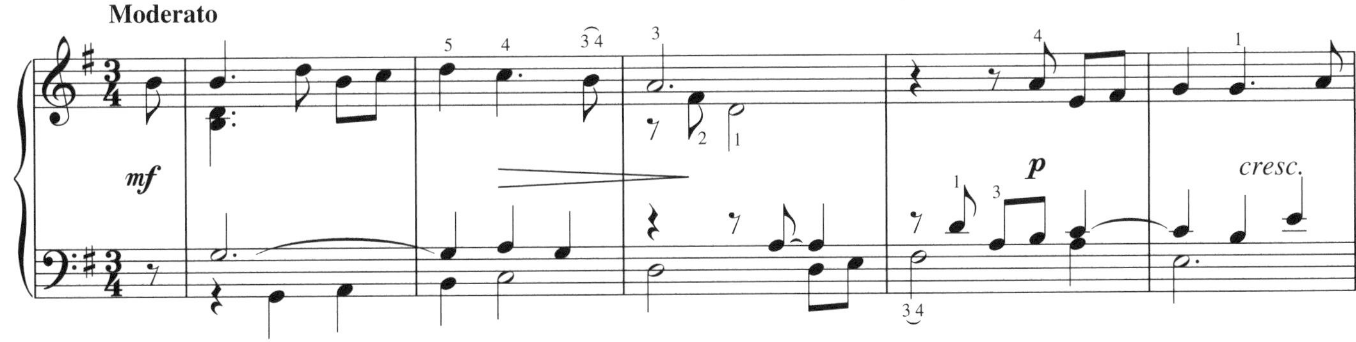

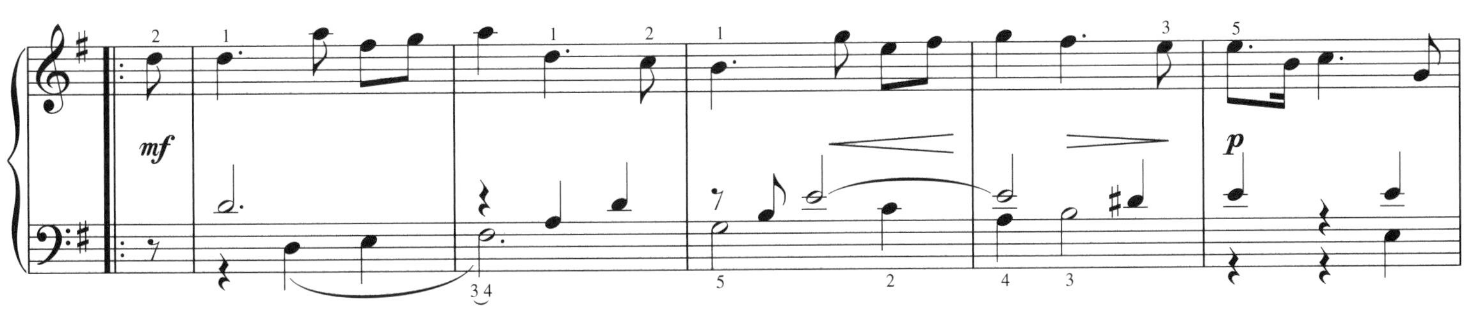

Minuet

Tambourin in E minor

Jean-Philippe Rameau
1683–1764

1
4
1
3
2
1
323

2
1
3232
2
1
3232
1

2
1
3131
2
2
1
1
2
1

5
4
3131
2
1
4
1
3
2
1
323
2
1

5353
3232
1
2
1
1 2

5353
(5353)
3232
3232
5353
3232

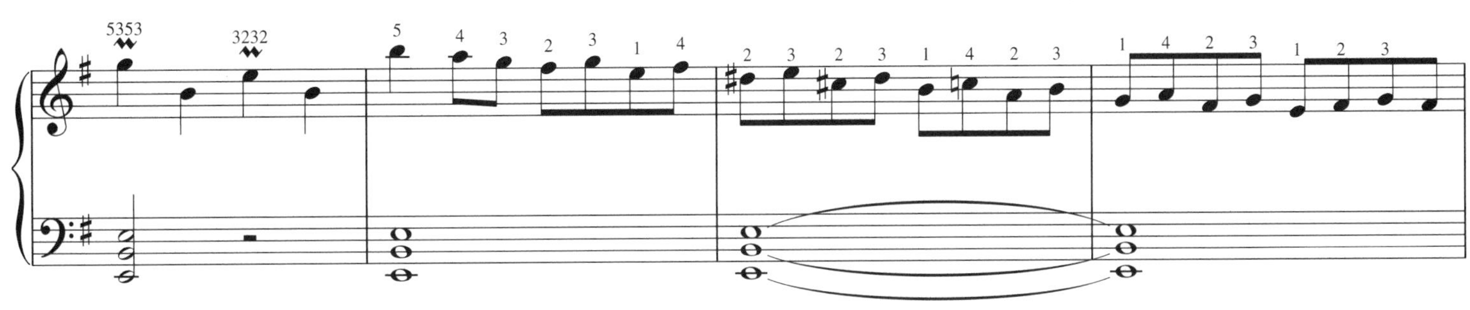
5353
3232

323

Gymnopédie No. 1

Erik Satie
1866–1925

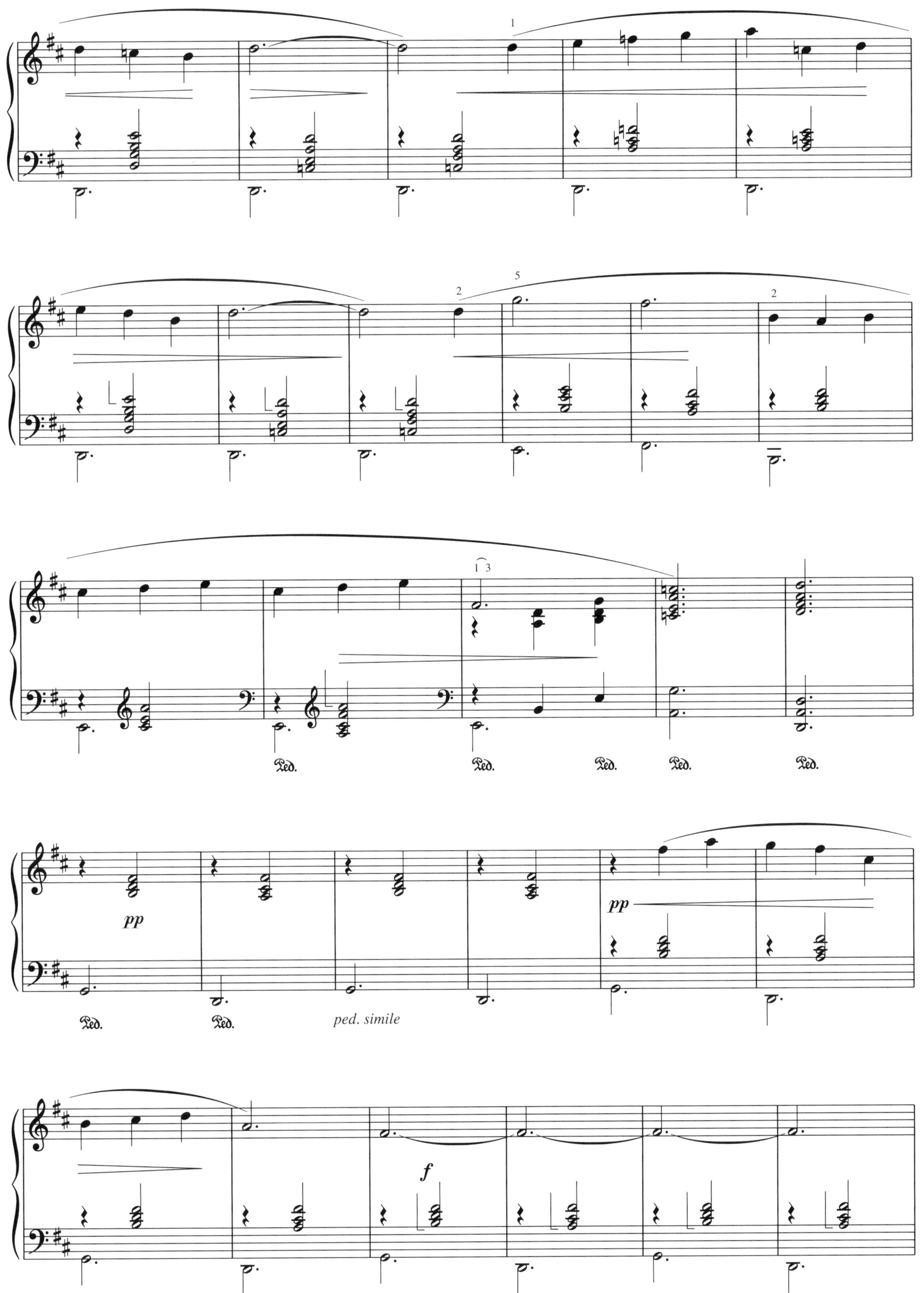
1
5
2
2
1 3
pp
pp
f
ped. simile

pp
p
Ped.
Ped.
Ped.
Ped.

Aria in D minor

Alessandro Scarlatti
1660–1725

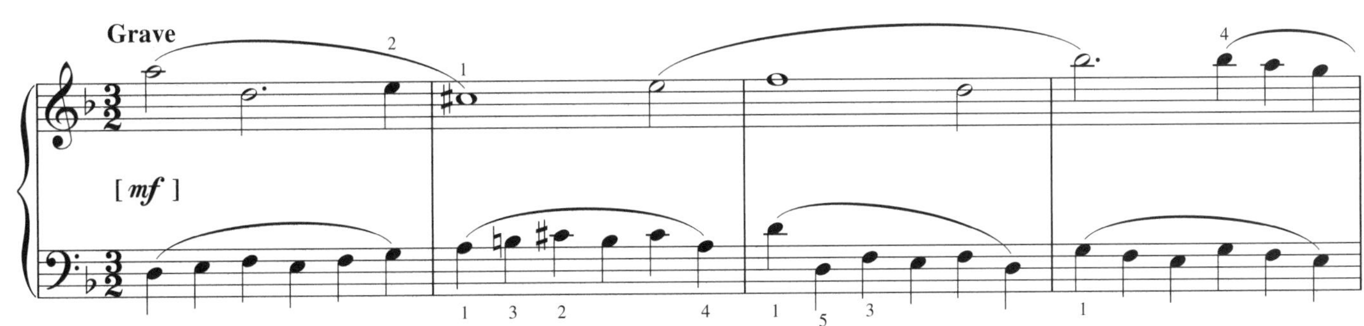

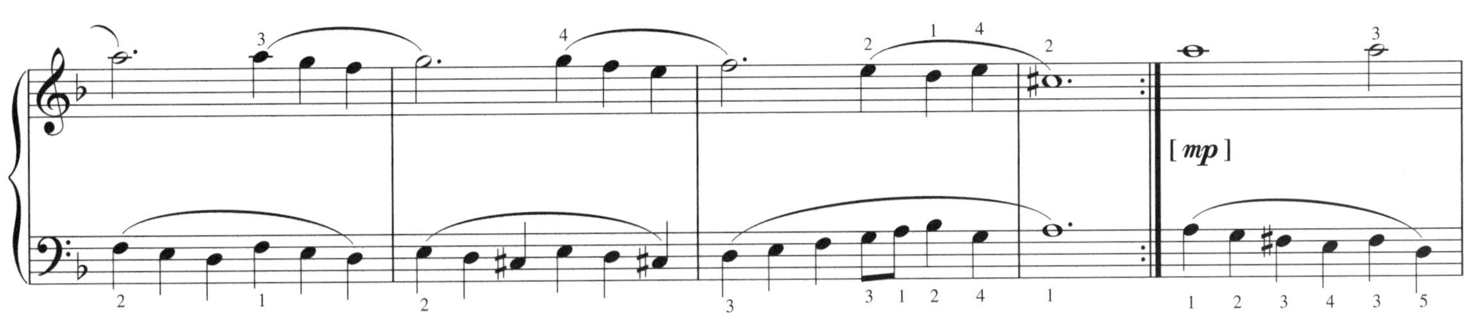

Sonata in G Major

L. 79 (K. 391, P. 364)

Domenico Scarlatti
1685–1757

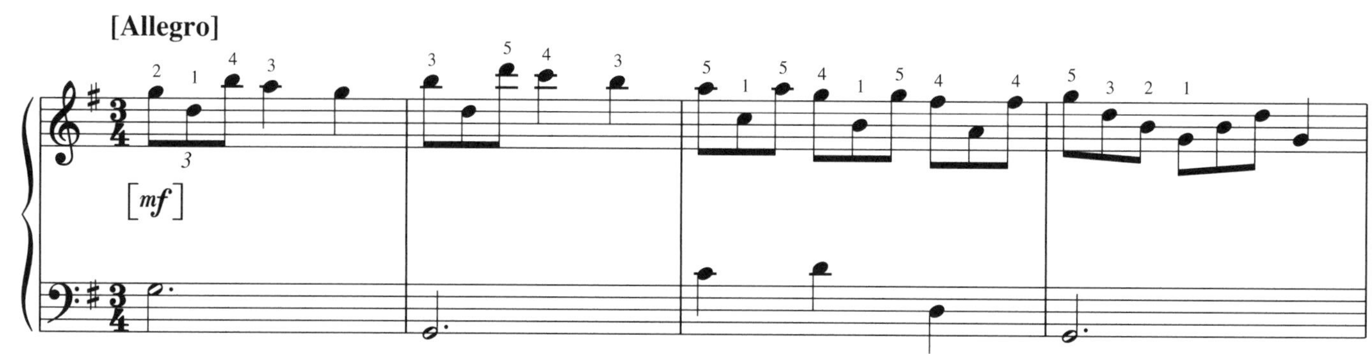

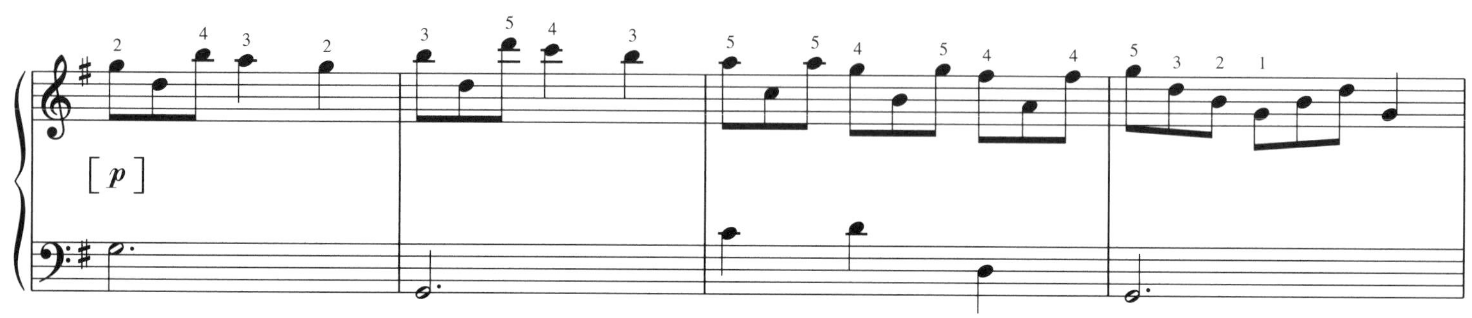

[mf]
tr
[p]
[mf]
[f]
[p]
[mp]

[p]

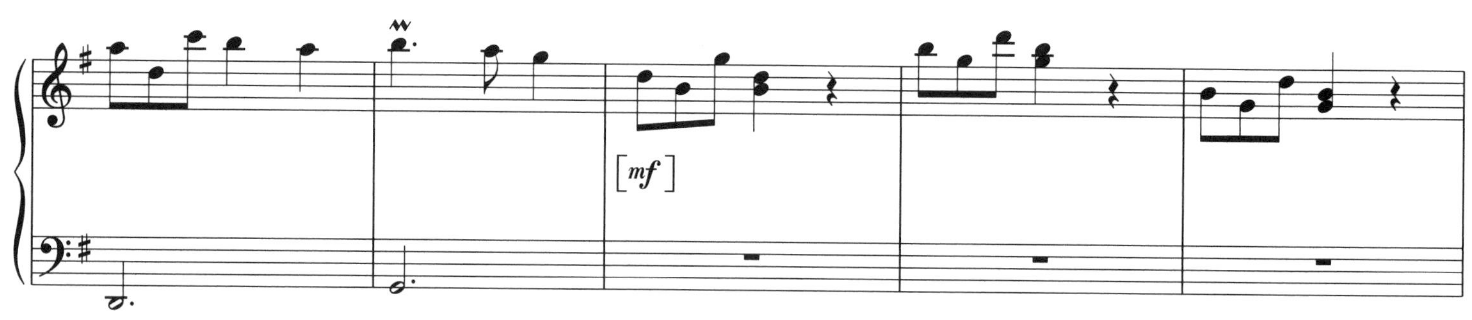
[mf]

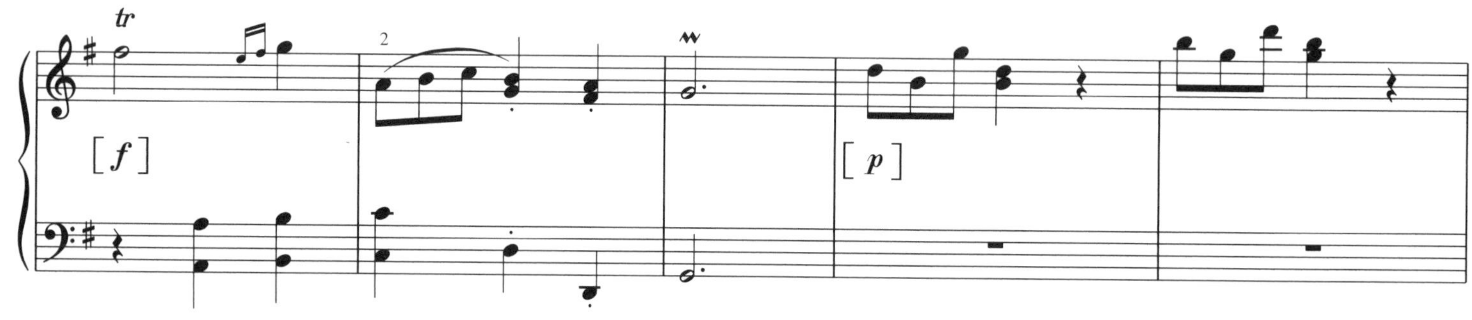
tr
[f]
[p]

tr
[f]

Sonata in C Major

L. 217 (K. 73b, P. 80)

Domenico Scarlatti
1685–1757

Sonata in A minor

L. 378 (K. 3)

Domenico Scarlatti
1685–1757

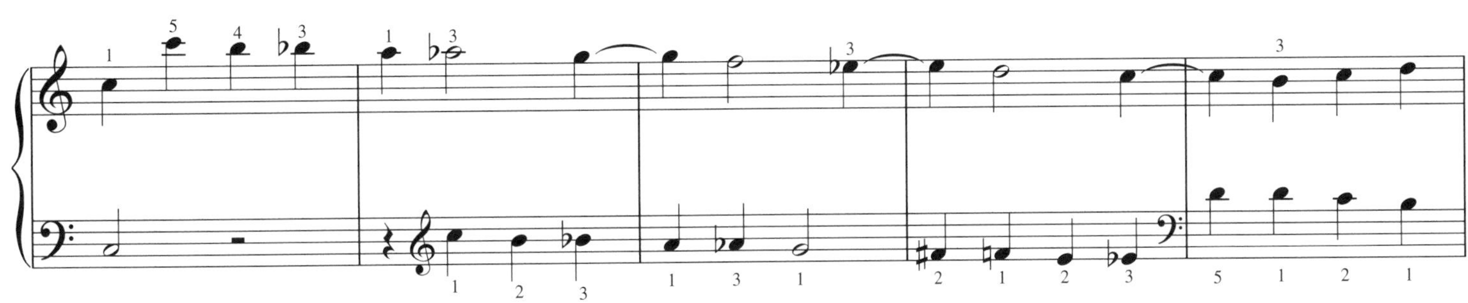

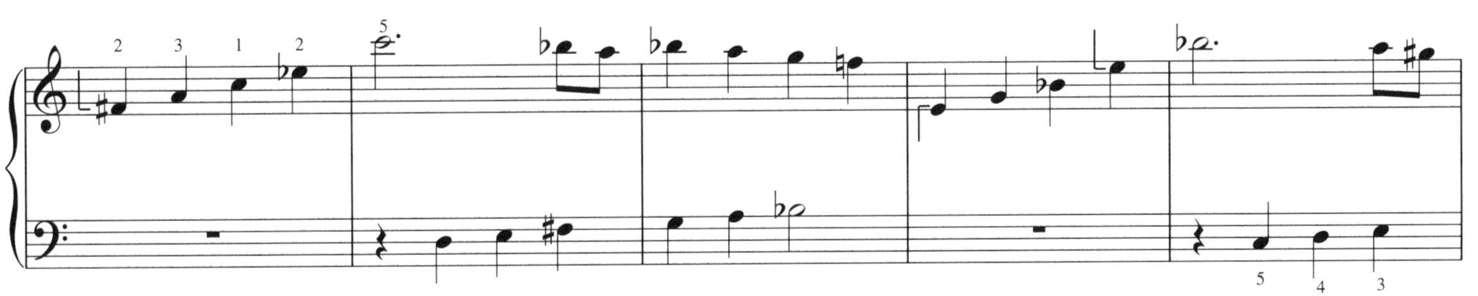

Sonata in A Major

L. 483 (K. 322, P. 360)

Domenico Scarlatti
1685–1757

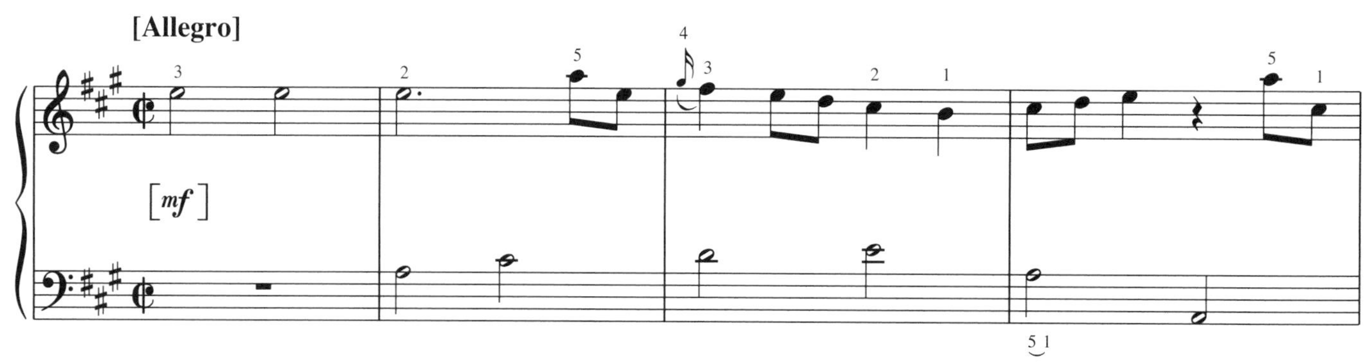

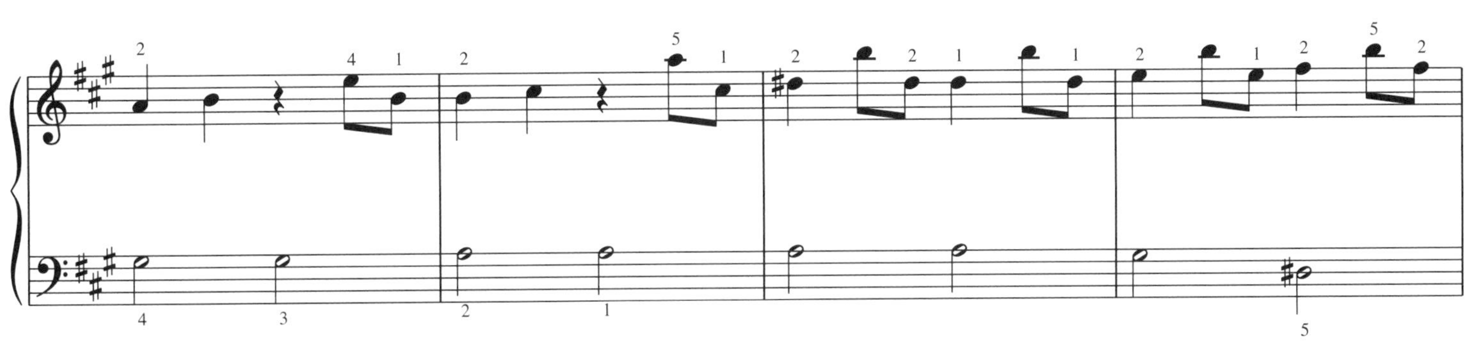

[p]

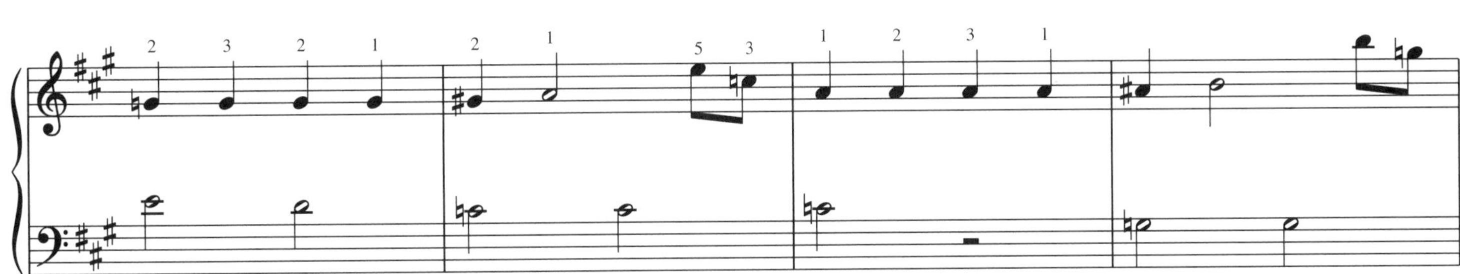

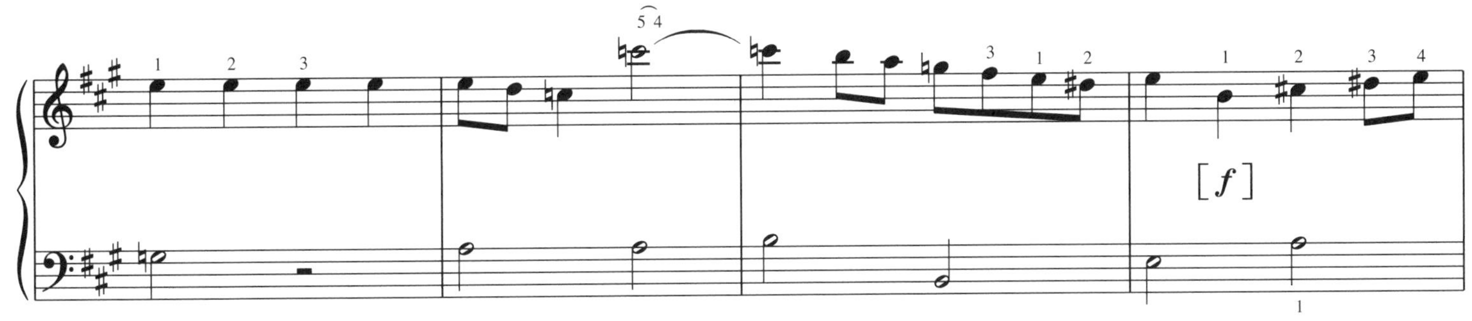
[f]

[p]

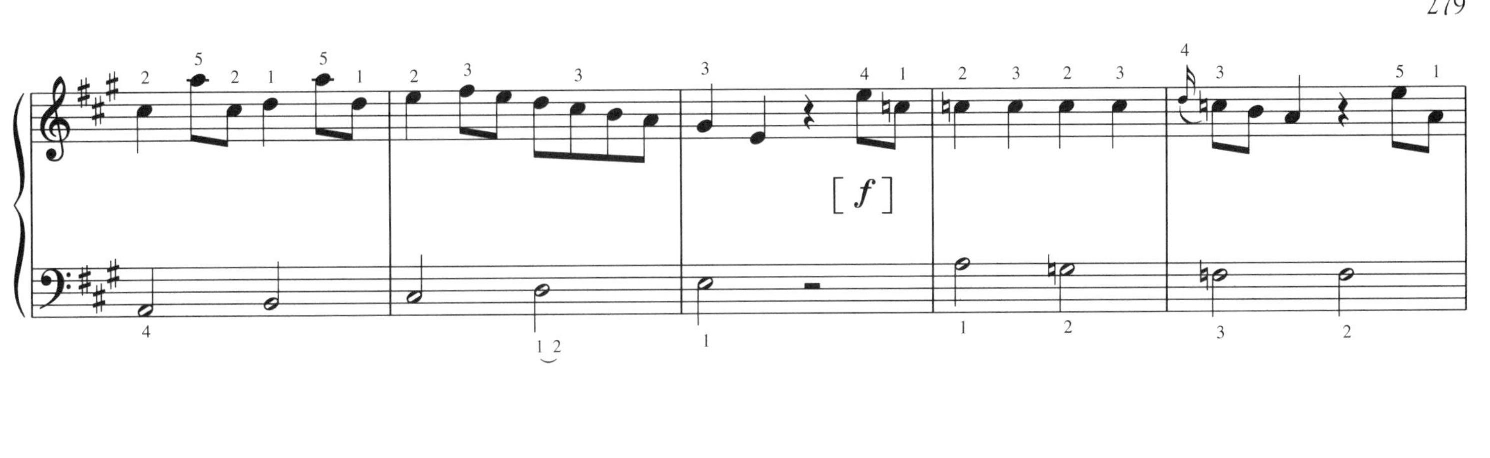
[f]

[p]

[f]

Sonata in D minor

L. 423 (K. 32, P. 14)

Domenico Scarlatti
1685–1757

Waltz in A-flat Major

Op. 9, No. 12 (D. 365)

Franz Schubert
1797–1828

Waltz in B minor

Op. 18, No. 5 (D. 145)

Franz Schubert
1797–1828

mf
p
mf
p
pp
mf
1
2

Waltz in F minor

Op. 33, No. 14 (D. 783)

Franz Schubert
1797–1828

Waltz in A-flat Major

Op. 33, No. 15 (D. 783)

Franz Schubert
1797–1828

An Important Event

from *Scenes from Childhood,* Op. 15, No. 6

Robert Schumann
1810–1856

sf
Ped.
Ped.
f
mf

Of Strange Lands And People

from *Scenes from Childhood,* Op. 15, No. 1

Robert Schumann
1810–1856

Melody

from *Album for the Young,* Op. 68, No. 1

Robert Schumann
1810–1856

Soldier's March

from *Album for the Young,* Op. 68, No. 2

Robert Schumann
1810–1856

Humming Song

from *Album for the Young,* Op. 68, No. 3

Robert Schumann
1810–1856

Little Piece

from *Album for the Young,* Op. 68, No. 5

Robert Schumann
1810–1856

Hunting Song

from *Album for the Young,* Op. 68, No. 7

Robert Schumann
1810–1856

The Wild Horseman

from *Album for the Young,* Op. 68, No. 8

Robert Schumann
1810–1856

The Happy Farmer Returning From Work

from *Album for the Young,* Op. 68, No. 10

Robert Schumann
1810–1856

Little Study

from *Album for the Young,* Op. 68, No. 14

Robert Schumann
1810–1856

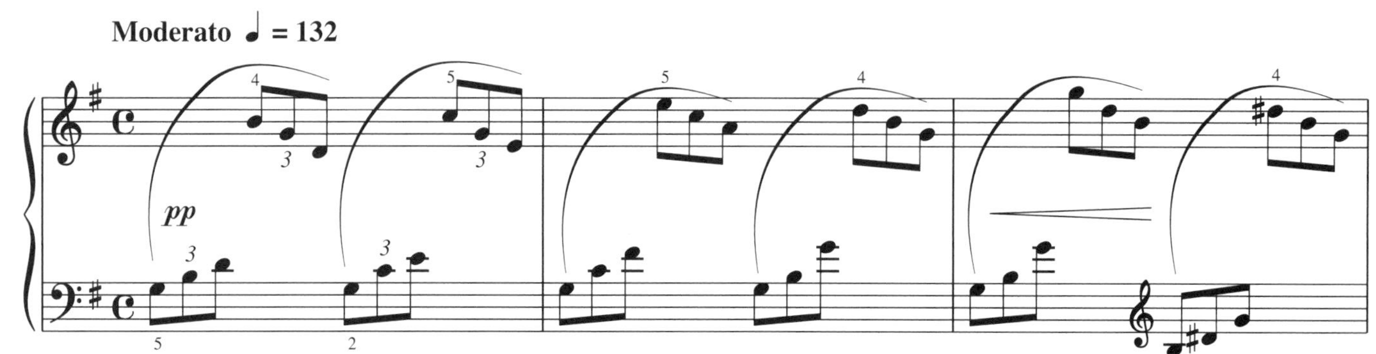

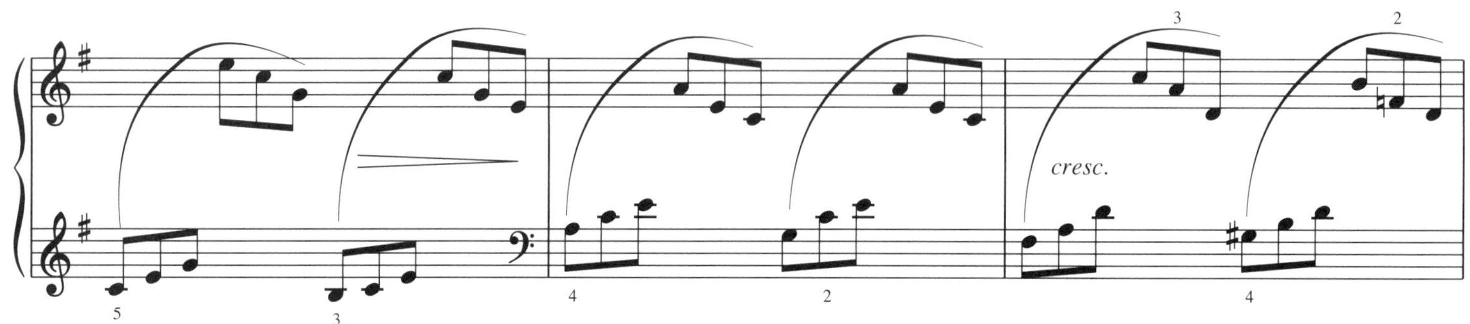

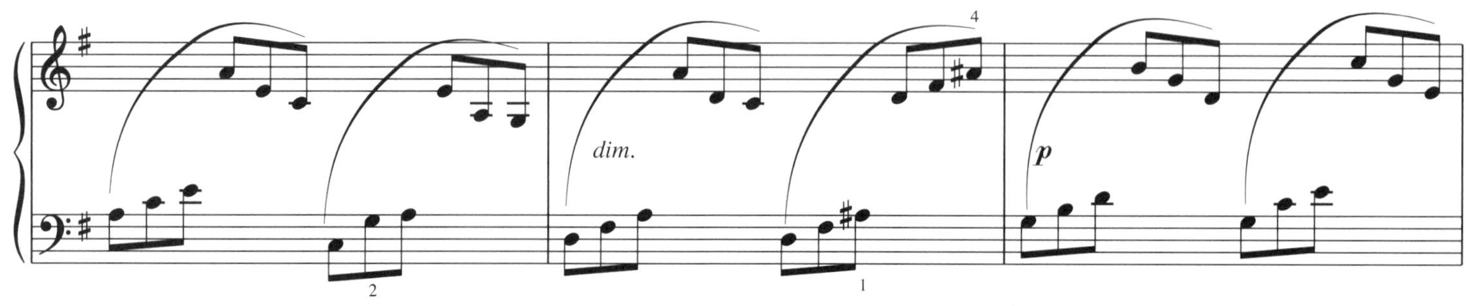

cresc.
dim.

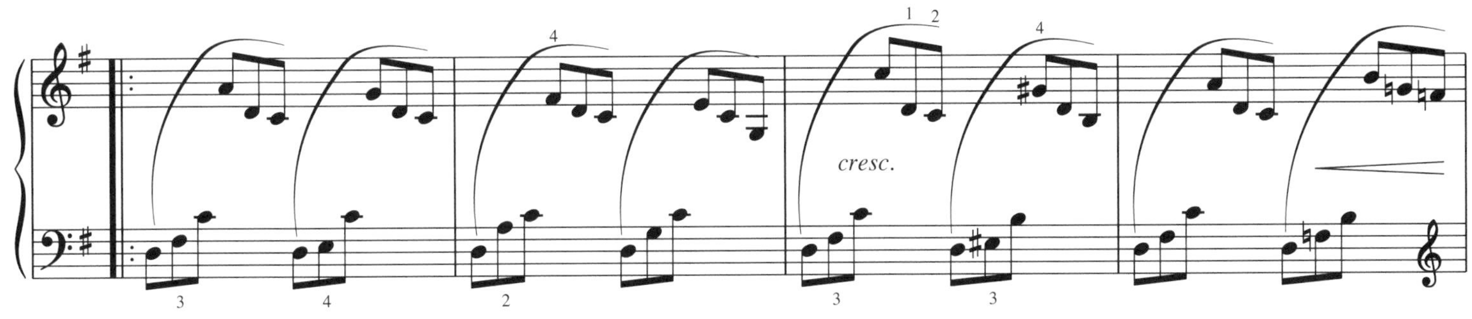
cresc.

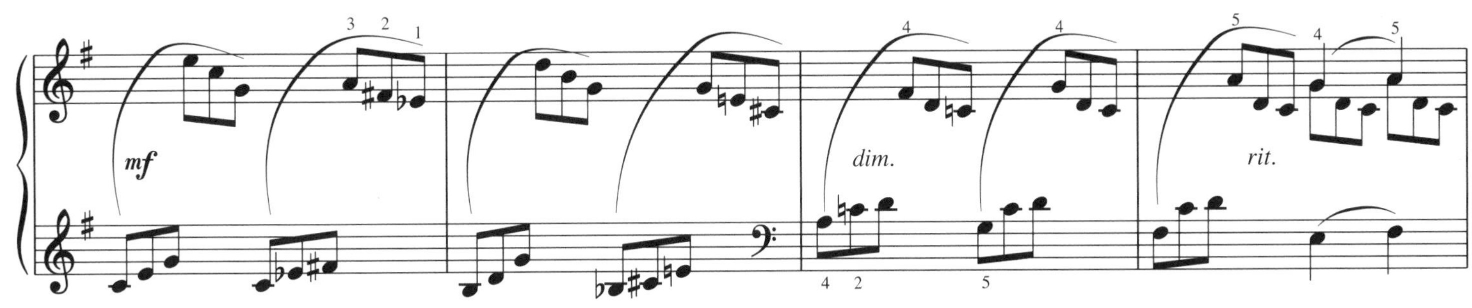
mf
dim.
rit.

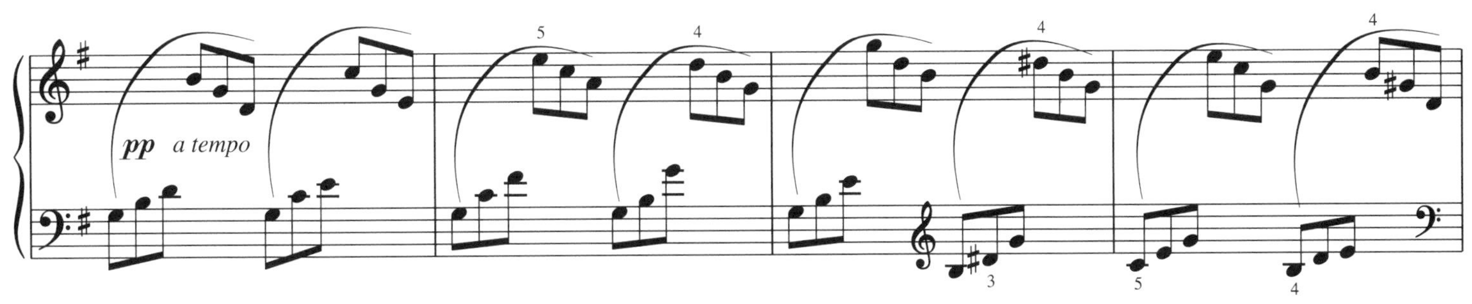
pp a tempo

The Reaper's Song

from *Album for the Young,* Op. 68, No. 18

Robert Schumann
1810–1856

p
mf
p
p

First Loss

from *Album for the Young,* Op. 68, No. 16

Robert Schumann
1810–1856

Morning Prayer

from *Album for the Young,* Op. 39, No. 1

Pyotr Il'yich Tchaikovsky
1840–1893

Mamma

from *Album for the Young,* Op. 39, No. 3

Pyotr Il'yich Tchaikovsky
1840–1893

p
mf
p
poco ritard
pp

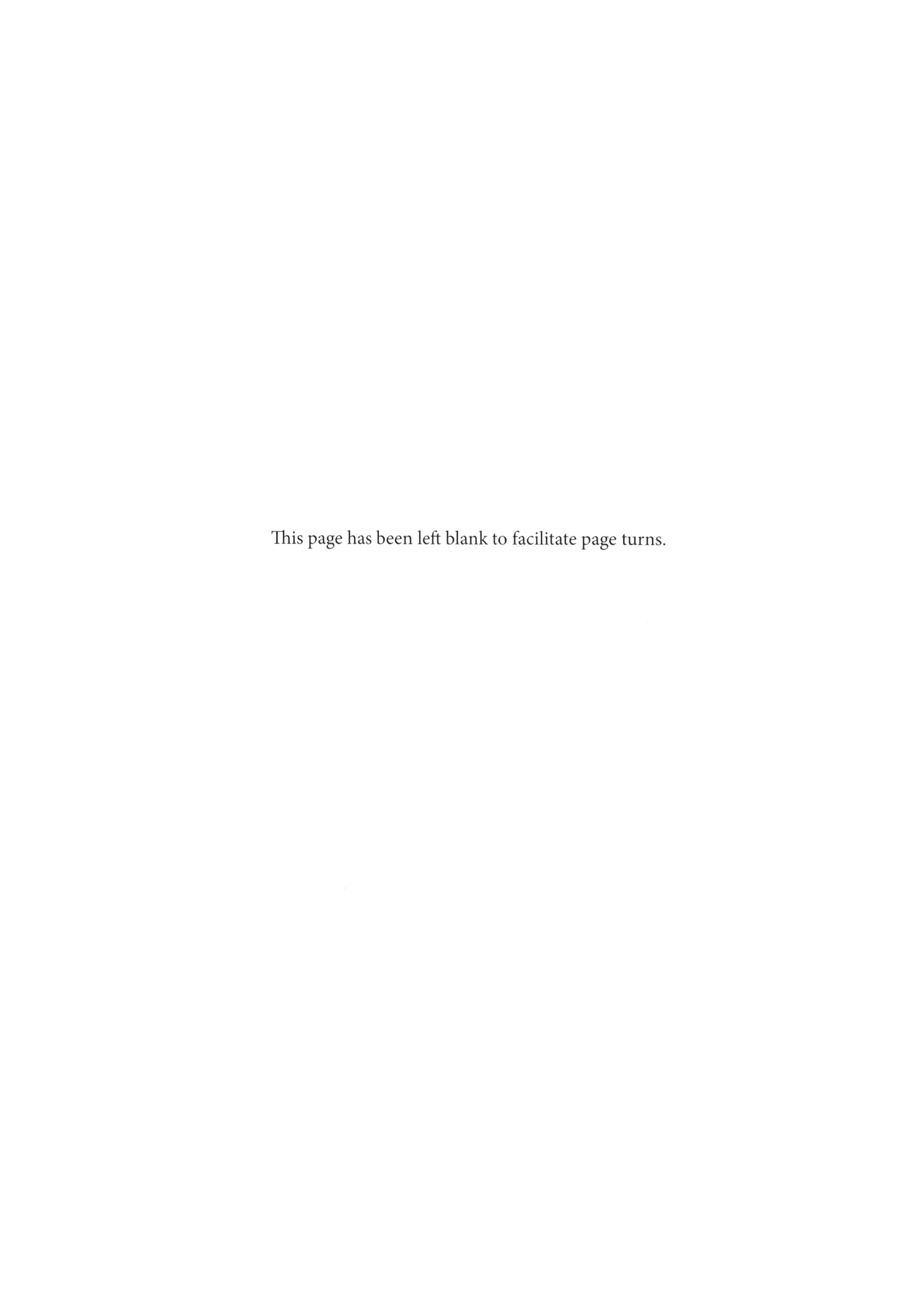

This page has been left blank to facilitate page turns.

The Sick Doll

from *Album for the Young,* Op. 39, No. 6

Pyotr Il'yich Tchaikovsky
1840–1893

The Doll's Burial

from *Album for the Young,* Op. 39, No. 7

Pyotr Il'yich Tchaikovsky
1840–1893

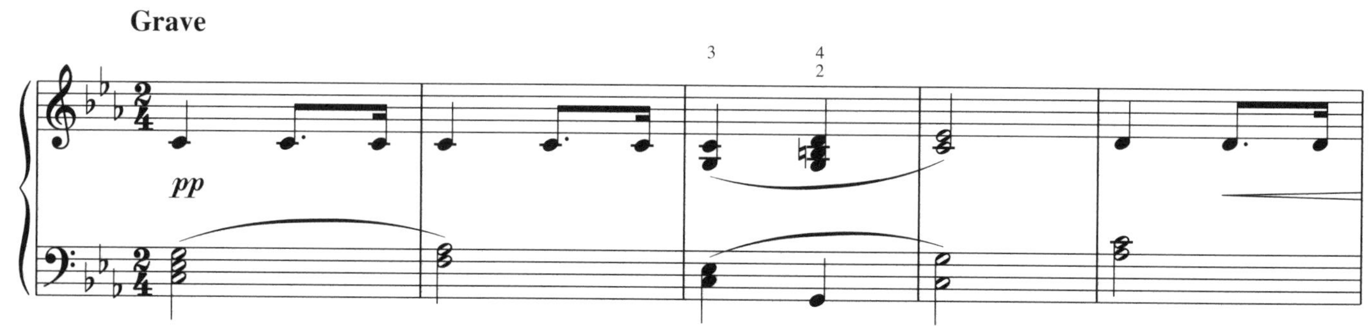

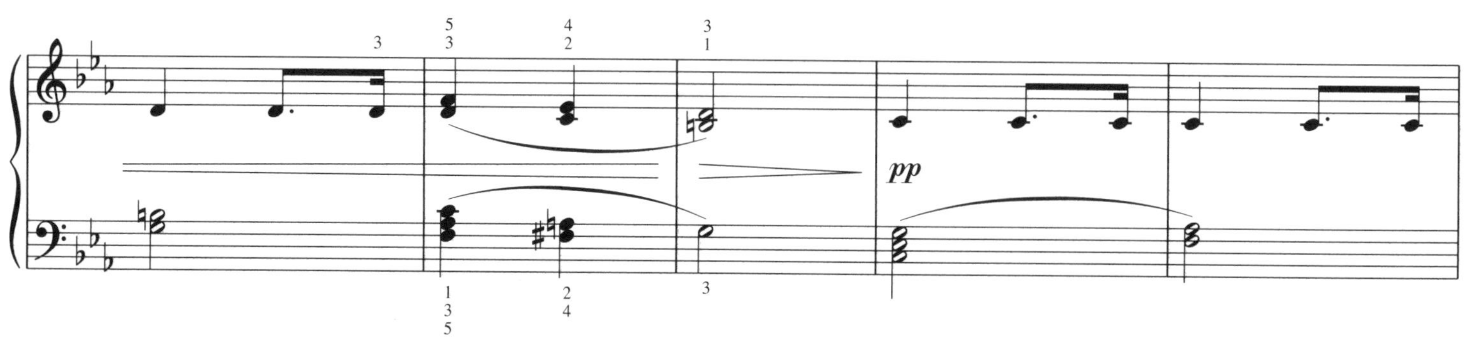

sf
p
pp

The New Doll

from *Album for the Young,* Op. 39, No. 9

Pyotr Il'yich Tchaikovsky
1840–1893

p
sf
p
p
pp

Russian Song

from *Album for the Young,* Op. 39, No. 11

Pyotr Il'yich Tchaikovsky
1840–1893

The Peasant Plays the Accordion

from *Album for the Young,* Op. 39, No. 12

Pyotr Il'yich Tchaikovsky
1840–1893

[Moderately]

mf

f

dimin. poco a poco

p

Italian Song

from *Album for the Young,* Op. 39, No. 15

Pyotr Il'yich Tchaikovsky
1840–1893

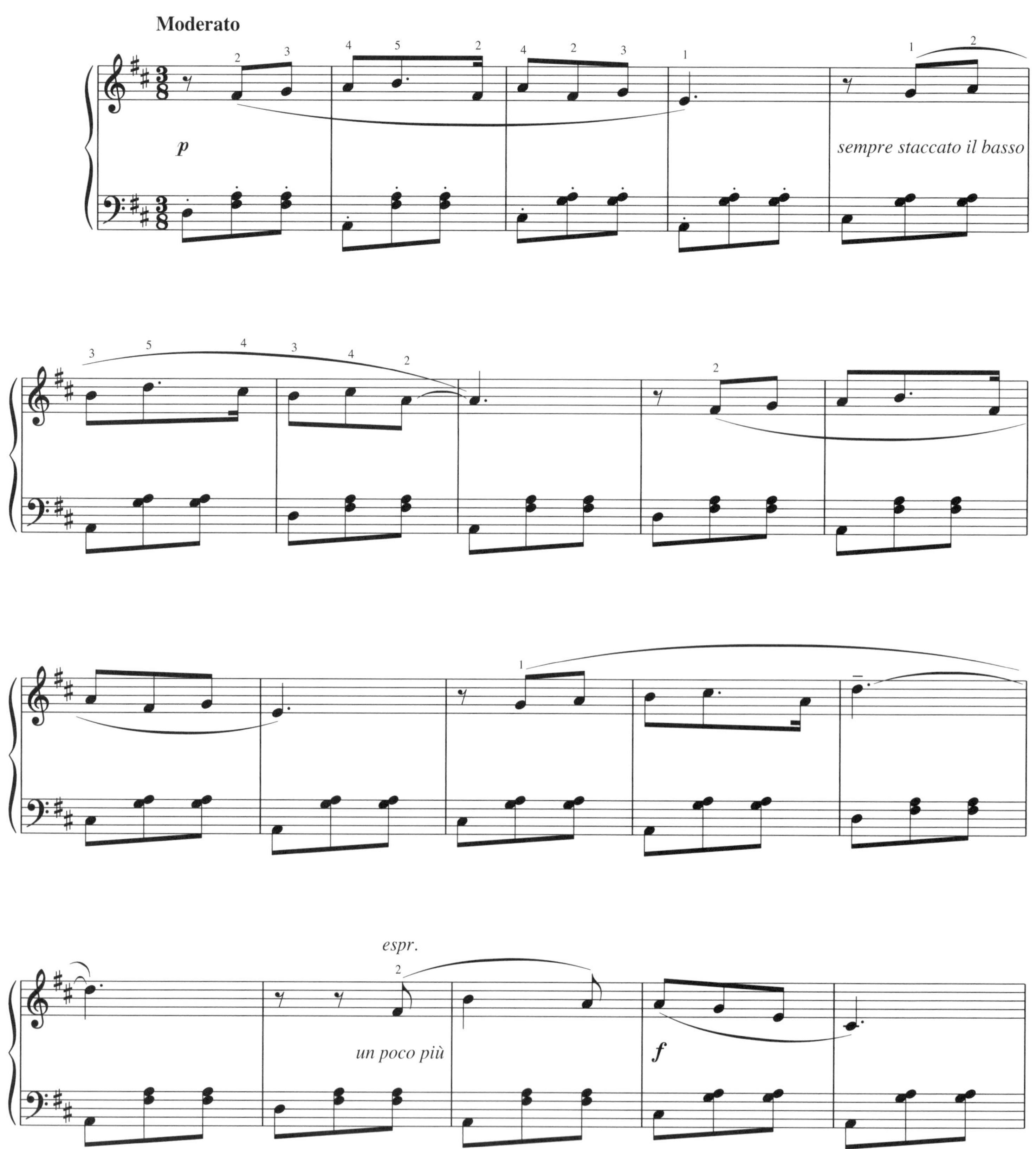

mf
mf
poco rit.
p
pp

Old French Song

from *Album for the Young,* Op. 39, No. 16

Pyotr Il'yich Tchaikovsky
1840–1893

Sweet Dream

from *Album for the Young,* Op. 39, No. 21

Pyotr Il'yich Tchaikovsky
1840–1893

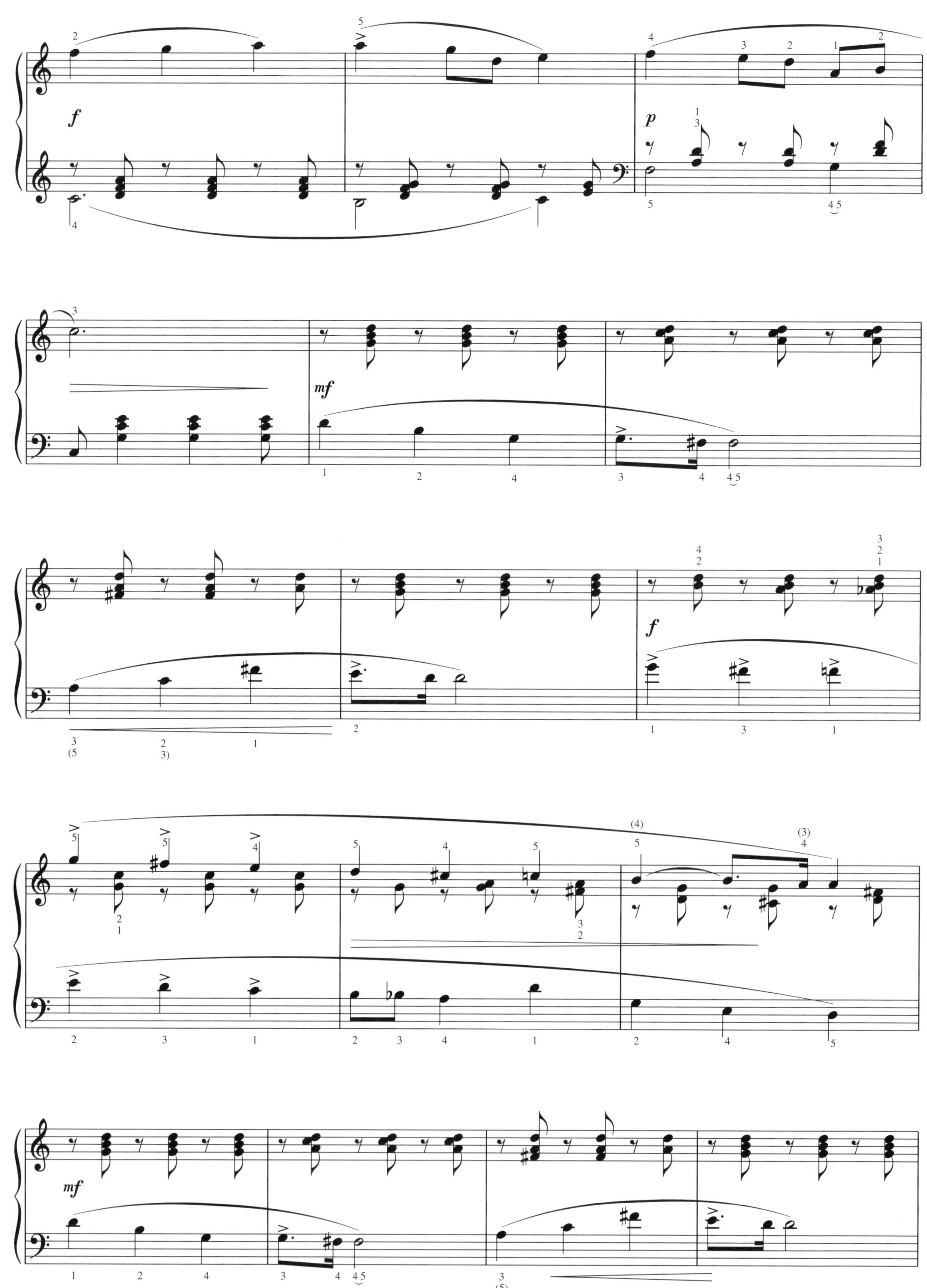

f
dimin. e rit.
a tempo
p
poco più f
p
poco rit.
p
a tempo
f
p

In Church

from *Album for the Young,* Op. 39, No. 24

Pyotr Il'yich Tchaikovsky
1840–1893

p
pp
pp
pp
perdendosi
ppp

The Organ Grinder

from *Album for the Young,* Op. 39, No. 23

Pyotr Il'yich Tchaikovsky
1840–1893

Dance in G Major

Georg Philipp Telemann
1681–1767

Children's Ballet

Daniel Gottlob Türk
1750–1813

The Dancing Master

Daniel Gottlob Türk
1750–1813

Allegro moderato

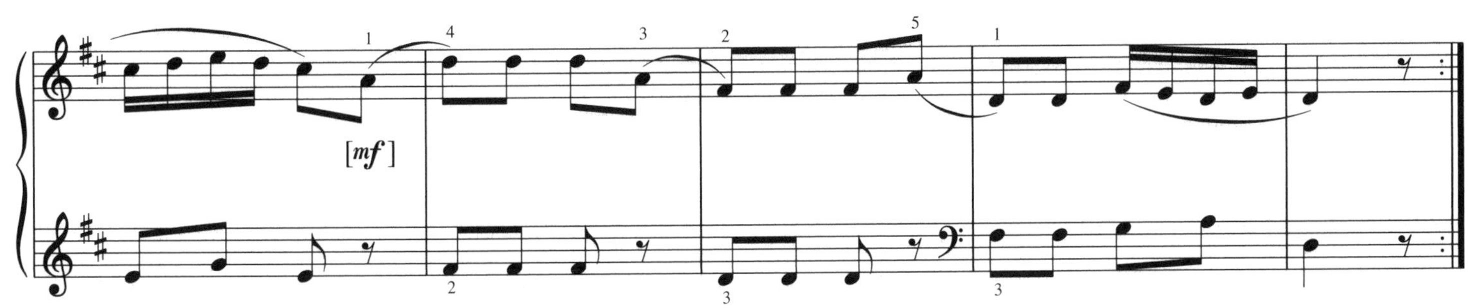

Little Rondo in F Major

Daniel Gottlob Türk
1750–1813

Simply

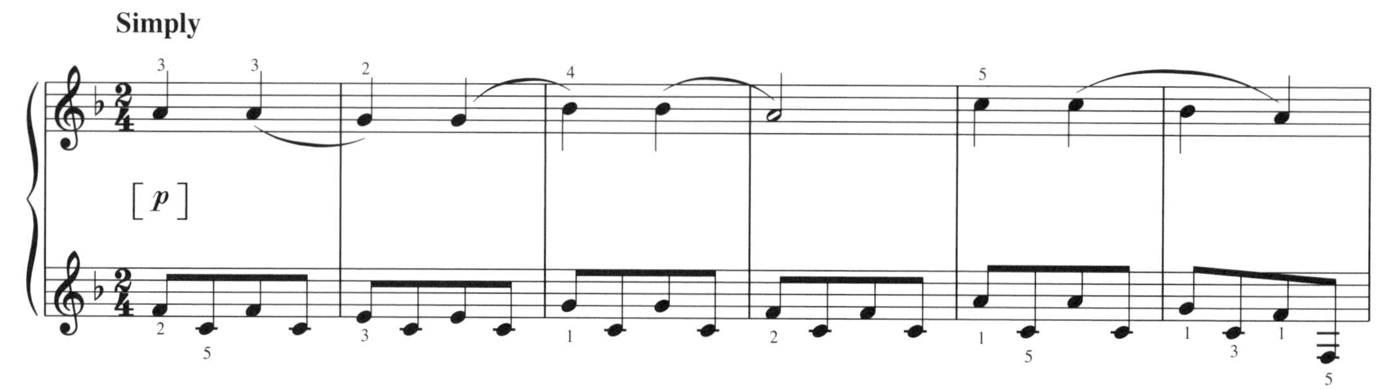

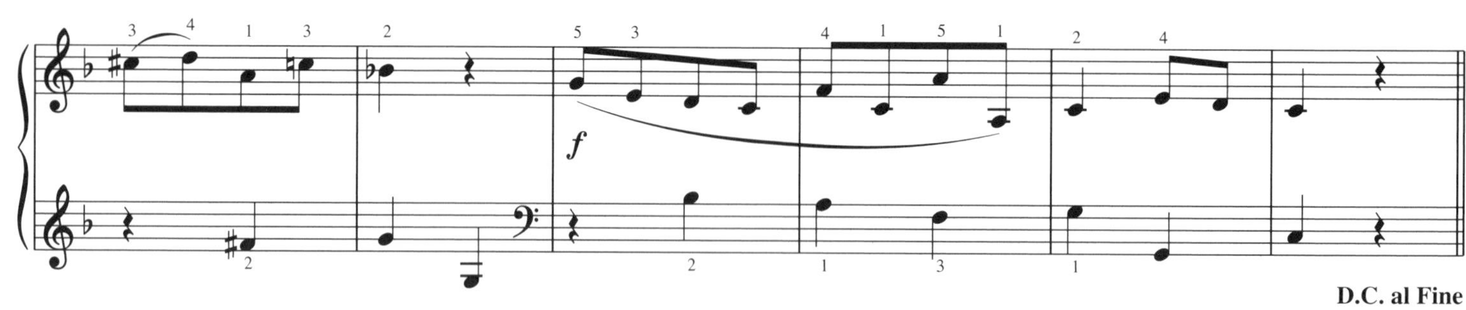